THE
CORPORATION
IN
MODERN SOCIETY

THE

CORPORATION

IN

MODERN SOCIETY

EDITED WITH AN INTRODUCTION BY

EDWARD S. MASON

HARVARD UNIVERSITY PRESS

CAMBRIDGE · MASSACHUSETTS

1960

Copyright © 1959 by the President and Fellows of Harvard College

Distributed in Great Britain by Oxford University Press, London

Second Printing

Library of Congress Catalog Card Number 60–5392

Printed in the United States of America

THE CONTRIBUTORS

KINGMAN BREWSTER, JR., Professor of Law, Harvard University

ABRAM CHAYES, Professor of Law, Harvard University

NEIL W. CHAMBERLAIN, The Ford Foundation

C. A. R. CROSLAND, Former Member of Parliament

ALEXANDER GERSCHENKRON, Walter F. Barker Professor of Economics, Harvard University

CARL KAYSEN, Professor of Economics, Harvard University

EARL LATHAM, Joseph B. Eastman Professor of Political Science, Amherst College

JOHN LINTNER, Professor in the Graduate School of Business Administration, Harvard University

NORTON E. LONG, Professor of Political Science, Northwestern University

EDWARD S. MASON, George F. Baker Professor of Economics, Harvard University

EUGENE V. ROSTOW, Dean of the Law School, Yale University

JACOB SCHMOOKLER, Associate Professor of Economics, University of Minnesota

RAYMOND VERNON, Professor in the Graduate School of Business Administration, Harvard University

W. LLOYD WARNER, University Professor of Social Research, Michigan State University

CONTENTS

Contents

FOREWORD

The industrial revolution, as it spread over twentieth-century life, required collective organization of men and things. To bring its human structure and physical plant into existence, to carry out its operations, to distribute its products, to meet the growing demands made on it in peace and war, proved wholly beyond the capacity of individual entrepreneurs. As the twentieth century moves into afternoon, two systems — and (thus far) two only — have emerged as vehicles of modern industrial economics. One is the socialist commissariat; its highest organization at present is in the Soviet Union. The other is the modern corporation, most highly developed in the United States.

The volume here presented contains, I believe, the best single collection of analyzed data that has yet appeared concerning the American corporate system. It is overdue, though the delay is understandable. Unlike the socialist commissariat, the American corporation is not a product of doctrine and dogma; it is an organic growth. Recognition of its institutional, causative qualities has been relatively recent among scholars. At the instance of the late Professor William Z. Ripley of Harvard, I gave some impetus to this recognition in a book written in association with Dr. Gardiner C. Means, *The Modern Corporation and Private Property*, published in 1932. In the ensuing decades, the United States achieved an explosive industrial expansion, familiar to all of us, in which the institutionalized corporation played a major and creative, perhaps a dominant, part.

Its role was not purely economic, though to be so was indeed its primary function, nor purely commercial, though profit was surely its purpose. It subtly changed both practice and theory of private property. It shifted substantial areas of production and exchange from a free market to an administered price system. It developed a vast, non-Statist organization of men and finance, an organization which increasingly raises problems of power. More recently we are beginning to see a pattern for distribution of its profits, suggesting an eventual non-Statist socialization of these profits unique in its institutional impact. Slowly — or perhaps not so slowly — industrial United States is moving toward a form of economic republic without historical precedent. A French philosopher, Jacques Maritain, observed that the system was in effect new, leaving nineteenth-century capitalism and European socialism far behind. A Dominican priest, Father Bruckberger, has recently elaborated this idea.

As a legal institution, the corporation has its roots in medieval history. It was used by Angevin, Tudor, and Stuart kings in England partly as a means of getting things done, partly as an extended arm of royal power. Speculation, dishonesty, and financial excesses caused the South Sea Bubble crash in 1720, and so discredited the corporation as an institution that for nearly one hundred years thereafter it was virtually outlawed in the English-speaking world. Grudgingly its use was resumed as the nineteenth century opened, both in Britain and in the nascent United States, though under severe limitations. It won its way to wide use in the mid-nineteenth century. As the century drew to its close, it had become a commercial instrument of formidable effectiveness, feared because of its power, hated because of the excesses with which that power was used, suspect because of the extent of its political manipulations within the political State, admired because of its capacity to get things done. From the turn of the twentieth century to the present, nevertheless, its position as a major method of business organization has been assured. Although it was abused, no substitute form of organization was found. The problem was to make it a restrained, mature, and socially useful instrument.

Perhaps the last great opponent of the large corporation as we know it today was my old master, Louis D. Brandeis, famous as a reformer–lawyer, and later as Justice of the Supreme Court. But he wanted, not socialized business, but good private business. The American corporations of his time exhibited a tendency to grow to dimensions of unforeseeable size, and he wanted to put limits upon them. His fear was that big business could never be good — and that its power, if allowed unrestrained expansion, could not be prevented from oversetting the principles of free democracy. He may have been right: time only will tell. Since his era, great corporations have grown even twenty times bigger than the size he thought impossible of efficient organization or effective restraint, yet the American political State still seems capable of coping with corporate power. The "curse of bigness" is still with us. But we see it now as a congeries of personal and philosophical problems rather than as an insoluble political dilemma.

Precisely because the great corporations had grown, because their power had become visible, and because this power fell outside the problems of power foreseen when American democracy was founded, the Fund for the Republic determined to study the question from our mid-twentieth-century stance.

This involved extending some classic premises. The Constitution of the United States, and peculiarly the Bill of Rights, was dedicated, among other things, to preserving the greatest single achievement of eighteenth-century thought. This was the conception of the free individual as the chief concern and also chief integer of organized society. He had lived under the menace of power; but the power-threat was that of the despotic State. Constitutional protections and limitations were therefore designed to shelter him from the rapacities, cruelties, or compulsion of arbitrary government power. May he not now need like protection from these non-Statist organizations of economic power? Yet, in the process, does he not also need the capacity to gather capital, to construct huge plants, to organize many men, to produce and to distribute, which these power centers have clearly demonstrated? Misery and poverty, we know now, can invade liberty as deeply as an oppressive State, and the corporate system obviously can provide, and even distribute, goods and services in volume sufficient to combat both.

But we know, too, that relative comfort and an "affluent society" (to use Professor J. Kenneth Galbraith's phrase) do not of themselves mean freedom either. This has led the writer to suggest that American problems of the latter half of the twentieth century will be as much philosophical as economic. Not that economics will cease to be important, or that all economic problems have been solved. We have still substantial areas of poverty to be dealt with. In prospect, also, the economic task of giving reasonable comfort to an American population, currently estimated to reach 350 millions by the year 2000, is certainly not small. But the corporate system appears to have evolved a method capable of providing goods and services sufficient to meet that problem — while it is not equipped, does not claim capacity, and probably should not be allowed to try, to solve the problem of the significance of individual human life. Lords Temporal rarely if ever make good Lords Spiritual.

The rule of law applied to the modern corporation is perceptively dealt with by Professor Chayes of the Harvard Law School and I commend his conclusions. I note two points. One is that some of his thinking emerges as a twentieth-century lawyer's parallel to canon-law thinking of the Middle Ages, when ethical considerations — notably that of a "just price" — were the imperatives. The other is an amusing incident which indicates how far we have traveled. My own book, *The Modern Corporation and Private Property*, was proposed to the faculty of the Harvard Law School in 1933 for recognition as one of the better books of that year in law. The faculty unhesitatingly turned it down: it was not in the field of "law." Professor Chayes and, I gather, the faculty of the Harvard Law School, now think otherwise; his studies are there to prove it. Rising to a point of personal privilege, I should not accept his view of the debate I had in that era with his predecessor, the late Professor E. Merrick Dodd. Dodd believed directors of corporations must (if they had not already) become trustees not merely for shareholders but for the entire community; this admitted them to a far greater power position than I thought they should have. In 1954 *(The 20th Century Capitalist Revolution)*, I conceded that Professor Dodd had won the argument: modern directors are not limited to running business enterprise for maximum profit, but are in fact and recognized in law as administrators of a community system. But when Professor Chayes suggests I conceded that Dodd was right all along, I must protest. It is one thing to agree that this is how social fact and judicial decisions turned out. It is another to admit this was the "right" disposition; I am not convinced it was. Things being as they are, I am unabashed in endeavoring to seek the best use of a social and legal situation whose existence can neither be denied nor changed.

More serious are certain observations made by Professor Lintner of the Harvard Business School. His chapter on the financing
of corporations is of prime importance; he is making, for the Rockefeller Foundation, a serious study of the methods by which industrial capital is gathered. Oddly, the so-called "capitalist system" knows relatively little about itself, and especially about its
central concept, "capital." Professor Lintner's study is not yet complete. The preview figures contained in this chapter more or less
confirm a pattern of capital formation indicated by an early and
extremely rough study I made in 1949 at the request of Governor
(then Mr.) Nelson A. Rockefeller. He was interested in this question, as indeed he still is. To conclude, as Professor Lintner does,
that the system has not changed may be debatable. In comparing
The Modern Corporation and Private Property (1932) with *The
20th Century Capitalist Revolution* (1954) and the more favorable
view of corporation managements in the latter with that in the
former book, he suggests that I must have had a "vision somewhere
on the road to Damascus," and changed position. I suggest that
the administrators of corporations may have seen some light (possibly somewhere on the road to the Pecora Investigation or the
Securities & Exchange Commission) since 1933. The principles
and practice of big business in 1959 seem to me considerably
more responsible, more perceptive, and (in plain English) more
honest than they were in 1929. The methods, morals, and social
education of the leaders of big business actually seem to have improved substantially in a generation. After all, the Graduate School
of Business Administration at Harvard (on whose staff I was
lecturer from 1925 to 1928) for thirty years has devoted itself to
making businessmen into professionals instead of privateersmen,
and toward making business the economic service-of-supply for
American society instead of the simpler art of exploiting human
need for private profit. Perhaps I overrate the achievements of
that very great institution; but I hope not.

Of more importance is Professor Lintner's argument that the
rates of industrial concentration — and the proportion of internal
accumulation of capital as contrasted with personal investment —
have not seriously changed. Therefore he suggests the system has
remained substantially unaltered in this century. Yet I wonder.

Further breakdown is needed. Because the ratio of concentration in industry is about the same now as it was when I made the early calculations in 1932, and because corporations internally generate about the same proportion of their capital now that they did in the earlier part of the century, Lintner thinks the present situation equates to the situation in the twenties or even earlier. This, it seems to me, ignores the results of growth in absolute size. A corporation with $400 million capital has one set of characteristics. That same corporation, expanding to $4 billion, is not the same: the pressures, stresses, power, potential, and impact have shifted all along the line. A "big corporation" of the year 1925 was still primarily a personal expression. In 1955 the same corporation — say, General Motors, or Aluminum Corporation of America, or (a less rapidly growing field) United States Steel — is quite obviously an institution. Again in the mathematical field of proportion, we should take account of the fact that in the forty-year period Lintner likes, the economy of the United States itself shifted. Relative to the whole, agriculture declined. Industry, in which the great corporations predominated, became the unquestioned dominant factor. The population dependent on it and on them in one form or another, and their corresponding power-factors, increased not only absolutely, but proportionally as well.

These asides, however, are merely incidental shoptalk between men who work in the same field. More significant is the fact that these non-Statist collectivisms which carry on the industrial revolution in the United States are now being studied as they are, and for what they are. The studies here presented, like evolutions of time, will confirm some of the older hypotheses, will overthrow others, and will establish new ones in their turn to be confirmed or overset. Increasingly we thus begin to understand the breadth, depth, and qualities of the economic society in which we live, which we daily help to create, and out of which we must build a civilization.

In a brilliant closing essay, Professor Gerschenkron describes the evolution of management and enterprise in the Soviet Union since the October Revolution. Communists also like to insist that their system does not change, has been excellent from the beginning, and is bound to continue as an artifact of ultimate truth.

Gerschenkron points out that the Communist–Socialist system in fact has evolved. If the United States has developed managerial power on the margin of the law, the Soviet Union has developed a degree at least of managerial freedom — also on the margin of its law. If Americans have cycles in their political–economic thinking, so apparently do the Soviets. The picture emerges of a very great industrial power struggling, in the ultimate, with many of the problems which America has faced in the past and with some (for instance, planning) which she must face in the future. Of interest is the fact that both peoples have still to master an enigma never wholly solved in history — that of power.

All of us, not least the Fund for the Republic, must be grateful to Professor Edward S. Mason for having assembled the best body of material on the American corporate system yet offered. It should prove of exciting interest not merely to businessmen and scholars but to Americans willing to face the conditions of the times and the polity in which they live, from which they must mold a good society.

Adolf A. Berle, Jr.

Columbia University
New York, New York

1

INTRODUCTION

EDWARD S. MASON

Everyone talks about the corporation, but, in the words of Mark Twain, no one does anything about it. And for this there are some pretty good reasons. In the first place, something very like the modern corporation is the inevitable product of an industrializing society, whether that society follows a capitalist or a socialist trend of development. Lawyers love to describe the corporation as a creature of the law, but law in a major manifestation is simply a device for facilitating and registering the obvious and the inevitable. Given the technologically determined need for a large stock of capital, the managerial requirements set by the problem of administering the efforts of many men, and the area of discretion demanded for the effective conduct of an entrepreneurial function, the corporation, or a reasonable facsimile thereof, is the only answer.

In the second place the business corporation is so much our most important economic institution and it is so thoroughly integrated into our business culture that to suggest a drastic change in the scope or character of corporate activity is to suggest a drastic alteration in the structure of society. If and when this comes about, it will take place not by radical changes in public policy toward the corporation but by radical changes much broader in scope. We are now a nation of wage and salaried employees and, in the main, we work for corporations. The days of Jeffersonian democracy are over and nothing can be done to resurrect them. We look to the corporation for the technical improvements that spark our economic growth. The corporation recruits our youth from college and provides them with pensions in their old age. It is the present support of community chests and other local charities and the future hope of institutions of higher learning. All this is to suggest not that the corporation cannot be touched but that to touch the corporation deeply is to touch much else.

In the third place, though many people have ideas on what to do about the corporation, there is little evidence of consensus. The "viewers with alarm" are approximately balanced by the "pointers with pride." On the one hand, we hear much talk of "a new feudalism," of "self-perpetuating oligarchies," of "irresponsible private power," and of "the euthanasia of the capitalist owner." But on the other, we are told of "the twentieth-century revolution," the "professionalization of management," the various "public" whose interests are sedulously cared for, and the beneficence of the "corporate conscience." It is not to be wondered that, to date, this cacophony of voices has not produced a very firm view on what to think or what to do about the corporation either in the general public or the minds of legislators.

The problem of what to think and what to do becomes the more difficult when one considers that, despite the fact that the United States has, over the last century, undergone a revolutionary change in which the rise of the corporation has played a dominant role, the rate of economic growth and the shares in which our increasing product has been distributed to the various recipients have remained remarkably stable. Under corporate dispensation the large economic classes in the community seem, over time, to be faring not much better and not much worse than they did before. Yet no one can doubt that the structure of our economy and our society has been profoundly altered. The mid-nineteenth-century nation of farmers, shopkeepers, and small manufacturers has become a highly industrialized economy dominated by organized groups. The percentage of the population in urban areas has continually increased and, despite the fact that it now approaches 60 per cent, the end is not yet in sight. Innovation at the hands of the small-scale inventor and individual enterpriser has given way to organized research. The role of government in the economy persistently increases. The rugged individualist has been supplanted by smoothly efficient corporate executives participating in the group decision. The equity owner is joining the bond holder as a functionless *rentier*.

If these changes had markedly accelerated or markedly diminished the rate of growth of which the economy seems capable or if they had profoundly changed the distribution between property and labor income, the popular attitude toward the corporation and all its works might be less ambivalent. But this has not happened. To be sure, employment under the combined influence of public policy and the policies of corporations and trade unions seems to be substantially more stable, a stability that may or may not turn out to have been purchased at the expense of persistent inflation. Furthermore, there is no doubt that the class conflicts and acerbities of business conduct of an earlier age have been substantially softened. But, so far as the essential rates and percentages that describe the performance of our economy are concerned, the key word is stability. What seems to have happened in our corporate society is that the prime movers of economic growth, the rate of capital formation, and the rate of technological improvement have become institutionally determined. And the political and economic balance among forces in society seems sufficiently resistant to change to prevent any marked redistribution of the fruits of growth. The stock of capital continues to grow at about twice the rate of growth of the labor force. The average yield per unit of capital falls slightly or not at all. The per capita real earnings of labor increase at about 2 per cent a year and the shares of property and labor in the division of the product change with a glacial slowness. *Plus ça change plus c'est la même chose.*

But if the inevitability of something like the corporate form, the degree of its integration with our culture, and the absence of any markedly adverse influence of the "corporate revolution" on the over-all performance of the economy help to explain the lack of a generally accepted bill of indictment against the corporation, this does not prove that all is well in Eden. Even A. A. Berle, who has done more than most to justify corporate man to his society — and incidentally, has thrown more light than any other man on the questions discussed in this volume — admits that he is afraid.[1] What Mr. Berle and most of the rest of us are afraid of is that this powerful corporate machine, which so successfully grinds out the goods we want, seems to be running without any discernible controls. The young lad mastering the technique of his bicycle may legitimately shout with pride, "Look, Ma, no hands," but is this the appropriate motto for a corporate society?

Almost every one now agrees that in the large corporation, the owner is, in general, a passive recipient; that, typically, control is in the hands of management; and that management normally selects its own replacements. It is, furthermore, generally recognized that, in the United States, the large corporation undertakes a substantial part of total economic activity, however measured; that the power of corporations to act is by no means so thoroughly circumscribed by the market as was generally thought to be true of nineteenth-century enterprise; and that, in addition to market power, the large corporation exercises a considerable degree of control over nonmarket activities of various sorts. What all this seems to add up to is the existence of important centers of private power in the hands of men whose authority is real but whose responsibilities are vague. At this point a confused medley of voices breaks in to assert the claims of various corporate "publics" — labor, owners, suppliers, customers, creditors, and so on — to whom management is *really* responsible; to point to the ever-widening scope of government jurisdiction and authority which managements must "take into account," and to extoll the emergence of a code of behavior generally recognized by professional managements, serving for the moment as a "corporate conscience," but in process of becoming a "rule of law."

All this is very interesting but very unsatisfactory, particularly to the intellectual who is bothered by apparent missing links in the chain of authority and by a seeming equilibrium of forces that by every right should be disequilibrating. The nineteenth century produced a social doctrine that not only explained but justified. But the functioning of the corporate system has not to date been adequately explained, or, if certain explanations are accepted as adequate, it seems difficult to justify. The man of action may be content with a system that works. But one who reflects on the properties or characteristics of this system cannot help asking why it works and whether it will continue to work.

The essays that make up this volume are in the main devoted to explaining various legal, economic, political, and social aspects of the corporate system. But they also raise questions of why, whither, and whether. In this introduction, borrowing heavily from the contributors, I shall attempt a brief statement of some of the principal questions that the rise of this modern leviathan are putting to us.

The one-hundred-and-thirty-odd largest manufacturing corporations account for half of manufacturing output in the United States. The five hundred largest business corporations in this country embrace nearly two thirds of all nonagricultural economic activity. These or similar figures are reiterated with such frequency that they tend to bounce off our heads rather than to penetrate. But by now we are all aware that we live not only in a corporate society but a society of large corporations. The management — that is, the control — of these corporations is in the hands of, at most, a few thousand men. Who selected these men, if not to rule over us, at least to exercise vast authority, and to whom are they responsible? The answer to the first question is quite clearly: they selected themselves. The answer to the second is, at best, nebulous. This, in a nutshell, constitutes the problem of legitimacy.

In the mid-nineteenth-century economy, corporate management was nothing if not legitimate. The generalizing of the privilege of incorporation was an aspect of a liberal movement that sought to give to all men equal opportunity under law. And the elimination of restrictions on the duration, size, purposes, and powers of corporations represented an attempt to convert the corporation from a special agency of the state into just another form of business enterprise. And indeed in the early stages of manufacturing development the corporation was just another form of enterprise, enjoying, it is true, limited liability, but functioning in essential respects like an individual proprietorship. The owner, if not the manager himself, selected the management, and the management was responsible to the owners. The traditional justification not only of private enterprise but of private property rested on that assumption. But those days are gone forever, and not even the assiduous efforts of the SEC can put ownership back in the saddle.

The phrase "self-perpetuating oligarchy" rings harshly to our democratic ears. But it must be recognized that some of our best people are oligarchs. The Harvard Corporation is self-perpetuating, and no one would deny — at least no one in my position — that this is an able and estimable body of men. The fact of the matter is that in some of the most effective and longest-lived organizations known to man, the management, in effect, is self-selected. So why not in the business corporation?

The answer, I would suppose, depends in part on how effective is self-selection as a method of assuring that the "best people" will continue to be chosen. But it also depends in part on whether good government, if assured, is an adequate substitute for self-government. A lot of people around the world have recently decided that it is not, and are now in process of discovering that self-government is not always an adequate substitute for good government. It would be nice to have both, but it may be necessary to give up a little of the one in order to secure an appropriate measure of the other.

The meaning of self-government within the context of corporate organization depends on who are considered to be "citizens." Some would say they are the salaried and wage employees and would devise plans of "industrial democracy" that lead straight toward syndicalism. But syndicalism has never had much appeal to the Anglo-Saxon mentality. Others consider the citizens to be members of the various corporate "publics" —owners, employees, customers, suppliers and creditors — and managerial spokesmen assert the responsibility of management to these "publics" without making it clear, however, how divergent interests are to be reconciled. This also is a quasi-syndicalist solution to the problem of legitimacy and one that inevitably assigns different weights to the "votes" of various constituencies. The consumer public, because of lack of organization, is obviously low man on the totem pole.

Legitimacy can ultimately be conferred only by the sovereign, and in the American tradition only the people are sovereign. But the sovereign acts through duly constituted representatives, and this opens the possibility for alternative routes to legitimacy. One possible route leads through court decisions to a rule of law designed to make equitable and tolerable the actions of inevitable private power. Another envisages an extended federalism, with corporations recognized as quasi-political entities properly legitimated. Still other routes move in the direction of public ownership or an expansion of the public-utility concept.

II. THE PROBLEM OF POWER

Legitimacy is a problem mainly because of the existence of private power. And private power now concerns us because that vision echoing Adam Smith, of an atomistic society no longer seems quite relevant to a corporate universe. In that society managerial control was made legitimate by ownership, and ownership was justified in part because of limitations on the power of ownership imposed by the competitive market.

Power, however, is a tricky concept, and it is even trickier to measure. There is a useful distinction between power to do (that is, a capability) and power over, which is anathema. Unfortunately, in any group or society there is little power to do without some power over. This is the dilemma of the philosophical anarchist. He cannot practice his faith, which is concerned with eliminating man's power over man, without becoming in fact a nihilist: one who is against all doing.

Faced with these and other difficulties, the search is directed toward ways of limiting or governing power that may be used against the interests of others while keeping as much as possible of the ability to act in his own or his organization's interest. Economists have been inclined to think of market power which they conceive, and sometimes try to measure, in terms of a departure from its opposite, an impersonal, and hence powerless, purely competitive market. But all markets that have ever existed inevitably contain certain buyers and sellers with some degree of market power. Consequently the search is for that degree of market power which is necessary to an efficient conduct of business but beyond which there is an inevitable divergence between the particular and the general interest. Some call this nirvana "workable competition," others prefer the term "effective competition," and still others draw a distinction between "reasonable" and "unreasonable" market power. Whatever the nomenclature, this concept embraces two ideas worth pondering. The first is that technological and organizational influences inevitably bring about, in a large sector of the economy, markets served by the few rather than the many and that not very much, really, can be done about it. The second is that in a dynamic economy, characterized by product changes, process innovation, advertising, and growth, competition among the few may not be so bad after all. This may be whistling in the dark, but the whistling is going to go on in any case.

But what if technological and organization considerations decree a size and a fewness — a type of competition — that not even a business economist would call workable? Under these circumstances, some would say, break them up even at the cost of some loss of efficiency. Others would turn to public ownership or regulation. And still others, I suspect, despairing of the first and dubious of the second, might prefer the known evil to the unknown consequences of action.

Even if competition among the few is "workable," the problem of private power is not exorcised. Industrializing economies inevitably move away from market relations among firms and toward administrative relations within the firm. Contractual relations between legal equals give way to relations between employer and employee within a bureaucratic hierarchy. This is an aspect of the "power over" that, in our industrialized society, seems inseparably connected with the "power to do." Furthermore, this exercise of power by management and the accompanying loss of freedom by the managed is independent of who does the managing. As Clark Kerr puts it,

> Some loss of freedom . . . is inevitable in an effective industrial system. It will occur, more or less, whether the system is run by the employers alone, by the State alone, or even by unions alone. Industrial society requires many rules and reasonable conformity to those rules. There must be a wage structure, a work schedule, and so forth, no matter who operates the system. This loss of freedom is one of the prices paid by man for the many benefits in income and leisure that can flow from industrial society.[2]

Labor has met this problem in part by the organization of

trade unions, whose most important function, undoubtedly, has been to assure labor a voice in determining those rules and regulations that affect working conditions. There remains, however, the question: how responsive are union leaders to the wishes of their constituents? Economic bureaucracy is not limited to the corporation. For the salaried employee there are all those pressures and subtle influences on the organization man — and his wife — so graphically depicted by W. H. Whyte.

Market power and managerial power reinforce each other in complex ways. In a vertically integrated enterprise economic processes are subject to managerial control from raw material to finished product, but with market power waxing and waning at different stages, depending on the vigor of competition. A large unintegrated firm buying from many small producers sometimes obtains what amounts to managerial control over these enterprises through the leverage of its market position.

Nor do managerial and market aspects exhaust the content of private power in the economy and the society. Large firms and large trade unions exert an influence on wages and prices outside the jurisdictions of their own managers and markets. Key wage and price bargains are made that affect the general level of wages and prices and wage-price relationships. If we are in for "creeping inflation," large corporations and trade unions are the principal creepers.

One is led on from this point to speculations concerning the political influence of large firms and other organized groups. Here we are offered a broad spectrum of choice ranging from "Business as a System of Power" [3] to the iniquities of a "laboristic economy." Does corporate size bring with it political influence or political vulnerability? Probably the first in some contexts and in others the second. Perhaps the safest thing that can be said is that politics inevitably reflects the structure of society and in a society characterized by large organizations, politics will be pressure-group politics.

III. THE MANAGERIAL REVOLUTION

Managerial direction is, of course, an aspect of bureaucracy, and its characteristic methods and attitudes have been with us for a long time. Before the rapid technological changes which we call the industrial revolution had confronted business enterprise with the need for complex administrative organization, the state, large municipalities, armies, the church, universities, and indeed all institutions bringing together the efforts of a sizable group of men had developed bureaucracies. Business bureaucracies as we know them, however, date from the industrial revolution, and the first area in which they significantly flowered was railway transportation. As late as 1900, three quarters of American corporations large enough to have their securities listed on the New York Stock Exchange were railways. But from the Civil War on, this form of organization made progress in other sectors of the economy.

People who talk about a "managerial revolution" usually have in mind, on the one hand, the increasing importance of large corporations on the American scene and, on the other, changes in administrative techniques that have continually increased the size of the enterprise that can be effectively managed. Those who doubt the significance of this "revolution" point to figures on economic concentration, and indeed it is possible to show that, during the last fifty years, there has been no significant increase, however measured, in the share of economic activity controlled by the largest corporations. The largest corporations have grown mightily, but so has the economy. This, in my view, does not dispose of the matter. In the first place, conclusions on the trend of concentration depend heavily on the date from which one measures the trend. If the date chosen is before the great merger movement of 1897–1903, it can be shown that concentration has, in fact, increased. In the second place, the phenomena we are concerned with are more a product of absolute size than of relative share. And about absolute size, however measured, there is no shadow of doubt. In the third place, there is probably a substantial lag between changes in the size of enterprises and changes in managerial techniques adapted to the new sizes. For these and other reasons, I conclude that, despite the lack of evidence of increased concentration during the last half century, there may well have occurred a profound change in the way industrial enterprises are managed. It goes without saying that in other broad sectors of the economy small-scale enterprise, managed in a traditional fashion, not only is holding its own but will continue to do so.

These changes in management are commonly grouped under the heading of bureaucracy. And bureaucracy, as the political scientists tell us, is characterized by a hierarchy of function and authority, professionalization of management, formal procedures for recruitment and promotion, and a proliferation of written rules, orders, and record keeping. All this is true of business administration in large corporations, but corporate bureaucracies also exhibit certain differences from typical government bureaucracies that are worth emphasizing. In the first place, corporate managements enjoy a much greater freedom from external influence than do the managements of government bureaucracies. As we have seen, management has pretty much escaped from ownership control, but though private ownership may no longer carry with it control, it does guarantee corporate management against most of the political, ministerial, and legislative interference that commonly besets public management. Perhaps in a corporate society this is becoming one of the primary contributions of private property. Needless to say, this independence of corporate management from any well-defined responsibility to anyone also carries with it the possibilities of abuse we have noted above in our discussion of the problem of legitimacy.

In the second place, corporate managements have traditionally been considered to have as their single-minded objective, in contrast to most government bureaucracies, maximization of business profits. And traditionally the incentives connected with profit maximization have been thought to constitute an essential part of the justification of a private-enterprise system. Now managerial voices are raised to deny this exclusive preoccupation with profits and to assert that corporate managements are really concerned with equitable sharing of corporate gains among owners, workers, suppliers, and customers. If equity rather than profits is the corporate objective, one of the traditional distinctions between the private and public sectors disappears. If equity is the primary desideratum, it may well be asked why duly constituted public authority is not as good an instrument for dispensing equity as self-perpetuating corporate managements? Then there are those, including the editors of *Fortune,* who seek the best of both worlds by equating long-run profit maximization with equitable treatment of all parties at issue.[4] But to date no one has succeeded in working out the logic of this modern rehabilitation of the medieval "just price."

Finally, since corporate managements work exclusively in the business area, which government bureaucracies ordinarily do not, it can be said that the possibility of monetary measurement in the former permits a closer adjustment of rewards to performance, and hence a closer observance of the causes of efficiency than is possible in the latter. This is true, and it is important, but the distinction is not between public and private efficiency but between the efficiency of operations susceptible to the measuring rod of money and the efficiency of those that are not. Furthermore, if equity rather than profits is the desideratum, even this advantage is lost. If equity rather than productivity is to determine the reward, what happens to the canons of efficiency?

One of the leading characteristics of well-ordered bureaucracies both public and private — a characteristic justly extolled by the devotees of managerialism — is the increasing professionalization of management. This means, among other things, selection and promotion on the basis of merit rather than family connections or social status, the development of a "scientific" attitude towards the problems of the organization, and an expectation of reward in terms of relatively stable salary and professional prestige rather than in fluctuating profits. This professionalization of management has, of course, been characteristic of well-ordered public bureaucracies for a long time. It helps to explain why able young Indians, for example, have in general preferred to cast their lot with a civil service selecting and promoting on the basis of merit rather than with the highly nepotistic business firms of the subcontinent. But it is a relatively new phenomenon in American business and one of increasing importance.

The degree of freedom enjoyed by corporate managements, in contrast to their governmental counterparts, has affected personnel as well as other policies. And no one who has observed at first hand the red-tape inefficiencies of the United States

Civil Service can fail to be aware of the superiority of corporate practice. This relative freedom from hampering restrictions on selection plus a high level of monetary rewards has brought the cream of American professional management into business corporations. No one doubts the superiority of American business management. Unwitting testimony, if testimony is needed, is supplied by the care with which Soviet planners examine American management practices.

But the process of managerial self-selection common in large corporations does raise certain questions worth pondering. Granting that we have been vouchsafed good corporate government, is the process of selection likely to assure us continued good government? Is good government enough or shouldn't we be permitted a modicum of self-government? Has corporate government, in fact, been as good as all that: aren't certain limitations in this process of recruitment already becoming visible?

If the truth be known, no very coherent account of how corporate executives are in fact chosen is available. This is one of those situations in which those who know don't tell, and those who tell don't know. C. Wright Mills, who, so far as I am aware, has had no experience in choosing corporate executives, asserts that advancement is "definitely mixed up in a 'political' world of corporate cliques." [5] This sounds very much like the process of promotion in a university department. Chester I. Barnard, who has had experience, strongly emphasizes the importance of "compatibility of personnel." Those are chosen who fit and fitness includes "education, experience, sex, personal distinctions, prestige, race, nationality, faith, politics, sectional antecedents," and "manners, speech, personal appearance." [6] This is a comprehensive list of qualifications and it recalls an alleged selection to a post at All Souls, Oxford, where the varied capacities of the two rival candidates were so evenly matched that the choice finally depended on the relative neatness with which each disposed of his artichoke.

Drawing on experience in other contexts, one would suppose that an able group of men in choosing successors would emphasize ability but that various considerations making for "togetherness" would strongly impinge. In the process of university selection, excessive concern for the old school tie is apt to be discouraged by the possibility of intervention from above and even more by active competition from rival institutions. University professors can and do move. So do corporate executives on occasion, but the increasing drag of pension rights and other endowments which ordinarily cannot be transferred seriously handicap movement. Nor is the process of executive selection subject to higher review. Since the managerial elite in our large corporations consist of a few thousand at most and since this elite has an influence that far transcends the immediate corporate jurisdiction, it is highly important that the process of selection be kept as competitive as possible even if this requires, as suggested by Brewster, some degree of government intervention.[7]

IV. THE CHANGING CHARACTER OF PRIVATE PROPERTY

Berle draws a distinction between "individual possessory holdings" and "power systems" and imaginatively sketches a cyclical development from feudal power systems to the seventeenth- — and eighteenth- — century emphasis on private property and from that into the modern corporate power system.[8] Certainly ownership of a local grist mill has a different economic significance than the ownership of 100 shares of United States Steel. And issues other than economic are involved. To a Jeffersonian society of small and relatively equal property owners, the "rights of property" was a phrase fraught with social significance. In a nation of wage and salaried employees, even though many are participants in stock ownership plans, the accent is apt to be on "privilege" rather than "right." Schumpeter contrasts the "full-blooded" capitalist owner of the nineteenth century, ready to fight for his property, with the stock-and-bond owner of the twentieth who has only the vaguest idea where "his property" is or of what it consists. The eighteenth-century philosophers considered property ownership as essential to the full development of personality, to the maintenance of individual freedom from the encroachment of those power systems represented by church and state, and to the formation of a citizenry capable of self-government. Corporate ownership is not usually defended in those terms today.

When questions are raised concerning a contemporary justification of private property, the ownership of one's house, its furnishings, and other consumer goods is not an issue. No one except a few communal crackpots and, apparently, the current Chinese Government is concerned with this type of property ownership. Nor are many people this side of the Iron Curtain unwilling to extend the eighteenth-century benediction to private ownership of agricultural land, of corner grocery stores, garages, and gas stations. The problem arises approximately where "individual possessory holdings" give way to "systems of power" — that is, at the point at which corporate size divorces control from ownership and converts owners essentially into *rentiers*. In Berle's terms, "The capital is there, and so is capitalism. The waning figure is the capitalist."

The fact that private property of this sort presents a "problem" does not mean that it is devoid of justification. But it does mean that the doctrines of Locke and Jefferson are no longer quite relevant. And it probably means that the content of the "rights" and "privileges" that may be justified will differ substantially from their eighteenth-century content. After all, it is a little difficult to see in the ownership of corporate securities the source of that invigorating moral, social, and political development that Jefferson saw in private property. And certainly the eighteenth-century economic justifications of private property based on the assumption that ownership carries with it control lack relevance to the corporate universe.

V. THE CORPORATION AND THE STATE

The economies of Western Europe and, increasingly, that of the United States are frequently described as "mixed" economies. This phrase is commonly interpreted to indicate a situation in which the role of government as owner and regulator has become sufficiently large to cast doubt on the validity of "capitalist" and "free enterprise" as appropriate adjectives but not sufficiently large to justify the appelation "socialist." Government ownership and regulation are important ingredients, but they inadequately characterize the "mixture" of public and private that the rise of the large corporation has produced. The growth of the modern corporation has been accompanied by an increasing similarity of public and private business with respect to forms of organization, techniques of management, and the motivations and attitudes of managers. Government has sought increasingly to use the private corporation for the performance of what are essentially public functions. Private corporations in turn, particularly in their foreign operations, continually make decisions which impinge on the public — particularly foreign — policy of government. And government, in pursuit of its current objectives in underdeveloped areas, seeks to use techniques and talents that only the business corporation can provide. Decidedly a *"verwickelte Verwand-schaft,"* as our German friends might say. Under these circumstances the classic arguments of the socialism-versus-free-enterprise debate seem a bit sterile, to say the least.

The increasing similarity of public and private enterprise has impressed both liberals and conservatives, though the conclusions drawn therefrom have tended to differ. In an early recognition of this trend, Keynes described it as a "tendency of big enterprise to socialize itself." A point is reached in the growth of big enterprises, he says, at which "the stockholders are almost entirely dissociated from the management, with the result that the direct personal interest of the latter in the making of great profit becomes quite secondary." [9] American managerial spokesmen supplement this thought by emphasizing management's responsibility to workers, customers, suppliers, and others, though they would hardly describe living up to this responsibility — as Keynes probably would — as behaving like Civil Servants. These and similar considerations have led elements in the British Labour Party to the conclusion that the form of ownership of large enterprise is irrelevant. "The basic fact is the large corporation, facing fundamental similar problems, acts in fundamentally the same way, whether publicly or privately owned." [10]

While large private corporations have been forced by their sheer size, power, and "visibility" to behave with a circumspection unknown to the untrammeled nineteenth century, government, on the other hand, has attempted to give its "business-like" activities a sphere of independence approaching that of the private corporation. Experience with the public corporation in the United States has, it is true, somewhat dampened an earlier enthusiasm for this type of organization. And even Britain, which has sought much longer and harder than we for a workable compromise between independence and accountability in its publicly managed enterprises, has not yet found a satisfactory solution. Nevertheless, it remains true that managerial practices and attitudes in the public and private sectors of most Western economies tend to become more similar.

Private ownership in the United States, however, still confers an immunity from detailed government supervision that a public corporation does not enjoy. And government takes advantage of the independence and flexibility of the private corporation to contract out the performance of what are essentially public services. Private firms become official inspectors of aircraft; various types of military "operations analysis" are undertaken by Rand and other privately organized corporations, and substantially more than half of public research and development expenditures go to private rather than public organizations. In commenting on these phenomena, Don Price observes, "If the question (of public versus private) is seen in realistic terms, we shall have to devise some way of calculating whether a particular function can be performed best in the public interest as a completely governmental operation at the one extreme, or a completely private operation at the other extreme, or by some mixture of the nearly infinite possibilities of elements of ownership regulation and management that our variety of precedents suggests. . ." [11]

If private corporations perform in certain areas services essentially public in character at the request of government, in other areas they perform services essentially public without being asked. It is probably true to say that not since the seventeenth century, when the Levant Company conducted Britain's foreign policy in the Near East as an adjunct to its business operations and the East India Company acquired India for the Empire "in a moment of inadvertence," have the activities of business corporations impinged so closely on foreign policy. Of course, the classic example is that of the oil companies in the Middle East, but in almost every overseas area in which large American corporations operate, their business activities either impede or advance the foreign policy of the United States. This is not because these corporations behave in a manner different from the way they would have behaved in the nineteenth century — although indeed they do — but rather because the foreign policy of the United States has become so comprehensive that it is touched by almost any sizable business activity. This picture of oil companies "making foreign policy" for the United States raises hackles in some quarters and stimulates demands for a bringing of private business activities under public control. But, in the first place, these are not "private business activities" in the nineteenth-century sense of the term, nor are they conducted as if they were. And second, although private and public relations in this area are probably in need of rethinking, further thought is unlikely to lead to a nineteenth-century type of solution in which authority was either private or public, with little or no commingling of the two.

How really mixed — and perhaps mixed up — our economy is these days can be clearly seen by casting one's eye on United States policy and practices in the so-called underdeveloped areas of the world. Our announced policy is to give substantial assistance to the economic development of countries whose economies have long been stagnant. And our preferred means are the stimulation of private enterprise in the underdeveloped areas and the encouragement of United States private investment abroad. But in many of these areas, the opportunities for foreign private investment are negligible, and our grants and loans inevitably flow through local government channels. At the same time, in the provision of technical assistance we depend heavily on contracts with American private firms. And we actively encourage mixed enterprise, private and public and foreign and domestic, as a means of getting enterprise moving. The effort is sometimes described as an exercise in government–business cooperation in the promotion of foreign economic development, and perhaps that is as good a description as any. In any case, it is a good example of a mixed economy in motion.

This lack of a clear-cut separation of public and private authority and responsibility offends some people. And indeed, the eighteenth-century political philosophers and political economists provided for their epoch a much more satisfactory intellectual framework than any vouchsafed to us today. The fact seems to be that the rise of the large corporation and attending circumstances have confronted us with a long series of questions concerning rights and duties, privileges and immunities, responsibility and authority, that political and legal philosophy have not yet assimilated. What we need among other things is a twentieth-century Hobbes or Locke to bring some order into our thinking about the corporation and its role in society.

VI. THE CONTRIBUTIONS TO THIS VOLUME

Pending the coming of such a one, the editor has done the best he can to assemble the views of a number of knowledgeable contributors to various aspects of this problem. These contributions have the virtues and defects of any symposium. Different points of view are duly represented, but there is lacking that nice articulation of argument that only a single author can provide. In default of this, it may be useful to give the reader some indication of the intellectual framework of the volume and what he may expect from the various contributions.

The first three essays are penned by lawyers. In a broad sense they all wrestle with the same problem: how is the wide scope of managerial discretion to be limited? But their answers are rather different. Chayes's paper, "The Modern Corporation and the Rule of Law," surveying the historical development of the corporation, emphasizes the facilitative rather than the proscriptive character of law. He suggests that, if the use of corporate power is to be made "reasonable" (that is, non-arbitrary), this is likely to happen through the legal invention of ways and means of representing the interests of groups affected by corporate decisions in somewhat the same manner as legal invention has facilitated the development of collective bargaining.

Rostow's general thesis in his essay, "To Whom and for What Ends are Corporate Managements Responsible," is that, despite managerial dicta alleging a responsibility to workers, suppliers, customers, and others, the primary responsibility of management is to the owners. It must be if we are to have a price system that will do its job. He believes that a firmly stated and widely accepted "rule" that the social duty of business management is to serve the best interests of the stockholders offers a better guide to corporate practice from the point of view both of the corporation and society than any of the current formulations of managerialism.

While Chayes seeks protection from arbitrary use of corporate power by strengthening the hand of those affected by corporate decisions and Rostow justifies the primacy of ownership interests and profit seeking within a competitive context, Brewster's paper on "The Corporation and Economic Federalism" turns toward governmental limitations of these "subsovereigns" on the analogy of political federalism. Viewing the large corporation as a kind of "state," he inquires what exercises of federal authority may be necessary to assure fair and equal treatment of the "citizens" of these "states" and the free movement of people and capital among the several "states."

The concern expressed by the legal contributors obviously arises from the fact of corporate power. Kaysen's paper on "The Corporation: How Much Power? What Scope?" is squarely addressed to this issue. The power of any actor on the social stage he defines as the scope of significant choice open to him. His examination of industrial structures leads him to the conclusion that the constraints imposed by market forces are, in the industrial sector of the economy, decidedly loose and that consequently the scope for managerial choice is substantial. Within this scope there exists a range of possible decisions that can markedly affect the efficiency, the stability, and the progressiveness of the economy and the equity with which its rewards and punishments are distributed. Market power, moreover, is the basis of substantial political and social power, the influence of which, particularly through the use of mass media of communication, is pervasive.

Since corporate managements indubitably have power, it would be interesting to know how managements are chosen and by what criteria. But, as I have suggested above, the literature on this subject is not very illuminating, and it is difficult to find a contributor who could and would effectively pierce this veil. Information, however, on the antecedents of corporate managers is much more available, and Warner, in his paper on "The Corporation Man," summarizes the results of long study of this subject. He presents substantial evidence for the proposition that the upward and downward social mobility of corporate executives has been increasing. If this is so, one of the principal contentions of the managerial school, that family connection is giving way to merit in the selection and promotion of executives, receives at least partial support.

Since the activities of the large corporation touch many segments of our culture, a complete analysis of the role of the corporation in modern society would take us into numerous byways. I have preferred to remain on the highways, and a number of essays have been devoted to what seem to me to be the principal highways of corporate action and influence. Chamberlain's paper on "The Corporation and the Trade Union" suggests that negotiation and conflict between management and labor have been essentially on ground chosen by management: within the business rather than the political arena. British experience has been interpreted by some people as indicating that greater labor gains might be secured in the latter field, and Chamberlain considers what range of circumstances might shift labor action in the United States in a political direction.

Schmookler's essay on "Technological Progress and the Modern American Corporation" evaluates the role of the large corporation in research and development. Revolutionary changes have taken place since the first American research laboratory in private industry was established by General Electric in 1900. But though private industry in 1957 spent $7.3 billion on research and development, of which $4 billion was their own money and $3.3 was contributed by government, this country exhibits a conspicuous weakness in basic research. One of the reasons is that basic research yields dividends that can to only a small extent be captured by a firm sponsoring this type of research. This argues for a heavy public investment in this area. Schmookler also has some interesting things to say about the relation of the patent system in invention and innovation.

Lintner's scholarly chapter on "The Financing of Corporations" undertakes a re-examination of certain theses originally propounded by Berle and Means in their volume on "The Modern

Corporation and Private Property" and later elaborated by Berle. There were three striking propositions in that classic study that have since received much attention. The first asserted an increasing concentration in the American economy. The second asserted the separation of control from ownership and foresaw a growing independence of management from stockholders' influence. The third related this independence to changing corporate behavior. The first proposition has turned out to be of dubious validity. The second has been generally accepted, and the Berle and Means study still remains the classic exposition. But while accepting the fact of a high degree of managerial independence in a highly concentrated economy, there has always remained the question, what difference does it make with respect to corporate behavior? Lintner's chapter suggests that, at least in the capital market, it appears to make very little difference. Large corporations, despite Berle's and Means's earlier expectations, rely no more on internal financing than they did fifty years ago. The response of management to changes in financial requirements have remained remarkably stable over time. And the investment considerations affecting the use of retained earnings appears to be about the same as those imposed by the market. Finally, Berle's later claims concerning the effect of pension-fund investment on corporate control are held to be exaggerated.

Large corporations are for the most part multi-plant firms. And the dependence of local communities on branch plants of national corporations managed by hired personnel who are here today and gone tomorrow raises a number of social and political problems discussed by Long in "The Corporation, Its Satellites, and the Local Community." A recognition by the central office of corporate responsibility to the local community, taking the form of directions to the branch plant manager concerning contributions to Community Chest and Red Cross, does not, perhaps, quite take the place vacated through the decline of the old owning families. There is, Long believes, a real and important conflict between "the corporation as an institutionalized center of loyalties and the local territorial community."

Latham's paper on "The Body Politic of the Corporation" presents a political scientist's interpretation of the corporation as a "rationalized system for the accumulation, control, and administration of power." Viewing it as a "government," he finds that power is distributed and used within the American corporation in ways that substantially violate the prevailing values of American democracy.

The operations of United States corporations abroad, it has been suggested above, have important implications for American foreign policy. Some of these implications are examined in Vernon's paper on "The American Corporation in Underdeveloped Areas." The contributions of United States private business to the economic development of certain underdeveloped parts of the world have been extremely large. In 1955 United States direct investors in Latin America produced sales of $4,400 million, paid local taxes of $1,098 million, undertook plant and equipment expenditures of $424 million, and financed an increase of $255 million in other local assets. United States private business activities are, however, very unevenly distributed over the underdeveloped world. Moreover, there are some conspicuous weaknesses in the contribution of private business — one of them the relative immobility of American technicians — that might be remedied. And the relation of United States government to private effort in the promotion of economic development abroad is relatively haphazard.

The volume concludes with two essays on foreign experience. In "The Private and Public Corporation in Great Britain," Crosland compares and contrasts the organization, objectives, managerial motivations, and external restrictions on management, in British private and public enterprise. He finds that despite the presence of a strong socialist party, the roles of both private and public management in Britain are rather similar to these in the United States.

Gerschenkron's essay on "Industrial Enterprise in Russia" examines that alternation between centralization and decentralization of authority that has characterized Soviet economic development since the revolution. One of the advantages of capitalism has traditionally been supposed to lie in a decentralization of authority to those in close contact with the act of production. And indeed as one studies the attempt in the Soviet planning process to act through a long chain of intermediaries, one can understand the trials and tribulations of a Russian plant manager. Gerschenkron quotes Marx's description of the essential spirit of capitalism, "Accumulate, accumulate! This is Moses and the Prophets," and observes that to no society does this more fittingly apply than to the Union of Socialist Soviet Republics. Indeed, he hazards the opinion that so firmly has the Soviet political system been wedded to the policy of a high and growing rate of investment that it is doubtful whether any other policy — for example, a higher and rising standard of living — is compatible with the maintenance of the Soviet dictatorship.

Despite the fact that numerous aspects of corporate activity and influence are here examined, it is obvious that certain fruitful fields of investigation have been neglected. There is no inquiry into the relation between large corporations and the media of mass communication, though Kaysen has noted the problem in passing. The tendency for the central offices of large corporations to cluster particularly in New York, but also in Chicago and San Francisco, and the consequences of this for the location of legal, public-relations, managerial, and other business services have been neglected. Corporate influence on various "freedoms" and the independence of the "corporation man" has been barely suggested.

Neglect of these problems is less serious than it might be in view of the fact that this volume is, in a sense, a part of a larger inquiry now being undertaken by the Fund for the Republic. The Fund has in process a re-examination of our liberties within a modern context. Since the business corporation, as we know it, did not exist when the Bill of Rights was written, no account was taken of the impact of this and other important institutions, including trade unions, on the rights and duties of the citizen. If the constitution were to be rewritten today, how would rights and duties be redefined, what role would be assigned to the business corporation, and what limitations imposed? I hope these essays may be considered to make a modest contribution to the larger study.

2

THE MODERN CORPORATION AND THE
RULE OF LAW*

ABRAM CHAYES

I. THE MODERN CORPORATION

"The modern corporation" is the big business enterprise in corporate form. The type, even before Peter Drucker made it explicitly so,[1] is General Motors — or DuPont or General Electric or any one of the top hundred (two hundred, if you are Mr. Berle, five hundred, if you are *Fortune*) that are the princes and kings of our corporate economy. The reason for concern with them is obvious. They are repositories of power, the biggest centers of nongovernmental power in our society.

What is meant by power? The ancient complaint against monopoly identifies with fair accuracy at least a part of it: the ability to control, within relatively broad limits, the price and quality of products made and offered for sale. This is traditional market power, the power of concentrated economic resources in a particular industry. It is by no means free from tricky conceptual and definitional problems, but it will serve in a general and nontechnical way to mark one kind of significant power which major corporations exercise.

Beyond the conventional power of the monopolist or near monopolist has been the power of the big company to affect economic levels outside the particular markets in which it buys and sells. U. S. Steel's wage settlement sets a pattern, taken directly by other steel producers, becoming a target in other major manufacturing industries, like the automobile industry, and spreading indirectly to influence wage rates, working conditions, and other terms of labor–management agreements throughout the country.

* This paper is based on a Reynolds Lecture delivered at Amherst College in the fall of 1958.

Steel's power over its wage bargain is not unlimited. Many factors, not least among them the United Steel Workers, have a good deal to do with the final terms. Yet, when full allowance is made for these other forces, a respectable residue of power, power to make an effective choice within a significantly broad range of alternatives, is left with the managers of the Steel Company.

To take another example, we have become sharply aware of the broader, systemic consequences of the price policies of major producers of basic products. Each wave of price increases over the past five to ten years has been led off by steel or other industries in which the great modern corporation is the characteristic unit. There is no need to get into the controversy about the wage-raise chicken and the price-rise egg. For present purposes, it is sufficient to note that the price decisions in these industries rather consistently had system-wide consequences extending far beyond the firms which made them.

Again, take levels of investment. In 1954, the announcement by General Motors of a $1 billion expansion program was largely credited with heading off the then threatening recession. GM's management might as easily, and perhaps with equal justification, have put the $1 billion in dividends or wage increases or price cuts. Yet the choice, having such profound public effects, was a corporate decision.

Economic power is not the whole story, however, nor perhaps even its most important part. Concern with the modern corporation is intensified to the extent that its activities have necessarily ramified beyond the economic sphere of production of goods and service.

Across a widening range of activity, the large corporations have become principal factors. They are the chief agencies of private research. They are the hope of fund raisers for institutions of higher learning and the principal consumers of the products of those institutions. Their advertising supports newspapers and sponsors TV programs. They are a leading, if not *the* leading, purveyor of influence and pressure on public officials in Washington and state capitals.

It follows that in these spheres and others they bear large responsibility for the quality and tone of American life. The neglect of basic research, the dilution of the college degree, the organization man, the dullness and superficiality of the mass media, the level of political morality — all these offspring, wanted or unwanted, find their way in the end to the doorstep of the modern corporation.

This attribution of responsibility is not a token of hostility to the large private corporation. What has been said amounts to no more than that the great corporation is the dominant nongovernmental institution of modern American life. The university, the labor union, the church, the charitable foundation, the professional association — other potential institutional centers — are all, in comparison, both peripheral and derivative.

This much is claimed by the most articulate and perhaps the most thoughtful spokesmen for the corporation. Mr. William T. Gossett, vice-president and general counsel of the Ford Motor Company, tells us:

> The modern stock corporation is a social and economic institution that touches every aspect of our lives; in many ways it is an institutionalized expression of our way of life. During the past 50 years, industry in corporate form has moved from the periphery to the very center of our social and economic existence. Indeed, it is not inaccurate to say that we live in a corporate society.[2]

More than a decade ago, Mr. Peter Drucker set this style when he said:

> What we look for in analyzing American society is therefore the institution which sets the standard for the way of life and the mode of living of our citizens; which leads, molds, and directs; which determines our perspective on our own society; around which crystallize our social problems and to which we look for their solution. What is essential in society is, in other words, not the static mass but the dynamic element; not the multitude of facts but the symbol through which the facts are organized in a social pattern; not, in other words, the average but the representative. And this, in our society today, is the large corporation.[3]

The corporation has come to occupy this Siege Perilous because it is our society's institutional device for large-scale organization of energies and resources. One need not defend the size of some modern corporate giants on grounds solely of technical efficiency. Yet, as a matter of history, the corporate form of organization came to prevail in an industry when the enterprises in it came to require more capital than could readily be contributed by one or a few men. Increasing scale meant not only more machines and bigger workshops. It involved a different organization of human participation in the productive process. A more bureaucratic form of organization began to replace the modes of decision-making and supervision applicable to smaller, face-to-face operations. The corporate form fostered not only the aggregation of capital but the altered social organization for work implicit in large-scale enterprise.

In another and more subtle way, the institution has mediated between social and technical demands. The technology demanded that the wealth of society be immured in large, stable agglomerations of fixed assets. Yet a system of private property required that wealth be kept in highly liquid, readily transferable form. The alchemy of the modern corporation, with its satellite paraphernalia of securities markets, has permitted both ends to be served.

A final rarification may be this: the technological growth included enormous improvement in physical mobility and communication, attended by a like increase in social mobility and communication. The bonds which held together the geographical community were loosened, and the bench marks by which men could know and measure their place in the old community lost relevance and definition. Has the corporation supplied a new community, institutional rather than geographical, to replace the old?

Professor Adolph Berle, in a contemporary summary note, tells us: "Some of these corporations are units which can be thought of only in somewhat the way we have heretofore thought of nations." [4] All the instruments agree: the modern corporation wields economic and social power of the highest consequence for the condition of our polity. Let us resist this conclusion, or belabor it, no further. Let us accept it as our first premise.

II. THE RULE OF LAW

Much of the historic dialogue among reflective lawyers and legal thinkers has been devoted explicitly or implicitly to developing and refining the concept of the rule of law. To see how little it signifies outside our walls is an ironically humbling reminder of how far apart are the rooms in the mansion of the intellect.

The words, in their elementary signification, are likely to evoke a question: how does law (or how do laws) govern society — how do they rule men? To some, such a question may sound painfully simple. The law forbids, and who offends its prescription is subject to its pains and penalties. But a moment's reflection, enlivened if need be by reference to the course of the law in the South today, leads us to suspect that there is more to the problem.

Others will say that after Marx it is impossible to sustain the illusion that law "rules" in any real sense at all. It simply reflects the basic constellation of power in a society. Far from being governor, it is governed, a formal recapitulation of the underlying economic realities, shifting only as they shift.

Engels himself was not willing to push the argument so far.

> In a modern state, law must not only correspond to the general economic position and be its expression, but must also be an expression which is consistent in itself, and which does not, owing to inner contradictions, look glaringly inconsistent. And in order to achieve this, the faithful reflection of economic conditions is more and more infringed upon. All the more so, the more rarely it happens that a code of law is the bold, unmitigated, unadulterated expression of the domination of a class — this in itself would already offend the "conception of justice." [5]

To put it more broadly, any society has a wide range of purposes and functions. To these the legal system is related in two important ways. First, it is a chief and indispensable instrument for directing activities of individuals and groups along lines which support and further those purposes. Second, the legal order has its own institutional necessities, prominent among them a "conception of justice," to which it responds, which serves it as an organizing principle and which the system, in its internal workings, continuously clarifies and refines. Because the legal order is such a central institution in the society, this developing conception of justice impinges upon and colors the whole spectrum of social purposes.

The legal system, then, harnesses human action to social purpose, but to social purposes infused with a conception of justice itself defined, in large part, by the legal system.

Without making any claim to be advancing a definition which would be universally accepted, even among lawyers, I use "the rule of law" to import the propositions just set out. These propositions can be taken as descriptive. They are also to be seen as stating a norm, an ideal imperfectly approximated in society. Indeed, with only a little professional imperialism, it can be regarded as the defining ideal of western democracy.

Conventional discussion has often put forward a narrower view of the rule of law which conceives the central problem as control of governmental power. At the beginning, however (whether we take as the beginning a symbolic state of nature or what we can tell of the tribal and feudal states out of which our own legal institutions grew), the rule of law was juxtaposed to the arbitrary exercise not of public but of private power, the might which asserted itself as right. The most elementary injunction of the law — "Thou shalt not kill" — is addressed to private individuals.

Clusters of institutional arrangements centering often about an embryonic monarchy were eventually successful in bringing their force to bear against the private power which broke the peace. Through this successful effort to subdue and control private exercise of power, the king and his state won much prestige. By the end of the Middle Ages that prestige was great enough to make good the claim of the monarch of the nation-state that he alone could legitimately exercise coercive power in society. This monopoly position of the nation-state is still widely admitted as a theoretical matter, though perhaps with the substitution of some mystical sovereign for the fleshly king of old.[6]

In Anglo-American history, these developments evoked lively experiment on how to bring power in this new embodiment under the rule of law. Of this experimentation, the establishment of the United States was a significant, perhaps culminating stage.

Because public authority asserted a monopoly of coercive power, the subjection of *public* power to law became the preoccupation of legal and political theory. Exclusive concern with limitations on *government* power is thus seen to be a temporal phase of the rule of law ideal, corresponding to the historical period in which an effective monopoly of power was claimed and exercised by organized western nation-states.

But to the extent that we are prepared to recognize centers of significant nongovernmental power within our society, they too must be subjected to the rule of law. It is implicit in the ideal, as here defined, that the processes and institutions of the society be organized so as to give reasonable assurance that significant power will be exercised not arbitrarily, but in a manner than can be rationally related to the legitimate purposes of the society.

It does not necessarily follow from this that when less formal arrangements have failed to provide the necessary assurance, the offending power center must be subjected to some sort of public governmental control. A rigidly Austinian conception of law as command might require such a conclusion. But law, in any moderately developed social system, is a far more intricate matter. Indeed, only a little reflection is needed to make clear that generalized prescriptive commands are quantitatively and qualitatively only a small part of the body of our law.

This type of law, just because it is the most direct and brutal intervention of power into men's lives, can be employed only in a limited range of situations and for limited purposes. Even in relations which maximize the domination of one party and the subjection of another — as for example, that between officer and enlisted man — orders can be used to accomplish only quite simple things. When complex interrelations and coordinations of the kind inherent in any modern social arrangement become involved, only those purposes which are self-evidently basic and most pervasively and articulately shared can be secured by prescriptive command. "Thou shalt not kill" or the rules of the road thus ought to be seen not as the typical manifestation of law but rather as at the furthest reach of the spectrum.

Much more characteristic of the operation of the law in more complicated and indeterminate areas of social direction is the provision of facilities. To illustrate: it is possible to look at the law of contract as a command of the state not to break certain classes of promises. This is not, however, a very useful point of view if the object is to understand the role of contract law in the development of our society. For this purpose, contract must be seen as a way in which men dealing with each other can insure that their promises will outlast their transitory states of mind.

The law does not prescribe contract. It attaches no immediate normative value to the act of promising. It says only that if you wish to act, and more important, if you wish to make your action binding, in some sense, on the future, act in such and such a way. If you do not follow the approved path, the promise made to you may nevertheless be kept. But the law will lend you no aid to see that it is kept.

It will be seen that what the law of contract has provided is a device by which private persons are enabled to some extent to stabilize and make predictable — to control — the future. That is, they are enabled to make their own law to govern their own affairs. The state lends its judicial machinery to enforce this personal law, if necessary. The law appears to exhaust itself in defining the conditions on which the public force will be enlisted to effectuate the private end. And it is true that these conditions, in our system at least, are elastic enough to permit a wide range of autonomously directed private activity. The ideal of the rule of law dictates, however, that these conditions be not arbitrary, but must be rationally related to legitimate social purposes. By providing useful facilities on such condition, the legal system mobilizes powerful inducements to action in support of those purposes.

The rule of law, as here conceived, then, is concerned with regularizing and rationalizing the use of power. But it is concerned with power in both its faces — not only as an evil, to be restrained, but as a resource to be harnessed in the service of society. The creation of legal institutions which enlist the energies of men in the service of legitimate social purposes is the most important mode by which this dual end of the rule of law is approached.

III. AN EXCURSION INTO HISTORY [7]

It will not have escaped the reader that "corporation" is a facility provided by the modern American legal system, hardly less important than contract. It comes to this position, however, only after a process of historical development and adaptation which has important consequences for the contemporary form.

The notion of the corporation is well established in English law at least as early as the fourteenth century. It was applied chiefly to ecclesiastical bodies, to boroughs, and to guilds, both craft and mercantile. Its principal legal incidents were well worked out in the ensuing two centuries — the capacity to hold property, to sue and be sued — to persist beyond the lives of its members. Its principal function was to regulate the affairs of its members, and to this end it had internal legislative and judicial power. Especially with the guild and borough, the economic activity of the members bulked large in the affairs to be regulated, the more so since the corporate body was often the carrier of an economic monopoly, functional or territorial, in which only those who were members in good standing could share.

Corporate status was achieved by grant from the king (although Parliament later asserted authority to confirm such grants and finally an independent power to grant its own charters). From the Crown's point of view the corporation was an administrative organ. The townsmen and guildsmen, for their part, eagerly sought the privilege of self-government as a buckler against the baronage. The grant of incorporation was thus a principal device by which royal power was at the same time administered and expanded.

In the sixteenth and seventeenth centuries, this idea of the legal unity of a group fused with the financial device of joint stock trading to bring to birth the business corporation. At first it too is an organ for accomplishing things the monarchy, newly energetic, wants done. But in contrast to the earlier period when the royal object was the internal administration of a town or a trade, the adjustment of relations among its members or between a member and an outsider, the Tudor purposes were external to the corporation: the development of foreign trade, colonization, privateering, the development of native sources of munitions.

The charter of incorporation continues to include such incidents as monopoly of trade to particular parts or in particular goods, or exemptions from certain burdens and exactions. The function of the corporation, however, is no longer to administer the privileges but to exercise them. The corporation is necessary because the objects pursued are beyond the reach of the members as individuals. The needed amounts of capital are too great, the risk is too high, the duration of the enterprise too long. The corporation is the legal institution which can hold the aggregated capital of many over a period of time unaffected by the death or withdrawal of individuals.

These defining differences were not early recognized, for a variety of reasons, and the business corporation took over from its antecedents the idea that the membership of the corporation, assembled in "general court," was, in theory at least, its highest governing body. Because the functions of the corporation had changed and because the member was related to it simply as a contributor of capital rather than in the integral fashion of the burgess or guildsman, this idea of government by the membership progressively lost reality. The business of the corporation was managed by a few, relatively qualified men of affairs.

In other respects, the seventeenth-century corporation was an admirable instrument of a mercantilist economic policy. It could be given a precisely defined task tailored to a concrete state purpose. The grant of monopoly which often accompanied the assignment of the task was relatively easy to enforce with fair efficacy. It was, at least, calculated to enlist the energies of the company in the detection and suppression of unauthorized, and thus unregulated, activity. The activity of the corporation itself was relatively accessible to the most highly developed national organ of administrative control, the royal courts, through which it could be held within its granted privileges, and, if it failed to act, its privileges could be revoked. Finally, the corporation was a device for mobilizing private resources in the king's business. Incorporators would venture their own funds for the state's ends, and indeed would pay for the privilege.

These potentialities of the mercantile corporation dictated the principal features of political and legal policy toward it: first, that each corporate charter be granted only on grounds of high policy, after careful and searching scrutiny and evaluation; second, that limitations on the size and, more especially, on the scope of activities of the company be laid down precisely in the charter and be enforced with considerable rigor.

Just as internal self-government atrophied in the transition from the medieval to the mercantile corporation, so it was necessary to strip away the characteristics that had defined the mercantile form in order to make the corporation a serviceable instrument of a liberal economy. What had been a rare, privileged entity existing at the will of the sovereign, exercised deliberately for great ends of policy, became in the course of hardly a half-century's development, from 1800 to 1850, a form of organization available almost of right to easily qualified people feeling the need for it.

The spread of incorporation, as has already been remarked, accompanied the growth in the scale of enterprise. With the industrial revolution and the consequent increase of the capital which could usefully be committed to single ventures, industry after industry reached the position where corporate organization of its component units was desirable. And so arose a press for corporate charters in which the notion of deliberate legislative examination of applications became progressively fictionalized. The idea that the grant was a special privilege in return for an undertaking to do a special task of importance to the state became equally illusory.

In most important American states, the system of special grants of corporate charters fell toward the middle of the century before more or less general incorporation acts under which the corporate form of organization for business became "a right justly accessible to any competent petitioner." [8] Like its near relative the contract, the corporate charter was now freely available on condition that it be used for business purposes.

At first these general incorporation laws contained in generalized form restrictions which it had been customary to put on companies in the old mercantile days, and which had been carried into the period of special legislative charter. These were, as we saw, restrictions on size and limitations of the corporate activity to the purposes expressed in its charter. These restrictions had functional significance when the corporation was in its mercantile setting. They were meaningless in the new context, unless we accept the Jacksonian hypothesis that they represent crude efforts to control the new monster.[9]

The restrictions were progressively abandoned or neutralized by one means or another. It seems to me dubious, both as history and as polemic, to regard this as a series of unbroken defeats for the defenders of yeoman's democracy. More properly, these restrictions were simply fossilized remnants of the characteristics appropriate to the institution in its earlier phase. Businessmen and their lawyers grew more confident of their ability to operate in corporate form. As the scope and scale of these operations increased they bumped against the old limitations and, disclosing them to be without the strength afforded by function, simply shucked them off.

The theoretical framework under which this development proceeded was that of contract, the most powerful stream of nineteenth-century legal growth. The charter, which had once drawn its force from the grant of the sovereign, became a bargain among the enterprisers. Who was to limit the terms of their bargain? As in other areas of the law which came under the sway of contract thinking, it came to be assumed that the bargainer knew best his own interest and how to secure it, and that the sum of the interests of the bargainers equaled the interests of the whole society.

This change in the legal character of the corporation meant the abandonment of the effort to subject business decisions to state review through the mechanism of court enforcement of the limits of a sovereign grant. It did not imply, however, that business activity was deemed free of limitations on the arbitrary exercise of power. The force of the market was substituted increasingly and explicitly for the force of law to achieve desired organization and regularization of power.

The market can be viewed as a planning device, an allocator of resources. Or it can be seen as a sensitive register of a society's choices and values. From the point of view of the nineteenth-century legal system, its character as a sanction against undesired activity assumed importance. The surveillance of the economy by market forces could be taken as assuring the rule of law ideal. The market punished arbitrary exercises of power, or so it was thought, by economic failure: that is, by the withdrawal of power.

A reasonable approximation of the economist's model, the market, requires a rather large number of relatively equal participants, able to adjust their actions rather flexibly in response to changing short-term judgments of a fluid and uncertain situation. Expansion in scale and extension of the time horizon of enterprise — increases which the corporate form of organization helped make possible — progressively diluted this approximation. As the nineteenth century neared its end, it became harder and harder over broad sectors of the economy to regard the market sanction as operative. Corporate enterprise, in effect, undercut the conditions which made it possible for the market to regulate the exercise of economic power. In the process, the modern business corporation emerged as the first successful institutional claimant of significant unregulated power since the nation-state established its title in the sixteenth and seventeenth centuries.

The response to the new problems of power began to take shape as the century closed. The Sherman Act, passed in 1890, prohibited combinations in restraint of trade, attempts to monopolize and monopolization — that is, certain predatory exercises of economic power. It thus sought to restore the hegemony of the market whence the corporation had already escaped. The Interstate Commerce Act of 1886 put railroads at the head of a steadily lengthening list of industries of which we said, "The market cannot be restored here." Instead, public power was invoked to review businessmen's decisions on prices, schedules, investment.

Ever since, antitrust and public regulation have, broadly speaking, been the characteristic response of American politics, government, and law to the problems posed by the modern corporation. It is not my purpose here to review this experience. It is by no means all of a piece. It certainly would be foolish to deny that both antitrust and public regulation have influenced, and fairly profoundly, the last fifty years of economic development. The most obviously antisocial activities of large-scale economic power have, perhaps, been meliorated. But the general problem that was addressed — the domestication of the private social and economic power derived from the new technology organized in corporate form — this continues unabated.

IV. AN INSTITUTIONAL APPROACH TO CORPORATE POWER

It is instructive to contrast the response of the American political and legal order at the end of the nineteenth century to institutionalized power in its new corporate guise, with that of their ancestors to power in the monarch of the nation-state at the end of the eighteenth century. The founders of the Republic proceeded by analyzing and altering the structure of the institution in which power was vested, the monarchical nation-state. They were not content to prohibit the specific exercise of government power which, in their experience, had been abused by the British king. They concluded that these abuses — or similar ones more or less intense — were implicit in the institutional organization of state power under which they had lived. It was that organization they set out to modify. In consequence, the original Constitution contains few substantive limitations on the sum total of public power. The Bill of Rights added only a few more.

The principal reliance of the Framers for the organization and regularization of state power was an elaborate pattern distributing that power among a wide variety of government organs. They emphasized the representative character of the government they built. They saw the governed not as a homogeneous mass with undifferentiated interests and relations to state power. They saw differences both in the kind and importance of the interests cherished by different constituencies in the body politic. Their achievement can be regarded as a success in identifying those constituencies and, for each, building an organ of government designed to crystallize and reflect its interests and with a "say" — often a power to veto decision — appropriately graduated to its importance.

I would suppose that history's verdict, by and large, confirmed this judgment of the Constitutional Convention that limitations of structure rather than limitations of substance would best secure our liberties. The work of the Framers has proved effective, durable, adaptable. By contrast the nineteenth century ignored the institutional arrangement of corporate power, and concentrated on forbidding specific exercises of economic power which were seen as abuses. It is at least possible that this difference in approach contributed to the difference in the quality of the result.

If we were to seek to reorganize the structure of the corporation so as to assure more responsible exercise of power, what would be the starting point? What is the institutional structure of the modern corporation?

The analogy between state and corporation has been congenial to American lawmakers, legislative and judicial. The shareholders were the electorate, the directors the legislature, enacting general policies and committing them to the officers for execution. A judiciary was unnecessary, since the state had kindly permitted the use of its own. Shareholders and directors each had functions which could not be exercised by the other. The directors managed. Shareholders could not directly affect most business decisions. The prescribed mode of review of directoral decisions was by the ballot. Only when proposed changes reached constitutional dimensions — charter amendment, merger, dissolution — was the shareholder given a direct voice in the decision. Only where a director's conduct was ground for impeachment could the body of shareholders recall its representatives before the appointed term.

This version of the corporation as the Republic in miniature could be applied with tolerable accuracy to the mid-nineteenth-century corporation with a substantial but reckonable body of stockholders, each with a significant stake in and fairly intimate knowledge of the concerns of an enterprise carrying on relatively localized activities. But like the simple conception of representative democracy which it paralleled, it was destined to be left behind by a reality which at once organized activity on an increasingly large scale and fragmented the individual's relation to that activity.

The corporate form was par excellence the form of large-scale enterprise. As scale expanded, the shareholder was less and less the capitalist, risking funds and exercising supervisory authority over a business with whose physical and financial workings he had informed and sophisticated acquaintance. He became an investor, separated in time and understanding, insulated by distance and the proxy machinery from the business activities of the enterprise which used his money. Suffrage was exhausted of reality since it was neither informed nor organized. Despite the forms of electoral control, management became in all but rare instances "an automatic self-perpetuating oligarchy" in Adolph Berle's phrase.[10] The reality of the internal corporate structure had changed from democratic to bureaucratic.

The one explicit legal response in terms of structure to the big corporation has nostalgically striven to reverse this process. It has consisted in efforts, supported by legislation, judicial decision and more than a dash of sloganeering, to restore meaning to the shareholder's vote. Elaborate rules for policing proxy solicitation are administered by the SEC with a view to revitalizing "shareholder democracy." With the parody of the honest vote has come the parody of the election campaign: the proxy contest with its attendant minstrelsy of public-relations counselors, professional solicitors, lawyers, ad-men.[11]

I submit this effort is misconceived. Of course the shareholder — and others interested in corporate doings — should be assured of full information about those doings; and certainly purchasers and holders of corporate securities should have protection against fraud and manipulation by those in control of corporate machinery. It is unreal, however, to rely on the shareholder constituency to keep corporate power responsible by the exercise of franchise.

Quite the reverse. Of all those standing in relation to the large corporation, the shareholder is least subject to its power. Through the mechanism of the security markets, his relation to the corporation is rendered highly abstract and formal, quite limited in scope, and readily reducible to monetary terms. The market affords him a way of breaking this relation that is simple and effective. He can sell his stock, and remove himself, qua shareholder, at least from the power of the corporation.

Shareholder democracy, so-called, is misconceived because the shareholders are not the governed of the corporation whose consent must be sought. If they are, it is only in the most limited sense. Their interests are protected if financial information is made available, fraud and overreaching are prevented, and a market is maintained in which their shares may be sold. A priori, there is no reason for them to have any voice, direct or representational, in the catalogue of corporate decisions with which this paper began, decisions on prices, wages, and investment. They are no more affected than nonshareholding neighbors by these decisions. In fine, they deserve the voiceless position in which the modern development left them.[12]

A concept of the corporation which draws the boundary of "membership" thus narrowly is seriously inadequate. It perpetuates — and presses to a logical extreme — the superficial analogy of the seventeenth century between contributors to a joint stock and members of a guild or citizens of a borough. The error has more than theoretical importance because the line between those who are "inside" and those who are "outside" the corporation is the line between those whom we recognize as entitled to a regularized share in its processes of decision and those who are not.

A more spacious conception of "membership," and one closer to the facts of corporate life, would include all those having a relation of sufficient intimacy with the corporation or subject to its power in a sufficiently specialized way. Their rightful share in decisions on the exercise of corporate power would be exercised through an institutional arrangement appropriately designed to represent the interests of a constituency of members having a significant common relation to the corporation and its power.

It is not always easy to identify such constituencies nor is it always clear what institutional forms are appropriate for recognizing their interests. The effort to answer those questions is among the most meaningful tasks of the American legal system.

The trail is not without its blazes, however. Among the groups now conceived as outside the charmed circle of corporate membership, but which ought to be brought within it, the most important and readily identifiable is its work-force. It is instructive to observe how, almost unconsciously, our legal and political system has worked to give this "constituency" a "say" in the governance of the corporation.

The importance of the workers' constituency was early recognized in American corporation law. Massachusetts and some other states did and still do authorize places on the board of directors to be held by persons elected by employees.[13] Direct worker representation on the managing board, however, has not proved fruitful in this country, although it is being experimented with in a variety of forms by different European nations.

Here, instead, workers have organized their own unions, which, after a painful struggle, won ultimate legal recognition as bargaining representatives for all workers in a designated bargaining unit. This was essentially the structural and institutional invention of the Wagner Act. It said nothing or very little about substantive terms and conditions of employment. It imposed fresh duties and obligations on the corporate employer only insofar as they were deemed necessary to preserve the integrity of the bargaining process. The corporation had to bargain in good faith, for example. It could not discharge or otherwise discriminate against employees for union activity. But as to the content of the bargain, the Act said nothing. That was to be worked out between representatives of two constituencies — management and workers.

The periodic wage negotiation between giant unions and giant companies is the feature of the collective bargaining process of which we are most aware. In these negotiations, the parties are made to appear as hostile antagonists in a kind of legalized class-warfare. But the negotiation of a labor contract can equally, perhaps more fruitfully, be seen as an effort to adjust the relations of both parties so that their common ends may be pursued jointly and they will not needlessly interfere with each other in the pursuit of their separate ends. Thoughtful analysts of labor relations have seen this, and often explicitly have regarded the contract as a legislative enactment to govern the activities of the plant.[14] The bargaining sessions, then, are no more a continuation of war by other means than are the sessions of any other legislative body. Instead, they are an invitation to what Professor Lon Fuller calls "the collaborative articulation of shared purpose." [15]

Union leaders, representing the workers' constituency, have used these lawmaking sessions to harness and regularize corporate power in significant respects. In addition to wage increases, for example, they sought first to secure the jobs of their members against arbitrary discharge. Contracts now generally contain a provision preventing disciplinary action without just cause. The justice of the corporation's cause can, under the contract, be tested before an independent arbitrator, a kind of private judiciary. Thus, the power of the corporation, in its potentially most fearful form, the power to hire and fire, has been by contract subjected to the conditions of rational exercise demanded by the rule of law.

In many other particulars, the power of corporate management to make decisions on the use of its resources — scheduling of production, training and promotion policy, vacations, plant location — has been limited by the necessity to consult with, or even to convince, the representatives of another interested constituency. A revision of the internal distribution of power has gone a long way toward assuring that corporate power, in one large group of its manifestations, will be responsibly exercised. At the same time, private autonomy of decision has been retained.

This does not mean that the growth of strong unions has been free of problems. It may be said that the bargain can too easily become an agreement to pursue joint ends at the expense of unrepresented parties. Such "collusion" has been said to characterize wage negotiations in the "administered price" industries.[16] Again, union members no less than shareholders may need protection against fraud and manipulation by those who are in control of the organizational machinery. In a more fundamental sense, "union democracy" may raise as many difficulties as "shareholder democracy."[17] These problems admitted and given the fullest weight to which they are justly entitled, they do not seriously detract from the force of the conclusion: by any reckoning, the legalization of the bargaining representative must be regarded as a significant piece of institutional invention.

This version of the participation of the workers in the government of the corporation has been developed at length because it is suggestive of a neglected approach to the pervasive problem of corporate power in our society. The work force, as I have said, is self-evidently a constituency of the corporation, requiring representation in its government. We should be sensitive to the emergence of other groups equally entitled to a voice. And we should be imaginatively seeking institutional arrangements appropriate to recording that voice.

That the emergence of the employee constituency is not an isolated phenomenon is suggested by a somewhat analogous development, though on a considerably smaller scale, among automobile dealers. Nominally, they were independent entrepreneurs, trading in the market with the manufacturing companies for their supply of automobiles. In fact, they were satellites, all but impotent before the pervasive exercise of the companies' superior bargaining power. Grievance brought political protest and, eventually, political response in the form of legislation forbidding the cancellation of the dealer's franchise without cause.[18]

Thus far, at least, there has been no rush of aggrieved dealers to the courts. This does not mean that the legislation was either unnecessary or ineffectual. As yet unnoticed is an apparently significant growth of intra-enterprise mechanisms for adjustment of relations with dealers. For example, GM's internal system for "adjudicating" individual dealer grievances has substituted an independent umpire, a retired federal judge, for the former panel of top management. More important, perhaps, General Motors Dealers' Councils, comprised of representatives apparently freely elected by dealers, have replaced earlier Councils hand-picked by management. These new Councils seem to have had some success in articulating and securing recognition of the dealers' position from divisional and company management. At least they seem to excite the dealers more than the prospect of a "day in court" or an independent umpire to review the cancellation of franchises.[19]

The dealer-franchise legislation is too recent and the data too spotty for even a confident preliminary judgment of its effects. But, like the experience with labor legislation, its suggests a more fruitful and complicated interaction between public authority and private response than the positivism of an undiluted regulatory approach. Protection of the dealer at the point of maximum vulnerability to corporate power — against arbitrary cancellation of his franchise — has provided room for the forces of self-organization to begin to work within the dealer constituency to make its voice heard on a wide range of issues affecting dealer interests.

Here is an additional perspective from which to examine proposals for softening the impact of corporate power. For example, it has been suggested with growing frequency that management pension rights should be "vested" so that the organization man *can* take them with him when he leaves for another organization.[20] May it not be, however, that the most important consequence of such legislation would be other than to improve his mobility as between all but identical corporations? May it not instead be to promote self-organization and self-assertion on his part within the corporate community in which he finds himself, tending toward an appropriate voice in the governance of that community?

In an accompanying paper, my colleague, Kingman Brewster, has persuasively advanced the federal analogy as a useful one for testing the relations *among* large companies.[21] The thrust of the present argument suggests that the *internal* structure of the corporation can also be fruitfully seen as a federation of associational groupings.

Perhaps all this proves only that lawyers today are prone to see federalism everywhere as an organizing principle, as, a century ago, their predecessors saw contract. I am well aware that, just here, where it is supposed to prescribe for the ills it has been describing, the mode of this paper has shifted from declarative to interrogatory. Though our problem is elusive, however, we ignore it at our peril. Like societies before us, we will be ill-advised to rely exclusively on the conscience or benevolence of the wielders of power to secure that it be exercised for ends we value. Power in its manifold guises must be submitted to the rule of law: that is, to the governance of reason. To this end, it seems to me, the prescriptive nay-saying side of the law in the past proved ill-adapted and will continue so. The problem of power in its new institutional setting of the corporation is as of old a problem of institutional organization and needs to be met in these terms.

3

TO WHOM AND FOR WHAT ENDS IS
CORPORATE MANAGEMENT RESPONSIBLE?

EUGENE V. ROSTOW

I

The very words "corporate raider" imply a volume of values, all unfavorable.

Who is a "raider," and what is so bad about what he does? In normal financial usage, a "raider" is a man who tries to "seize" or "capture" [1] control of a corporation against the will of its management, by buying up or otherwise mobilizing a working majority of its common stock. The raider may use his own money or credit for the purpose, often in large quantities. Or he may proceed by organizing a "raiding" party of like-minded stockholders, employing all the techniques of political persuasion to attain his goal. He may be a long-time stockholder, restless under the rule of weak management. More often, he is an "outsider," eager to gain the privileges and perquisites of management for himself and his friends — the salaries, expense accounts, chauffeur-driven Cadillacs, stock options, and pension rights; and the attractive patronage, too, which goes with corporate power even more dramatically than with high office of the political variety. The raider may be a corporation in the same field, seeking an advantage in competition, a hedge against tariff change, a foothold in another market. Or the marauder may be a stranger to the line of business, seeking to build up a fashionable "conglomerate" empire, on the unlikely but popular assumption that skill in one kind of work is readily transferable to another. His interest may be in power or in pelf. He may be a freebooter of the most noxious kind, or a serious-minded businessman, bent on canny, prudent, and well-calculated gain.

Whatever the raider's motives may be — and they are diverse

in practice — the raider depends upon the ordinary legal machinery of corporate decision in order to displace the management. Where control of a publicly-held corporation of the familiar kind [2] is at stake, the raider persuades the stockholders for once to act is if they really were stockholders, in the black-letter sense of the term, each with the voice of partial ownership and a partial owner's responsibility for the election of directors. This is the essence of the raider's offense: to attack the established management and to treat the fictional legal structure of the publicly-held endocratic corporation as if it represented reality.

In such circumstances, it is reluctantly conceded that the raider is exercising his historic legal rights as a stockholder in voting for one slate of directors rather than another. It would be agreed with equal reluctance that an investor who seeks out undervalued stock is helping the financial market to fulfill its classic function in guiding the allocation of capital. And it might be acknowledged, too, that the raider who replaces poor management with good is advancing the social cause of effiiciency in the use of resources.

When all these concessions are made, however, the verdict remains clearly adverse: the act of raiding breaches a standard of business propriety with an even stronger claim to the loyalty of respectable opinion. Incumbent management, especially in the great endocratic enterprises, seems to have a half-acknowledged "right" to continue in power until it decides to change itself. This implicit power of managerial self-perpetuation is accepted the more readily when the challenge comes from men who buy stock in a corporation in order to participate in its control.

Raiding is regarded as something more than uncouth: increasingly, it is treated as almost illegal. Is it an accident, for example, that the three most severe cases holding mergers illegal under the antitrust laws all concern attempted raids? [3] Statutes and judicial decisions frown on the purchase of stock for the purpose of exercising what the textbooks treat as one of its most fundamental privileges — that of voting.[4] Even Professor Bayless Manning, Jr., in his recent brilliant review of the problem,[5] seemingly approves an expansion of the doctrine "that shares improperly [6] acquired for fighting purposes only may not be voted." [7]

The development of this view measures an extraordinary paradox. Many of the men who adhere to it most strongly are also and almost equally incensed about the apathy of the average stockholder in endocratic corporations. Many studies confirm the impression that the common stockholder in such companies tends to ignore and subordinate his voting rights, whether he is an individual, an investment trust, a pension fund, or a university.[8] The typical modern shareholder is often a well-informed and well-advised investor, who carefully studies his stocks in the interest of prospective dividends or capital appreciation. But increasingly, he regards the selection of directors as beyond his proper ken. It is difficult to persuade him even to return his proxy favoring the existing management.

It is hard to imagine what canon of the capitalist ethic could be considered violated by the decision of the investor to buy corporate stock in order to vote it. But a powerful current of opinion, representing views widely and deeply held, regards raiding as wrong. Naturally, this view is coloring the older law. The prevailing business code goes well beyond the conventional image of the corporation as an entity "owned" and controlled by its stockholders. That code is having an increasing impact on our corporate mores, and on the law of corporations.

These comments are not meant to imply that corporate raiding is on the whole a Good (or a Bad) Thing. We know that under the indefensible New York decisions it is a procedure absurdly expensive to the enterprise;[9] we know, too, that it is often neutral, or negative, in its effect on the enterprise's business policy. All I do mean to say is that so long as the incumbent management acquires its office by a stockholders' vote, it is in no position to object in principle if others seek to do likewise.

The common attitude of repugnance towards the ethics of corporate raiding is mild, however, when compared with the general distaste for the stockholders' suit. "Strike suit" and "blackmail" are among the kindest words heard in higher business circles to describe the most important procedure the law has yet developed to police the internal affairs of corporations. The stockholders' suit is an imaginative creation, particularly in its American forms, intended to protect the corporation against fraud, overreaching, and other breaches of fiduciary duty on the part of officers and directors. It is true that in this area, as in some others, the law still relies on the seventeenth-century device of the private attorney general, who expects to be paid for his work in exposing and undoing the misdeeds of management. And it is true, also, that the law has always had a strong prejudice against those who stir up litigation, or engage in fights which are not, strictly speaking, "their" business. For these reasons, many rules have developed, some embodied in statutes, denying the right to sue against corporate wrongs to stockholders who acquired that status only for the sake of starting or joining the fray.[10]

The stockholders' suit is not a uniformly effective remedy for the misdeeds of directors — indeed, it is not often an effective remedy for such misdeeds at all. Sporadic in its incidence, costly in its procedures, it has been, from time to time, a vehicle for extortion as well as for purification.

Nonetheless, one would expect those concerned for the integrity and future of private business institutions to applaud the intrepid souls who ferret out corporate wrongdoing, and risk their own time and money against a contingency of being rewarded, if in the end sin is found to have flourished. Not at all. Such men are not treated as honored members of the system of private enterprise, but as its scavengers and pariahs. Their lawyers rarely become presidents of bar associations, or trustees of charitable bodies. They receive no honorary degrees. At best they are viewed as necessary evils, the Robin Hoods of the business world, for whom a patronizing word may sometimes be said, when they succeed in revealing some particularly horrendous act. Even courts and legislatures are unfriendly to stockholders' suits. Many judges dismiss them on any plausible technical ground. Procedural obstacles bristle, and are relentlessly enforced. The substantive doctrines of law, and especially the wide scope given to the directors' "business judgment," make liability infrequent. Both statutes and judge-made law treat as dubious, or worse, the professional stockholders' suit against those who misuse other peoples' money.

II

But are corporate funds "other peoples'" money, so far as the directors are concerned? Or, in the emerging ethos of the second half of the twentieth century, is corporate property really that of the directors and the management, to dispose of, as many suggest, in accordance with their own standards of business foresight, social statesmanship, and generalized good citizenship? The modern endocratic corporation embraces immense pools of capital and skill. Whatever its past, has it become a free collectivity, divorced in its business life from significant public or private control, save the will of the small group which happens to have inherited its management?

It is a pool of property, it is true, held in a vaguely defined trust for vaguely defined economic purposes. In terms of the accepted rules of the game, we should expect society to react, through its courts or legislatures, if the Board of Directors of General Motors began openly to spend corporate funds on a large-scale effort to propagate the doctrines of Social Credit or Buchmanism, to build dog-and-cat hospitals, to send Peace Ships to Archangel, or to restore Williamsburg. So long, however, as corporate property is employed in ways which the directors think will advance the long-term economic interests of the enterprise, broadly defined, does society wish to raise any questions, or allow any questions to be raised by private litigants, about the judgment of the management?

In the twentieth century, the modern corporation has been transformed beyond all recognition. Its ancestors included giants like the East India Company, devices of business and government which gave rise to deep-seated fears. The earlier private companies of the eighteenth and nineteenth century were puny institutions by comparison. Until recent times, corporations received restricted powers from the state. And they were generally viewed by the law and by public opinion with the suspicion which Anglo-American law has always reserved for potentially dangerous accumulations of private power. Their business activities were narrowly confined to certain designated lines of business, firmly written into their legislative charters or, later, into corporate charters granted by public officials. In some states, the absolute amount of property corporations could own was limited by law, well into the twentieth century.[11] A few such limitations survive as curiosities, even today.

All that has been changed, in a series of developments which began around 1880, and have continued without basic modification. Corporate charters are granted routinely, without substantial supervision. They normally confer, or can readily be amended to confer, almost unlimited freedom to engage in any kind of business. The problem of a company acting *ultra vires*, that is, beyond its authorized powers, has almost disappeared as a practical issue in business or law.

The corporation in its familiar form has become an accepted instrument of social policy, — indeed, the chosen instrument of the law for carrying on a large part of the economic life of society.

Corporate directors are endowed with immense discretion. In endocratic corporations, where no stockholders own more than a few percent of the stock, the directors normally control, or come close to controlling, the electoral process from which their powers nominally derive. Where the board of directors consists largely or wholly of corporate employees, dependent upon the president for every step of their future careers, the board is simply a fictional projection of the president himself, whose power is diluted only by the possible presence on his board of bankers, representing creditors' interests, or directors representing important customers, or of an occasional so-called "Public" director.

The directors must, of course, comply with national and state legislation and the rules of securities exchanges, requiring the disclosure of their financial affairs. The antitrust laws, labor legislation, and other laws impose certain patterns of conduct, and define boundaries of power. Consciousness of fiduciary duty, and fear of the stockholders' suit, have genuine influence. And occasionally, the dread figure of the raider may appear.

With these qualifications, the endocratic corporation is an autonomous body politic in a legal order of decentralized power. Its directors do not have quite the degree of freedom from public oversight which the law has afforded to clubs, churches, charitable foundations, universities, and, until recently, to trade unions. And, given our philosophy of property, corporate directors have decidedly less freedom in disposing of corporate property than individuals who happen to possess "private" fortunes. One who has inherited or accumulated even a very large and potentially important estate is considered to have an unchallengeable option about its use, unless he is committed as insane — a risk against which great wealth affords a measure of protection. But it is not a distortion of perspective to view the modern corporation against the background of such institutions, as part of a spectrum of arrangements which the law has developed regarding the ownership and control of property. That spectrum ranges from the relative freedom of individual owners of property, at one extreme, past charities, clubs, ecclesiastical bodies, universities, philanthropic foundations, trade unions, and then business corporations, to the strictly supervised affairs of governmental and semigovernmental corporations, at its other end. Governmental bodies, of course, when duly authorized, can spend funds for any purposes deemed by legislatures to be for "the general welfare."

Viewing the corporation from this vantage point, it is immediately apparent that endocratic business enterprises and huge endocratic trade unions, too, present a problem in genealogy which does not arise in the other cases. The individual may acquire his wealth by economic success, or by devolution, legal procedures of ancient lineage, acknowledged as unquestionably right in the moral universe of the society. The property of churches, universities, clubs, and foundations is accumulated under protective custom, common-law doctrine, or legislation, as the gifts of persons interested in their declared and defined purposes. These bodies corporate are managed with great freedom; but they are managed as trusts, by men selected through established procedures of choice. While it is rare to have the courts review the decisions of such trustees, in order to determine whether they have used trust property for an unauthorized purpose, suits of this kind are not unknown. And finally, of course, the mayors and aldermen, the governors and legislators, and the President and Congress, who handle the funds of governmental corporations and other public bodies, acquire their powers by political election, a source of authority which the society accepts as fully legitimate. But those who control trade-union funds, or the funds of endocratic corporations, often have much cloudier title-deeds to their offices. So far, however, they too have enjoyed wide and undisturbed latitude in the exercise of discretion vested in them by elections which may or may not have been convinc-

ingly authentic. And there is formidable resistance to any proposals for bringing such institutions under closer and more sustained
supervision by the state.

Many decry this state of affairs; others rejoice in it, as an imaginative expression of our genius for pluralism.

III

The critics of managerial autonomy have long preached democracy as the manifest remedy for feudalism: if only stockholders could be more fully informed, protected by better proxy rules,
and given cumulative voting and easier access to stockholders'
lists, they urge, the stockholders' annual meeting would become
a meaningful source of authority for the directors, and a meaningful procedure for reviewing their stewardship.[12]

It is becoming clear that such hopes for corporate "democracy" are bound to be disappointed, in the case of many, perhaps
most of the endocratic enterprises which have become so important a feature of the economic scene. They are not addressed to
prevailing reality. In comparatively few large publicly-held corporations, managerial control is in fact exercised by or for considerable stockholding interests — as in the familiar instances of corporations where Ford, Rockefeller, Mellon, or duPont investments
are dominant. In such companies, practice corresponds to the
legal forms, as it does, by and large, in the case of smaller, closely-
held companies: responsible ownership, using the voting powers
of the common stock, provides a classically legitimate base for
the power of the directorate. But cases of this kind are growing
rarer every year. The estate tax, the antitrust laws, the process of
dilution through growth — these and other forces tend to disperse
large stockholdings formerly held by individuals, groups, or families who were willing to participate in management, or take responsibility for selecting it, in order to protect their investment.
The current prototype, increasingly, is that of a corporation with
stock widely scattered among individuals, investment trusts, or
institutional investors, who faithfully vote for the incumbent
management, and resolutely refuse to participate in its concerns.
In such companies, the stockholders obey the management, not
the management the stockholders. Most stockholders of this class

are interested in their stock only as investments. The prevalence of this view makes it almost hopeless to expect that the electoral process can ever become anything more significant than an empty ritual. The reforms of the Roosevelt era accomplished much, in requiring financial and corporate disclosure and in establishing procedures for enforcing these requirements. But no amount of disclosure can make corporate democracy effective where the corporate vote belongs to weak, scattered individual investors or to institutional investors who cannot or will not take an effective part in the corporate electoral process.

Many believe that the prevailing state of gloom about corporate democracy may have gone too far. After all, they point out, political elections often fall far short of the ideal, both in the motivation of voters, and in the level of discourse at which their franchise is solicited. Shortcomings of this order, if not too widespread, do not gravely impair the usefulness of the institution.[13]

But for the endocratic corporations, the corporate election is frequently not a partial but a total farce. Well-informed investors, analyzing the company's documents, often prefer to sell their stock, despite the tax and other costs of such sales, rather than to engage in lengthy and dubious battles for remedying managerial shortcomings. It is better business for them, they conclude, to shift capital to a profitable company than to conduct a quixotic struggle against the inherently powerful and entrenched position of the management. Thus far, investment trusts, welfare funds, and institutional stockholders have by and large refused to cross the line which in their view divides investment from management.[14] The few exceptions, like the Atlas Corporation, underscore the generality of the rule.

Various proposals have been put forward, intended to make corporate democracy more effective.

Mr. Justice Douglas, while he was a member and later Chairman of the Securities and Exchange Commission, urged the development of a new profession — that of full-time directors. Vigorous and well-paid directors, he thought, purged of all conflicting interests, would provide sustained supervision over the work of management, and protect the interests of those orphans of the business system, the scattered small stockholders, now doomed to impotence in most corporate environments. "The paid director," he wrote, "would revive and strengthen the tradition of trusteeship. His job would not be to represent the management or to represent himself. It would be primarily to represent the stockholder — to return to the stockholder the protection which today's stockholder has too frequently lost." [15] Unfortunately, the Commissioner did not indicate how most corporation presidents could be persuaded to elect, and then to re-elect, directors who would make their lives more difficult, perhaps even actually dangerous, or how paid directors could avoid becoming identified with the management which paid them.

Other critics have urged the formation of Small Stockholders' Protective Committees or Councils, to pool their voting strength, and to obtain representation on boards in behalf of their members.[16] The analogy of the Foreign Bondholders' Protective Council is sometimes invoked, as a private device for encouraging or accomplishing this end.

Some reformers look to salvation through the development of new attitudes by investment trusts and other large fiduciary investors. The astronomic growth of welfare funds, they point out, will soon compel the managers of such portfolios to assume a responsibility for corporate management which they have so far largely shunned.[17] Then we should face a situation to arouse Professor Mills' ire — one group of professional managers supervising another, in an atmosphere, as he would view it, of tacit conspiracy among the members of the Establishment against the rest of us.

Writers like Scott Buchanan go even further.[18] They would accept the *de facto* autonomy which economic and legal history has conferred upon the management of the endocratic corporations, but they would seek to make its internal procedures more democratic. Solutions of this type, like those espoused in earlier periods by syndicalists, cooperators, and Guild Socialists, would seemingly enfranchise not only stockholders, but also workers and perhaps bondholders, who would then determine corporate policy through "republican" forms of government. While Mr. Buchanan's prescriptions are vague, and difficult to isolate, he would apparently hope to cure the present shortcomings of corporate democracy in endocratic corporations by adding new groups of apathetic and disinterested voters to the masses of stockholders who now fail to exercise their franchise intelligently.

Such approaches would deny the possibility of public oversight for endocracies. After all, the endocratic corporation is an institution which deeply affects the public interest in many ways — not only as a potential monopolist or collaborator in monopoly arrangements, but as a reservoir of savings and a combination of men and skills, which for many purposes should be subject to publicly established rules governing the use of money, the modalities of finance, and even the pattern of business policy. General Electric and General Motors are private companies in form. They are also indispensable parts of the national defense establishment. Accepting the autonomy of the endocratic corporation would remit its government more and more completely to groups which have strong financial interests in certain lines of policy. These policies may, or may not, also serve the public interest.

IV

There is, on the other hand, a considerable opinion about modern corporations which welcomes the idea of self-perpetuating management, not genuinely based on the will of substantial stockholders' votes. Men of this persuasion question the relevance of the democratic model to the problem of organizing and conducting a business corporation or, for that matter, a trade union. And they find much to applaud in what they regard as a more civilized concept of corporate responsibility, which they detect emerging as the professional manager supplants the old style owner-manager in one business situation after another.[19] Dean Mason has recently characterized this literature as the "apologetics of managerialism." [20] While there is variety in detail among the prescriptions of those who have contributed to this general view, they share certain attitudes.

First, they believe that something should be done to provide a substitute for or, more often, a supplement to, the fading dream of corporate democracy in the large, publicly-held endocracy. As Professor Berle has said,

Whenever there is a question of power there is a question of legitimacy. As things stand now, these instrumentalities of tremendous power have the slenderest claim of legitimacy. This is probably a transitory period. They must find some claim of legitimacy, which also means finding a field of responsibility and a field of accountability. Legitimacy, responsibility and accountability are essential to any power system if it is to endure. They correspond to a deep human instinct. A man desires beyond anything else to have someone give him the accolade of "Well done, thou good and faithful servant," thereby risking the condemnation of "You have been no good — get out." If he has to say it to himself, or hear it from a string of people whom he himself has hired or controls, he is apt to die a cynical and embittered man.[21]

But no member of this school of thought would accept the proposals of the British Labour Party, that the government purchase shares of such companies, to achieve both legitimacy and accountability through socialism. Nor would many of them view with favor the postwar German practice of having workers' representatives on boards of directors, which Mr. Scott Buchanan seems to have had in mind in his recent pamphlet on the subject.[22] Most such reformers seem to be groping for a private device, or a device of state law rather than of federal law, which could give the managers a more tangible source of authority than the accident of their own possession of the seats of power, and a more serious and official procedure of accountability than the empty histrionics of the usual annual meeting.

Professor Manning has sketched the outlines of an idea which has intriguing implications and merits further exploration.[23] His suggestion is addressed primarily to the issue of accountability, rather than to the problem of providing corporate boards with a more tangible mandate. His article proposes to consider the large, publicly-held corporation as if it were in law what it often is in fact, a kind of voting trust, where the stockholder delegates all his rights save that of collecting his dividend to the directors — that is, to the management. Viewing the corporation in the light of this theory of itself, he points out, immediately brings certain problems into the foreground, and indicates certain possibilities for remedial action. In order to establish more effective procedures for visitation and control, he has in mind the development of a new device, public or private, which could carry out certain functions presently neglected, or relatively neglected. He seems to visualize this device as preferably private, and as a kind of "second chamber," distinct from the board of directors, and with more limited powers. This "extrinsic" body would presumably review decisions of the board where conflicts of interest arise, particularly with regard to the compensation of officers; it could also pass on other board and managerial decisions, notably where corporate funds are spent for charitable contributions not directly related to the company's business. It might well have broader powers, in enforcing a full disclosure of the corporation's financial and business affairs, for example. In a corporate world organized in this way, the stockholder would hold in effect certificates in a voting trust. He would "own" his stock, and not the equity of the corporation, save for such problems as the determination of creditors' rights, where Professor Manning would not alter the existing law of contractual priority.

Professor Manning's proposal is in its preliminary stages, and it is not now without ambiguities. He seems, for example, to contemplate the continuance of the present stockholder voting machinery, and even the occasional catharsis of a good proxy fight.[24]

This original line of thought might well offer much to protect the corporation, in that important group of cases where stockholders as a class are unable to function in accordance with the expectations of legal theory. The development of the idea might be most fruitful if it clearly separated the directors' function from that of monitoring their work, and provided a device which excluded management from any role in the selection of the "Second Chamber" — perhaps by delegation to a trustee under an indenture.

Professor Manning's proposal does not solve the problem of managerial legitimacy in large endocratic enterprises, as he frankly recognizes:

"Although the proxy system of electing directors is largely an engine of, rather than for, management control, someone has to select directors, and there would be no advantage in permitting them overtly to choose their own successors." [25]

Perhaps we can do no better, in a system of private property, where the claimants to the residual equity insist on delegating their interests to the managers. One can, however, visualize more constructive solutions. Building on a long if checkered experience with corporate trustees under bondholders' indentures, could we not consider requiring the issuance of stock in endocratic corporations in a form which gave small stockholders the option of delegating their voting rights to a trustee, who would act for them more effectively than they can ever hope to act for themselves?

v

In reviewing the literature about the current development of endocratic corporations, and about possible programs for their reform, one is struck by the atmosphere of relative peace. There seems to be no general conviction abroad that reform is needed. The vehement feelings of the early thirties, expressing a sense of betrayal and frustration at a depression blamed on twelve years of business leadership, are almost entirely absent. Ideas for reforming endocracy are not supported by anything like the sense of purpose which sustains the antitrust laws and the income tax.

I suspect that enlightened lay opinion could be summarized in these terms: "Yes, there are paradoxes and anomalies in the way boards of directors are elected in some large, publicly-held companies. But what of it? There are irrational moments in most of our legal arrangements, some more illogical than this one. The disclosure requirements of the Securities Act and the Securities Exchange Act do a lot of good. And most boards of directors are not so bad. Business seems energetic. There's a good deal of competition — not enough, but still a good deal. Corporate executives are overpaid, but the income tax must take quite a lot of their excessive salaries. All in all, the system may be illogical, but it works. And besides, any serious reform would have to bring government agencies more directly into the internal affairs of corporations, and that would be worse."

So long as the problem of corporate responsibility is viewed in this pragmatic light, change will come only from within the system, in response to moves which corporate management may consider prudential and protective in the long run. Many such moves have characterized the development of the corporation during the postwar period, most notably the spread of the idea of "public directors," [26] and the flowering of the view that the primary duty of the corporation is not to make as much money as possible for its stockholders, but to advance the public interest in some alternative sense.[27]

Many have proclaimed this doctrine as the dawn of a better day, in which the outworn maxims of Adam Smith have yielded at last to the higher virtue of responsible citizenship. Corporations have "souls" and "consciences," we are told. They no longer take a "narrow," "selfish" view of policy, but what passes for a more statesmanlike attitude towards their problems.

It is difficult to give any palpable meaning to these ideas. Mr. Frank Abrams, Chairman of the Board of the Standard Oil Company of New Jersey, has said that the managers of his company conduct its affairs "in such a way as to maintain an equitable and working balance among the claims of the various directly interested groups — stockholders, employees, customers, and the public at large." [28] In urging his proposal for paid directors, Mr. Justice Douglas said, while Chairman of the Securities and Exchange Commission,

Today it is generally recognized that all corporations possess an element of public interest. A corporation director must think not only of the stockholder but also of the laborer, the supplier, the purchaser, and the ultimate consumer. Our economy is but a chain which can be no stronger than any one of its links. We all stand together or fall together in our highly industrialized society of today. One function of the paid director would be to harmonize those various elements so far as possible. For, although those elements may superficially appear to conflict, the fundamental interests of all social groups are identical over the long term. The corporate officer frequently recognizes these principles; but he is so close to his work that it is hard for him to look beyond its immediate necessities. But the paid director need not be afflicted with such nearsightedness. It would indeed be one of the defects which he would be paid *not* to have.[29]

Others, welcoming statements of this kind in the speeches of corporate presidents, have cheered the birth of a more benign stage in the evolution of capitalism. They observe great companies making gifts for scholarships,[30] establishing welfare procedures, and participating in community affairs. The image of the corporation has changed. It is no longer symbolized by a grim and energetic tyrant, single-mindedly driving his staff on to new feats of money-making. Today the presidents of endocratic corporations wear buttoned-down striped shirts, not stiff collars; tweed jackets and flannels, rather than formal three-piece suits; wrist watches, not great gold repeaters at the end of heavy gold chains. In the public mind and in fact, the great corporation is more often than not a friendly committee of smiling bureaucrats, cheerfully sharing the burdens of the world around them.

Responding to these changes in atmosphere, public opinion has become far more tolerant of Big Business. In England, socialists say that the managers have already socialized capitalism, so that it is no longer necessary to invoke the cumbersome formality of public ownership of the means of production.[31] Besides, they note, the Russians are having lots of trouble conducting a system of unified control, and are moving to decentralize the direction of their business: that is, to give their managers something like the degree of free-floating autonomy the managers of great American and British endocracies already enjoy. The diseconomies of excessive scale are quite apparent, both in business and government. All over the world, the movement to decentralize is gaining momentum, as men seek to avoid being strangled by Parkinson's famous Law. The political consequences of the new model capitalism-with-a-social-conscience begin to emerge very sharply.

A classic debate on the question was conducted by Professor Berle and Professor Dodd almost thirty years ago, and Professor Berle has now concluded that Professor Dodd was right in the first place.[32] As is the case in many debates, the theses of the protagonists turn out on inspection to be quite compatible. Professor Berle starts with the proposition that all corporate powers are powers in trust, "necessarily and at all times exercisable only for the ratable benefit of all the stockholders as their interest appears." [33] In the light of this premise, he makes illuminating comments on a number of controversial issues of corporate law and practice. Professor Dodd agrees that corporate powers are powers in trust, to be sure. But the use of private property, he urges, is deeply affected with a public interest, and the development of public opinion is more and more acutely conscious of that fact. Recognition of the public interest in the use of corporate property, Professor Dodd contends, requires that directors be viewed as trustees for the enterprise as a whole — for the corporation viewed as an institution — and not merely as "attorneys for the stockholders." [34] To this Professor Berle replied by agreeing that the use of private property, notably in the case of large corporations, was indeed a matter of the highest public importance. But, he said, "I submit that you can not abandon emphasis on the view that business corporations exist for the sole purpose of making profits for their stockholders until such time as you are prepared to offer a clear and reasonably enforceable scheme of responsibilities to someone else." [35] We have no such directing rule. In its absence, the consequence of Professor Dodd's argument would be to remit the control of corporations, and the orientation of their policies, entirely to the management. The older rule, Professor Berle contended, offers the only chance of ordering business affairs in ways which would minimize managerial overreaching and self-seeking. With this position Professor Dodd then agreed, although he felt that the rule had lost all contact with reality, and with public aspiration.

> Profit-making for absentee owners must be the legal standard by which we measure their conduct until some other legal standard has been evolved. Granted — with some reservations that this is all that the law can do at present, the question remains as to how effectively it can do that. If trusteeship for absentee investors, in addition to being an ideal having little emotional appeal to managers, is an ideal that is losing ground in the community generally and if the signs are multiplying that our economic order is evolving away from it, the prospect of its effective enforcement as an interim legal rule of conduct is not encouraging. Abandon it, as yet, we dare not — enforce it with more than moderate success, it is to be feared we cannot.[36]

In 1954, Professor Berle accepted Professor Dodd's initial position, apparently because he concludes that the directors of endocratic corporations, as keepers of the public conscience, can now be safely trusted to exercise their vast powers in the public interest, without the safeguard of either stockholder control or effective public supervision.[37]

What content, if any, is there in the notion of directors' obligation first propounded by Professor Dodd, and now accepted by Professor Berle?

From the point of view of legal and economic orthodoxy, the New Capitalism is all bewildering balderdash. The law books have always said that the board of directors owes a single-minded duty of unswerving loyalty to the stockholders, and only to the stockholders. The economist has demonstrated with all the apparent precision of plane geometry and the calculus that the quest for maximum revenue in a competitive market leads to a system of prices, and an allocation of resources and rewards, superior to any alternative, in its contributions to the economic welfare of the community as a whole. To the orthodox mind, it is therefore unsettling, to say the least, to have the respected head of the Standard Oil Company of New Jersey equating the management's duty to stockholders with its obligation to employees, customers, suppliers, and the public at large.

The stubborn relics of an analytical tradition have difficulty translating the soothing formulas of managerialism into terms they can understand. And perhaps the task is impossible. In sectors of the economy more or less effectively insulated from direct dependence upon market pressures, as the economists have long known, the negotiated solutions of multilateral oligopoly, or even of bilateral monopoly, are neither so uniform nor so predictable as those of the straightforward competitive model. In such situations, it has been customary to conclude, there is no equilibrium position towards which the market tends to move, but rather a zone of possible solutions within which ignorance, accident, or other bargaining factors yield an oscillating and unstable result, explicable only in the tenuous terms of game theory.

Accepting this reservation, however, what does the "new" concept of corporate responsibility imply? Does it mean that the management of a great corporation should not bargain very hard in negotiations over wages or the prices paid to suppliers? Does it mean that a statesman-like and well-run company should charge less for its product than the market would bear, less than the prices which would maximize its short-term revenues, or what it conceives to be its long-term profits? Should it regard its residual profits, not as "belonging to" its stockholders in some ultimate sense, but as a pool of funds to be devoted in considerable part to the public interest, as the directors conceive it — to hospitals, parks, and charities in the neighborhood of its plants; to the local symphony or the art museum; to scholarships for the children of employees, or to other forms of support for the educational system of the nation at large? If what is good for the country is good for General Motors, as is indeed the case, does this view of managerial responsibility set any limit upon the directors' discretion in spending corporate funds for what they decide is the public good?

If the rhetoric of managerialism is properly interpreted in this way, two general classes of difficulties are immediately apparent, one economic, the other legal and political. The new corporate morality may result in prices and wages which sabotage the market mechanism and systematically distort the allocation of resources. Such pricing practices would make the task of monetary and fiscal authority in controlling general fluctuations of trade more expensive and more difficult, and could well make it impossible to sustain high levels of employment save at the cost of considerable price inflation. Secondly, the new theory of corporate responsibility may produce patterns of corporate expenditure which could disturb the present equilibrium of opinion about corporations, and invite public restrictions on the present freedom of corporate management.

If, as is widely thought, the essence of corporate statemanship is to seek less than maximum profits, postwar experience is eloquent evidence that such statesmanship leads to serious malfunctioning of the economy as a whole. In recent years, many industries having some degree of power over the prices they charge have tended for a variety of reasons to charge less, in all probability, than the market would bear in the short run. Prudence and a bias in favor of long-run price stability; the twin mottoes of "wait-and-see" and "live-and-let-live"; a concern for the firm's relations with government, labor, and the public; a fear of new entrants and of "excess" capacity — all these combine to persuade the firm and the industry that the upward movement is temporary, that demand is weaker than it is, that it would be better, on the whole, to pursue a cautious line than to risk being wrong about the new shape of the schedule of demand.[38]

Many economists and public officials have praised the great companies in markets of the few for their statesmanship in keeping prices low, or raising them relatively slowly, during periods of recovery. Indeed, President Eisenhower has preached this doctrine to both business and labor as their highest social duty.[39]

Viewed against the background of the flow of national income as a whole, a policy of profit abstinence seems neither tenable for extended periods, nor sound, especially during a recovery period of rising total spending.

The first consequence of such moderation in pricing is that demand is unusually high for the product of such industries, but prices rise less than in others. Relatively low profits are earned. The pressure of rising demand is diverted to other sectors of the economy, where prices and profits rise more rapidly. Thus capital is attracted to areas which would have claimed less if the market mechanism had been more accurate in measuring the comparative intensity of consumers' desires for different products. On the other hand, since demand for the product is high, public policy may intervene, as it has through accelerated depreciation and other policies, to subsidize expansions of capacity within existing firms despite their relatively low profits. Big firms having great advantages in any event in their access both to long- and short-term capital, may be able to finance expansion without subsidy, despite their relatively low profits during such periods. The result, as is perhaps the case now in the steel industry, may be the paradox of low profits and capacity which is genuinely, if temporarily, excessive in the real sense — that is, excessive at competitive prices, even at full employment levels of demand.

This kind of policy, in either of its aspects, records a failure of the market as the chief instrument for guiding the allocation of capital and labor. If long continued, policies of self-restraint may result in a serious distortion in the pattern of resource use. The classic example of French rent control represents an extreme case of this phenomenon. Rents in France have until very recently been frozen at their World War I levels. The result is that tenants pay less rent for their Paris apartments than they do for cigarettes. Leases, of course, are sold, at high prices. But landlords have no incentive to build new apartment houses, and the housing situation, after forty years, is almost insoluble, save through public action.

I do not suggest that we have yet reached this point in the great oligopoly industries which have been so widely applauded for price moderation during the postwar inflationary boom. But the phenomenon has been visible, in varying degrees, signaled by the appearance of occasional "gray" markets for certain key products. And it has been a major barrier to the possibility of entry by new firms, since the earnings of existing capital resources have often been lower than the return to be anticipated, at prevailing prices, on investment in totally new capacity.

One of the consequences of so-called moderate price policies has been to delay and prolong the process of adjustment to episodes of inflation — that is, to periods when demand is excessive in relation to full employment supply. During such periods, competition for scarce resources bids up prices, as businessmen persist in optimistic views about the future of demand, price and profit in their bailiwicks. Prices of raw material rise, inventories are accumulated, and wages of junior executives, foremen, and good machinists are pushed up by the offers of unusually efficient, productive, well-located, or optimistic firms. The entire economy must adapt its system of notations to the impact of such changes in the marginal product of work, the norm around which the general wage structure is crystallized. Price moderation, like other lags in the process of market adjustment, prolongs the agony. Long, slow-rolling movements of prices and wages have characterized the response of the economy to the pressure of such inflation-induced changes in the general wage level. The length of time required for these adjustments explains the apparent anomaly of costs and prices rising slowly during the early part of a recession, as they did in 1957 and 1958.

Of course even the latter-day policies favoring price stability in markets of the few cannot indefinitely postpone action to keep even short-run profit at a maximum. Pessimistic views about the nature of demand schedules do not usually survive for long. It is difficult for a firm, or even for an industry, to buck the tide. The result is that companies in this position take every opportune excuse, such as a labor negotiation, to raise their prices, and catch themselves up to a position which gives them as much as they could earn in their market. Guided by experts in public relations, the companies make matters worse by trying to blame others for their own mistakes of price policy.

The standards of corporate statesmanship so far announced do not, however, supply a price theory which could supplant the traditional lore of economics. I certainly do not object to corporate management which takes a civilized and democratic interest in the morale of its employees, treats them with dignity and respect, and deals with them as equals, through collective bargaining procedures and otherwise. Nor do I oppose trade-union leadership which is willing to acknowledge the common humanity of management. But the basic service for which society looks to business and labor is the production of goods and services at the lowest possible cost, and at prices which measure the comparative pressure of consumers' choices. This is a hard and demanding task. The literature of "managerialism," from Commons and Veblen to Drucker, Burnham, and Berle, suggests no criteria to replace the standards for judging the propriety of wages and prices which the economists have painfully developed during the last century or so.

We have tended to misconstrue the fascinating sociology of the modern endocratic corporation, with its divorce of ownership and management, and its hierarchical features. There is a rich literature which describes corporations and trade unions as institutional entities. These studies have much to contribute to our understanding of the dynamics of economic life. But studies of social and human relations, however valid, do not provide a substitute for the competitive norm in defining an acceptable social goal for the process of price-making. Indeed, the literature of managerialism has not so far squarely faced the issue. I doubt very much whether it can produce a standard for "fair pricing" which expresses the idea of efficiency in the use of resources otherwise than in the familiar guise of the concept of competitive equilibrium. It is an ironic comment on the problem that many of the younger socialist economists, especially in England, propose procedures for pricing under socialism which would in fact achieve the classic purposes of competition, both in distributing goods, and in determining which branches of the economy should expand or contract. Their effort comes perilously close to the thought that the first task of a socialist society should be to restore competitive markets — the traditional hallmark of capitalism, and its most characteristic institutional ideal.

The political and legal aspects of corporate statesmanship present vistas which are quite as disturbing as its economics. The endocratic corporations are accepted as powerful and effective instruments for carrying on the business of society. If their directors begin to act as if they really were general trustees for the public at large, they may well imperil their present freedom. Corporations are not accepted in public opinion as institutions through which society makes its educational policy, its foreign policy, or its political policy. Programs which would give reality to the idea of spending corporate funds to advance the general welfare, as the directors visualize it, will sooner or later invite the critical attention of legislators, governors, and presidents, who consider that they have been elected by the people to advance the general welfare, and know more about it than the directors of endocratic corporations. As Professor Ben W. Lewis has recently said, commenting on the thesis that "the corporation, almost against its will, has been compelled to assume in appreciable part the role of conscience-carrier of twentieth century American society":

> It is not going to happen; if it did happen it would not work; and if it did work it would still be intolerable to free men. I am willing to dream, perhaps selfishly, of a society of selfless men. Certainly, if those who direct our corporate concentrates are to be free from regulation either by competition or government, I can only hope that they will be conscientious, responsible, and kindly men; and I am prepared to be grateful if this proves to be the case. But, I shall still be uneasy and a little ashamed, with others who are ashamed, to be living my economic life within the limits set by the gracious bounty of the precious few. If we are to have rulers, let them be men of good will; but above all, let us join in choosing our rulers — and in ruling them.[40]

The responsibility of corporate directors requires redefinition. It may give us a warm and comfortable feeling to say that the director is a trustee for the community, rather than for his stockholders; that he is a semipublic official, or a quasi-public official, or some other kind of hyphenated public officer. It would be more constructive, however, to seek redefinition in another sense: to restate the law of corporate trusteeship in terms which take full account of the social advances of this century, but which direct the directors more sharply to concentrate their efforts on discharging their historic economic duties to their stockholders. The economic job of directors and management is quite difficult enough to absorb the full time of first-rate minds, in an economy of changing technology, significant general instability, and considerable competition, both from rival firms in the same industry and from those which steadily offer rival products.

Similarly, watching the investment of trade-union funds in a variety of banks and other business enterprises, one wonders whether the public interest is really served by their present freedom. Is it sound public policy to allow unions to accumulate funds not required by their primary needs, and to invest those funds at will, in ways which often lead to grave conflicts of interest?

VI

Would such a redefinition of goals for large endocratic business units and trade unions serve any useful purpose? How could such rules be enforced? Could they have any impact on the flow of events? Is "the long-run economic interest of stockholders" any more meaningful, as a standard to guide the deliberation of directors, or the decisions of courts or other public bodies reviewing what the directors have done, than "the interests of the enterprise as a whole," or "the interests of the community"? Such a "rule" would comfort the few remaining adherents of the older orthodoxy. What else would it accomplish?

The Dodd–Berle exchange and its sequels are strongly colored by economic and social views popular during the NRA era, when the trend toward "planning" was viewed as necessarily involving something close to the direct control of business enterprises by the state. The climate of opinion has been greatly altered by thought and experience since that time. Another view of the relation of the government to the economy has become ascendant. This theory of "planning" contemplates government control of the level of employment, through fiscal and monetary policy, which could provide a favoring environment for the effective functioning of comparatively free and competitive markets for goods and of comparatively free markets for labor.[41] The controversy over managerial responsibility should be viewed in this context, which significantly alters perspective.

In this setting, does the debate over competing "rules," exemplified in the Berle–Dodd exchange, and the subsequent literature, have any substance? Save in the area of managerial salaries, options, and pension plans, and perhaps that of charitable contributions, is endocratic Big Business really doing anything which the directors could not justly claim was in the best long-term interests of stockholders? The conduct of pricing policies is more a matter of antitrust enforcement than of alternative doctrines of managerial discretion. So long as enterprises are not subjected to the pressure of effective market competition, they will have considerable discretion as to the prices they charge, and will be tempted, in perfect good faith, to make plausible "mistakes" in resource allocation. If they do function in the matrix of effective competition, their opportunity to pursue price policies of "philanthropy" or "public welfare" rather than of "profit seeking" will be correspondingly reduced. The conduct of labor relations, again, is more directly a function of the law and economics of the labor market than of rival philosophies of corporate management.

The function of rules of law is both descriptive and normative. Such rules reflect the pattern of accepted behavior and the standards which the community seeks to have upheld in the daily conduct of business affairs. They are at best hypotheses, articulated to guide and explain the wayward course of events. As an abstract statement of the social duty of business enterprise in the middle of the twentieth century, I believe the "rule" I have suggested — that of long-term profit maximization — conforms more concretely than any alternative both to the image of preferred reality for business behavior in public opinion, at this state in the evolution of our legal and economic order, and to the ends business enterprise is expected to fulfill as part of the nation's system of law for governing the economy.

But how can such policies be enforced? Are the votes of stockholders, or of some agent for stockholders in endocratic corporations, such as the optional voting trustee suggested earlier, a better guide to the long-term economic interests of stockholders than the business judgment of directors? Are minority stockholders' suits, even if brought by a public officer in the name of the inherent visitorial powers of the state, a suitable or sufficient remedy? Such devices, backed by strong policies of required disclosure, may help curb overreaching, the wrongful taking of corporate opportunity, excessive managerial compensation, trading on inside information, and other abuses. Professor Manning's "second chamber" is a provocative thought which deserves extended consideration in this connection. It can hardly be assumed, however, that any of these procedures, or all of them in combination, would provide a better basis than the directors' judgment for determining the long-term *economic* interest of the stockholders.

The voting of active stockholders, or, in the case of endocratic corporations, voting by an independent trustee for stockholders, would have one advantage over the present rule of untrammeled managerial discretion: it would provide a less dubious base for the authority of directors and officers of great enterprises, now almost cut off from their source of power.

On the other hand, a clear acceptance of profit maximization as a legal principle might well do something, perhaps a good deal, to order the pattern of corporate policy. Legal rules are not always fully self-enforcing, of course. But they do exert an influence, even though procedures of enforcement are not comprehensive. Adequate means for surveillance and accounting can and should be developed, to minimize abuses of corporate power. The more important problem, however, is the orientation of legitimate business policy: should it be essentially economic in purpose, or should it become an ambiguous amalgam of economic and noneconomic themes? I, for one, conclude that a clear-cut economic directive should help directors to discriminate more effectively among competing claims upon them, in carrying out their public trusteeship for the economic system as a whole.

4

THE CORPORATION AND ECONOMIC FEDERALISM

KINGMAN BREWSTER, JR.

The political interpretation of economic institutions seems to be taking its place alongside the mellowing economic interpretation of politics.[1] Both can easily be overdone. When the focus is on corporate power, the temptation to political tub-thumping is spurred by deep populist roots of antipathy to private economic power.[2] Phrases like "private government" which were a past generation's metaphor are legitimate tools for the analysis of today's reality. Concepts of an economic market are no longer adequate to describe the "constituency" "governed" by the modern large business firm. At the risk of overplaying political analogy, this paper seeks to explore some of the economic as well as non-economic dimensions of corporate power in terms of values more generally associated with the allocation of political power.

The affirmation that only the people are sovereign, and that government is legitimate only when it is the explicit delegate of that sovereignty, has a peculiar reality for Americans, whose government was a conscious constitutional creation on a slate wiped clean by revolution. We are bound to become increasingly uncomfortable when we contemplate the modern corporation as a power with many of the trappings of sovereignty.

There is small practical consolation in the historical fact that corporations did originally derive their being from legitimate government — were in fact recipients of a limited delegation of public powers, for limited public purposes. For in practice the ability to incorporate is a right, not a privilege; not limited in purpose, not readily made forfeit. And "shareholder democracy" is no consolation either; in part because it does not exist,[3] partly because the modern corporation "governs" a constituency whose interests are different from, and often at odds with, ownership. Nor is the "countervailing power" of organized workers much solace to the corporation's other constituents: the customers, the suppliers, the competitors. If price is a tax which brooks no evasion. the rates are no more palatable because they must pay off both the original and the countervailing powers.[4]

Since corporate power seems to defy traditional external check and balance, it is not surprising that the holders of the power and its victims alike should increasingly be tempted to find comfort in the discovery that even corporations have a "conscience"[5] — they may even have a "soul"![6] If there cannot be a rule of law, it is tempting to seek consolation in the hope that you can have good government if you have good governors. The classic response would be that benevolence cannot in the long run ever be a satisfactory justification for despotism. But to cast the problem of the modern corporation in terms of wickedness is to obscure it. Egregious abuse can be brought to book even by the law's ancient crude standards of evil conduct and malevolent intent. And it is probably true that even if the flamboyant claims of hucksterism are discounted, corporate self-consciousness can be counted on to afford at least a tolerable decency; especially if prodded from time to time by jawbone regulation, legislative investigation, and organized critical opinion. However, even if corporate power is shorn of the tendencies inherent in all power, it is neither corrupt nor absolute, there are both economic and social values and expectations which may be jeopardized by a concentration of power. The central question is how power that is necessary can be made as tolerable as possible. This question finds its measure not only in terms of welfare economics but also in terms of other values. Freedom for self-determined self-fulfillment is vastly more fundamental than mere protection against exploitative abuse.

The economic expectations associated with a dispersion of competing power centers are well understood: quasi-automatic allocation of resources according to popular priorities, and the spur to progressiveness through hope of gain and fear of loss. Perhaps most important of all the virtues of a dispersed political economy was that the painful process of sloughing off the obsolete and the inefficient was accomplished with an impersonality and fairness which prevented resentment from either festering into upheaval or obtaining payoff in unjustified protection or wasteful support.

Now that technological and economic factors seem to make corporate power inevitable, there is much constructive effort to demonstrate that the *economic* objectives of competition can be achieved even if many firms (or industrial constellations of firms presenting a common front out of mutual self-interest) have in fact achieved an indispensability to those from whom they buy or to whom they sell. The countervailing power of large buyers [7] or the competition of substitute products may still be a spur to productivity.[8] Law might itself add to the spur by having legality turn in part on good performance.[9] Or law might still achieve a measure of deconcentration without imperiling the capacity to be efficient.[10] Exhortations to "industrial statesmanship" might be given legal significance if the government enjoyed unbridled discretion to intervene whenever the "public interest" was outraged by sins of corporate commission or omission.[11]

There is some validity to all these approaches. Business decisions are subject to a host of pressures beyond the mere number of rivals in any given product line. But the less perfect the substitutes the less perfect the competition.[12] The more powerful the power that countervaileth, the more likely that it will pocket rather than pass on the profits it bargains away from its supplier across the table.[13] Legal ingenuity probably could devise instruments for a more effective deconcentration policy without impairing efficiency.[14] But the closer you get to making power itself illegal, the more uneasy is the law's concern for values of administrative fairness and feasibility.[15] Even without creating a single, plenary, discretionary, jurisdiction to regulate or intervene in business affairs, the "public interest" does make itself felt in the desire of every firm to avoid being made a political whipping boy. But the political whip is too often a tool of a demagogic ambition rather than a rational instrument of the public interest. The fact that these "controls" are haphazard is not out of keeping with our tradition. The trouble with them is that, even taken together, there is wonder whether they are adequate even for the purely economic job of assuring competitive performance in the absence of competitive conditions.

It may be that the modern corporation can be allowed to wax even more powerful and still be counted on to do a productive job of a high order. However, the social expectations, more correctly the political expectations, associated with a dispersion of economic power have a significance of their own. Pluralism has its claim quite apart from economic performance. The widespread sense of personal choice and lack of dependence, the widespread feeling that success is related to effort, remain important even if welfare is assured. Indeed, the more "affluent" the society, the greater the relative importance of the fact and the feeling that opportunity is not dependent on the benevolence of others. Captivity without escape, exclusion without redress, are evils in themselves. If corporate power is to be tolerated in the name of economic necessity, it must be made as tolerable as possible in terms of the noneconomic values of an open and mobile society.

Professor Berle opened up new perspectives upon the vindication of political and social values in the context of the political power of the modern corporation. He has drawn heavily and imaginatively upon the King's Conscience and the rise of equity for analogy.[16] I rather prefer an earlier suggestion of his, directing attention to some of the lessons of federalism.[17]

The virtue of leaving considerable economic power in private hands is not too dissimilar from the virtue of leaving considerable political power in the several states of a federation. In the negative sense both reject centralism because of the bureaucratic overload at best, the political and moral overload at worst, which total accountability to central authority portends. More important, both the exponents of states' rights and those who would leave economic power in private hands are affirming that more socially constructive energies will be released in the long run if problems can be attacked by and left to the final decision of those living closest to them. Even if they are problems which the subsovereigns have in common, the more experimentation the better. There may be more error through independent trial. But in the long run, more success whose lesson is available to all will be generated by leaving play for diverse solutions to comparable problems.[18]

So much for the common perspective which an approach to the problem of corporate power shares with the approach to the problem of the sovereignty of states within the State. However, so much is really no more than excuse for tolerating the corporation's "sovereignty" for the simple reason that gathering it under central control would be worse. More significant for our dilemma would be anything in the organization of federated pluralism which throws light on the appropriate limitations on corporate power once it is decided that corporations are to remain private even though they are powerful. Analogy is dangerous. As Whitehead once pointed out, the very fact that it is analogy means there is a difference, and perhaps the difference is more important than the similarity. However, if the corporation is to be viewed in political perspective, political analogue may serve to suggest lines of further constructive thought and inquiry.

At least three attributes of workable federalism may be brought to bear on the modern corporation. One is the assurance that some power exists outside the constituent state to vindicate minimal standards of fair and equal treatment of citizens and residents and strangers. Another is the insistence that there be no serious barriers to the coming and going of people among the several states. A third is the insistence that capital and goods be free to move into and out of a state.

Subjecting "corporate sovereignty" to a "Fourteenth Amendment" is the essence of the Berle prescription.[19] Such analogy poses verbal problems, to say the least. Corporations do not have residents or citizens, unless it can be said that those under contract of ownership or employment are "citizens," those under commercial contracts, "residents." But despite such verbal awkwardness, the Berle thesis is, if anything, understated. The urge to protect competitors or suppliers or buyers who are satellites of a corporate "concentrate" (Berle's word) is the nub of most of the laws which, although called antitrust laws, are at odds with the competitive policy. The Robinson-Patman Act's prohibition of discrimination in price or service is the most crucial symbol of such legislation.[20] That Act defies economic rationalization precisely because it is motivated by an "equal protection" spirit, not the rationale of competitive economics. It affirms that if the economic ability to discriminate unreasonably is to be tolerated, then the exercise of such power must be directly regulated. To borrow the constitutional lingo, the classification must be reasonable, else the difference in treatment must fall. Parenthetically it might be suggested that frank acceptance of the noneconomic motivation of the Robinson-Patman Act might do much to facilitate the cure of its anachronisms, by confining its application to situations of unreasonable economic power and articulating its classifications of the justified and the unjustified discrimination in more comprehensible terms. Seeing it as a politically motivated response to the unenforceability of competition rather than as an instrument of the competitive policy might make it better understood, administered, and complied with.

The recent automotive-dealer franchise legislation [21] comes closest to bearing out the Berle "due process" prescription for corporate accountability. No doubt arming a dealer with the power of legal complaint if his franchise is terminated without cause flies in the face of competition's traditional reliance on freedom of customer selection and rejection.[22] But if the laws designed to enforce competition cannot prevent centers of dependence, if bargain has to such an extent given way to ultimatum, then other avenues of redress will be found. Maybe "equal protection" considerations will one day become the explicit policy basis of more rigorous insistence that the vertically integrated firm cannot favor itself against those who compete with it at one stage and deal with it at another. Such was part of the objection to A & P's insistence on discounts not available to competitors [23] and the rationale of the case which forbade Eastman Kodak to cut off an old distributor when it decided to go into distribution for itself.[24]

Again it is quite correct to say that such protections, privileges, and immunities tend to freeze commercial relationships and patterns in a manner absolutely contrary to the economic prescriptions of competition. But if economic efficiency is a justification for not disturbing or dispersing the power of the modern corporation, perhaps efficiency will have to give way a bit and accommodate itself to increasing requirements of compulsory nondiscriminatory dealing. Maybe regulation would be more rational, less of a hodgepodge of conflicting laws, perhaps even more tolerable for those living under it, if it spoke frankly in terms of an ultimatum: "Either restore effective competition or subject yourself to the burdens of having to deal with all comers on a nondiscriminatory basis." But whether by legislation of general applicability like the Robinson-Patman Act, or by the tailor-made "legislation" of antitrust consent decrees, or by some more straightforward process yet unborn, corporate power can expect to spawn techniques of redress against its discriminatory exercise.

A second condition associated with a workable federalism is the insistence on freedom to move into and out of the constituent states without prejudice. In the interstate context the barriers are most often barriers of exclusion, or requirements or burdens, which put the nonresident, the stranger, or the newcomer at a disadvantage. In the context of the modern corporate "sovereignty" the barriers to personal mobility are more likely to be barriers of captivity which impose penalties or forfeitures on shifts in employment. There is some dispute about the seriousness of barriers to mobility of wage earners among companies.[25] But there can be no dispute about the tendency of many compensation and retirement schemes to hold executive and technical personnel within the "jurisdiction" of the corporation in which they first choose to reside.[26] Indeed that is usually their purpose.[27] Deferred compensation and stock-warrant and retirement plans with a "you can't take it with you" feature seem to be successful in their purpose of reducing the horizontal mobility of talent.[28]

Even before their recent accelerated growth, the restrictive tendency of such schemes was noted by one of the more comprehensive studies of such plans, their operation, and their actual impact. Mr. Hall's concern was primarily the misallocation of human resources that would result. Such concern would seem to take on more significance if, as is often said, shortage of executive and technical personnel sets a much lower ceiling on a firm's capacity for growth than does its financial resources, and in a time when the allocation of scientific, engineering, and technical personnel is one of the nation's most important rationing jobs. However, as long as there is such furious competition in the placement offices of technical, professional, and business schools perhaps there is no economic loss of really national significance in relative immobility after the first choice is made. Moreover, the economies of having talent captive are not wholly private. There may be efficiency justifications for allowing the large corporation to order its managerial and technical personnel from one sector of the industrial front to another with the same assurance that a General Staff enjoys in knowing that it has the battalions to carry out its battle plans. The economies of continuity which come from having talent integrated for keeps rather than continually bargained for would seem to be even greater than the economies of vertical integration which have so long commanded the sympathy of industrial economists.[29] So, weighing the immobility of talent on the scales of purely economic effects and purely economic justifications, there may not be much to fuss about.

We return, however, to our initial concern with the political and social consequences of the "sovereignty" of the modern corporation. Most of the sociological concern with mobility has been focused on the chances of changing status in the vertical dimension over the cycle of a generation.[30] On this score it would seem that perhaps because of rather than in spite of the professionalization of modern corporate management, the chances are better than ever to get on the escalator that leads to the top.[31] The new barriers, if any, are barriers resulting from the greater premium put on higher education, and the increasing shortage of higher educational opportunity relative to the demand for it.[32] It would be pretty farfetched to look to the corporation or its regulation to solve this problem or to shoulder the blame for lack of its solution.

However, social or political concern about mobility among corporate sovereignties is not exhausted by finding that the chance to improve your status vertically is, if anything, better now than it was. Certainly moving around under orders is not of itself an index of the voluntary character of a society. Voluntariness is the crux; mobility may or may not be its measure.

Not only actual change but the continuing ability to choose to stay or leave is important. The feeling of continuing choice is not less important than the fact of initial choice. There might be real gains if both the highly subjective and the ludicrously objective standards of promotion had to meet the continuing test of impersonal competition in the personnel market. The perfect allocation of human resources may, in the ultimate analysis, be less important than the maintenance of a widespread confidence throughout the society that the allocation is at best self-determined, or at least not rigged.

Removal of barriers to quitting a particular corporate jurisdiction might even do something to revive and release the energies of "organization men." Freedom to entertain alternatives without prejudice or forfeiture might keep the horizon of interest broader. No matter what the score was at any given time, the game would not be over so soon. Walter Mitty images may be healthier than the rut of the "yes man." If restlessness can seek reward without penalty it may be more creative. Even if the self-dependence of individual proprietorship must give way before the inevitabilities of corporate size, at least its values should be maximized within the salaried society.

There is, of course, some danger of overdrawing both problems and possibilities. Quite likely there is no really adequate way to realize fully the desired goal of a continuing sense of choice. But if corporate sovereignty is to be made as tolerable as possible, it may well be that the state must take positive measures to lower barriers to mobility; first, by removing the tax encouragements to methods of compensation which tend to personnel captivity; second, by positive prohibition of private arrangements which penalize leaving one corporate jurisdiction for another. Like teachers' insurance and annuity, compensation plans, including retirement benefits, might be required to be transferable or at least not forfeited. Emphasis on the values of mobility among subsovereignties can be no more than suggestive, but it may serve to remind those who might object to such "interference" with the "prerogatives of management" that it is a political and social corporate system we are faced with, not just the organization of industrial economy.

Insistence on the mobility of capital among the constituent states of a federation may also have some bearing on both the economic and social problems posed by the modern corporation. Again, while many interstate barriers to commerce are primarily exclusionary, the intercorporate barriers are primarily those of captivity. Again, there are at stake both the economic concern for efficiency and the political or social concern that corporate power be as tolerable as possible.

To the extent that success breeds success too automatically the economist may be worried that a company's chance to grow will depend more on accumulations from its past than on potential for its future. The predominant role of retained earnings and depreciation reserves as a source of postwar industrial expansion [33] would indicate that the built-in bias in favor of inherited corporate success is very great.[34] The advantage is not limited to internal financing. The large corporation has great advantages in tapping not only the funds but the promise of high leverage which fixed interest financing affords. Debt financing is now concentrated very largely in large savings institutions, insurance companies, and pension funds. Often by law, almost always by habit, the managers and trustees of such institutions seek security more than they seek return at the price of risk. As a borrower, the more you have the more you can get. The immunity from accountability to the financial market which the captivity of retained earnings affords is not measured solely by the assets such earnings themselves can buy.

The economist may quite rationally assert that the judgment of a corporate finance committee about a proposed use of corporate reserves or surplus should not be any different from the judgment of the loan officers of a creditor institution, the investment committee of a corporate trustee, or, for that matter, the collective judgment of the professionalized money market appraising a new stock issue. The financial power in any case is derived from profitability, and would not be lost by requiring the corporation to distribute its earnings and then buy them back again. Surely if nothing is to be gained, why suffer the obvious losses and costs of recycling the earnings through the external capital market?

Even in economic terms the answer may be that a wider dispersion of investment judgment would be more conducive to a variety of objective appraisals. Internal finance committees are few, always tempted to bail out their vested mistakes or to seek growth for reasons of power and prestige and managerial outlet which may bear inexact relation to purely economic potentialities and priorities. At best, allowing the industrial corporation to be investment banker may encourage a diversification by acquisition or otherwise which increases concentration without relation to operating efficiency. At worst, it is open to all the abuses of self-dealing to the advantage of the control group at the expense of "outsiders," which was the target of the banking reform of the thirties.[35]

Any drastic requirement to distribute all earnings would, of course, call for offsetting adjustments in corporate and personal income-tax laws. Even if taxation's incidence upon investment could be equated to what it is now, still there might be a very different pattern of investment than now obtains. Some might well fear that if all earnings had to be cycled through the pockets of individual shareholders, the pattern of reinvestment would be even more conservative, even more concentrated in the "blue chips," than it is now when earnings may be retained for reinvestment by the corporation which earns them. One might wonder, however, whether such a tendency might be somewhat offset by the developing investment-management profession and the growth of risk capital funds.

If one foresees an inevitable increase in the public direction and channeling of economic activity generally, then the requirement to distribute earnings may take on further significance. Surely it is preferable to bring about the allocation of resources in the public interest with a minimum of direct government intervention in managerial affairs. The guaranty of mortgages on private low-cost houses seems preferable to government building and operation of dwellings, to the extent that it will accomplish the same job. Also, provision of financial assistance and tax favors to those who will put together a special investment company to invest in small business seems preferable to direct government lending to particular enterprises. In short, subsidies and favors to investors who will invest in activities decided to be of public priority seems a far better way to direct private energies in the public interest than to increase government intervention in the actual conduct of enterprise itself, either by public regulation, contract, or ownership. If this has any validity, then forcing all investment to be made through a dispersed capital market would seem to facilitate the accomplishment of public purposes through investment rewards and incentives by government loan, loan insurance, or tax favor. If investable private capital can be deconcentrated, then government should be better able to influence the pattern of investment in the public interest without resort to public investment.

Such optimistic, or (to some) probably horrendous, potentialities should not obscure the host of problems and economic costs which would inevitably flow from compelling the distribution of corporate earnings. However, the assessment of pros and cons should not either start or stop with purely financial or economic consideration, nor should it be primarily concerned with allegations of corporate wickedness. The focus is on corporate power and how to make it as tolerable as possible, just as it is when considering the modern corporation's external satellite relationships, or the power of the corporation over its salaried managerial and technical personnel. Even if market power cannot be significantly reduced, it is important that it should not either be or seem any more self-justifying or self-perpetuating than necessary. "Shareholder democracy" cannot be achieved in the direction of management, but perhaps the power of corporate governors would be more acceptable if they had to stand for re-election in the constituency of a free capital market.

Political federalism may provide more metaphor than analogy to the problems and possibilities of handling corporate power. Certainly it does not offer a prescription. However, it may serve to cast thought as well as verbiage in line with a perspective on the modern corporation as a *political* fact. It suggests that in order to preserve the noneconomic values of pluralism as a social and political species of organization it is necessary to assure the political as well as the economic acceptability of corporate "sovereignty." This may require the devising of prohibitions and requirements which would outrage inherited notions about the "normal" prerogatives of management and finance not less than did the compulsion to bargain fairly with organized labor. It may also require acceptance of standards of behavior in the market which would flout the precepts of unbridled "hard" competition.

By dint of technological and economic circumstance rather than predatory avarice the "kingly prerogative" which was Senator Sherman's target [36] may have outgrown the bounds of enforced price competition which he set for it. Discriminatory conduct, barriers to mobility of talent and capital, may deserve more direct legal action precisely because the power to restrain trade cannot any longer be effectively prohibited.

5

THE CORPORATION: HOW MUCH POWER?
WHAT SCOPE?

CARL KAYSEN

The proposition that a group of giant business corporations, few in number but awesome in aggregate size, embodies a significant and troublesome concentration of power is the cliché which serves this volume as a foundation stone. I propose here to analyze this proposition, both to trace out what I consider its valid content to be, and to reflect briefly on its possible implications for social action. Let me anticipate my conclusion on the first point by saying that its familiarity is no argument against its truth.

The power of any actor on the social stage I define as the scope of significant choice open to him. Accordingly, his power over others is the scope of his choices which affect them significantly. Our fundamental proposition thus asserts that a few large corporations exert significant power over others; indeed, as we shall see, over the whole of society with respect to many choices, and over large segments of it with respect to others. It is worth noting that this sense of "power" is not that in which we speak of the "power" of a waterfall or a fusion reaction, or any other transformation in a fully deterministic system; rather it is appropriate to a social system in which we see human actors, individually or in organized groups, as facing alternative courses of action, the choice among which is not fully determined without reference to the actors themselves.

We usually demonstrate the concentration of power in a small number of large corporate enterprises by showing what part of various total magnitudes for the whole economy the largest enterprises account for. The statistics are indeed impressive: I list a few of the more striking below.[1]

(1) There are currently some 4.5 million business enterprises in the United States. More than half of these are small, unincorporated firms in retail trade and service. Corporations formed only 13 per cent of the total number; 95 per cent of the unincorporated firms had fewer than twenty employees.

(2) A recent census survey covered all the firms in manufacturing, mining, retail and wholesale trade, and certain service industries: in total some 2.8 million. These firms employed just under 30 million persons. The 28 giant firms with 50,000 or more employees — just 0.001 per cent of the total number — accounted for about 10 per cent of the total employment. The 438 firms with 5000 or more employees (including the 28 giants) accounted for 28 per cent of the total. In manufacturing, where large corporations are characteristically more important than in the other sectors covered, 263,000 firms reported just over 17 million employees: 23 giants with 50,000 or more employees reported 15 per cent of the total, 361 with 5000 or more, just under 40 per cent.

(3) The most recent compilation of the corporation income-tax returns showed 525,000 active nonfinancial corporations reporting a total of $413 billion of assets. The 202 corporations in the largest size class — each with assets of $250 million or more — owned 40 per cent of this total.

(4) The last survey of the National Science Foundation reported some 15,500 firms having research and development laboratories. The largest 7 among them employed 20 per cent of the total number of technical and scientific personnel in the whole group, and accounted for 26 per cent of the total expenditures on research and development. The largest 44, all those with 25,000 or more employees in total, accounted for 45 per cent of the total number of technicians and scientists, and more than 50 per cent of the total expenditures.

(5) The one hundred companies that received the largest defense contracts over the period July 1950–June 1956 received nearly two thirds of the total value of all defense contracts during the period. The largest ten contractors accounted for just short of one third of the total value of all contracts. These were General Motors, General Electric, American Telephone and Telegraph, and seven large aircraft manufacturers.

Large corporations are not of the same importance in all sectors of the economy.[2] In agriculture they are of no importance; in service, trade, and construction, proprietorships and partnerships and small corporations that are essentially similar in all but legal form predominate. Conversely, activity in the utility, transportation, mining, manufacturing, and financial sectors is overwhelmingly the activity of corporations, and predominantly that of corporate giants. The share of total business accounted for by corporations in these sectors ranged from 85 per cent for finance to 100 per cent of utilities; by contrast it was between 50 and 60 per cent for trade and construction, less than 30 per cent in service, and less than 10 per cent in agriculture. The five sectors in which large corporations predominate produced 51 per cent of the total national income, and 57 per cent of the privately-produced national income. Moreover, the strategic importance of these sectors as compared with trade and service — the largest part of the small-business part of the economy — is greater than their contribution to national income would indicate. The relative share of giant corporations in these sectors was larger than in the economy as a whole. The corporate income-tax returns for 1955 showed the relative importance of the largest corporations, as in the accompanying table.

Many more figures similar to these could be added to the

The Relative Share of Giant Corporations in Various Sectors of the United States Economy.

Sector	All corporations		Corporations with assets of $250 million or more	
	Number (thousands)	Assets (billions of dollars)	Number	Proportion of assets of all corporations (percentage)
Manufacturing	124.2	201.4	97	42
Mining *	9.7	13.3	5 (19)	17 (32)
Public utilities	4.8	62.9	56	72
Transportation	21.9	43.5	30	61
Finance	214.6	474.9	218	46

* The figures in parentheses show the number and share of corporations with assets of $100 million or more, since the number of mining corporations in the largest size class is so small.

list. They show clearly that a few large corporations are of overwhelmingly disproportionate importance in our economy, and especially in certain key sectors of it. Whatever aspect of their economic activity we measure — employment, investment, research and development, military supply — we see the same situation. Moreover, it is one which has been stable over a period of time. The best evidence — though far from complete — is that the degree of concentration has varied little for the three or four decades before 1947; more recent material has not yet been analyzed. Further, the group of leading firms has had a fairly stable membership, and turnover within it is, if anything, declining.[3] We are thus examining a persistent situation, rather than a rapidly changing one, and one which we can expect to continue into the future.

Disproportionate share alone, however, is not a valid basis for inferring power as I have defined it. In addition, we must consider the range of choice with respect to significant decisions open to the managers of the large corporation. The disproportionate share of the sun in the total mass of our solar system would not justify the ascription to it of "power" over the planets, since in the fully-determinate gravitational system the sun has no choice among alternative paths of motion which would change the configuration of the whole system. Though the relative weight of the sun is great, its range of choice is nil, and it is the product of the two, so to speak, which measures "power." It is to an examination of the managers' range of choice that we now turn.

Our economy is organized on a decentralized, competitive basis. Each business firm, seeking higher profit by providing more efficiently what consumers want, is faced by the competition of others, seeking the same goal through the same means. Coordination and guidance of these activities is the function of the system of markets and prices. These form the information network that tells each manager what is and what is not currently profitable, and, in turn, registers the effects of each business decision, of changes in consumers' tastes, and the availability and efficiency of productive factors. Ideally, in a system of competitive markets, the signals would indicate only one possible course for any particular manager consistent with profitability. Nor would this depend on the degree to which the manager was committed to the goal of profit-maximization; margins between costs and prices would be so narrow as to make bankruptcy the alternative to "correct" choices. In practice, of course, no real firm functions in markets operating with the sureness, swiftness, and freedom from frictions that would eliminate the discretion of management entirely and make the firm merely an instrument which registered the forces of the market. But firms operating in highly competitive markets are closely constrained by market pressures, and the range of economic decision consistent with survival and success that is open to them is narrow.

By contrast, there exist much less competitive markets in which firms are insulated from these compulsions and the range of discretionary choice in management decisions is correspondingly widened. There is a wide variety of situations which can confer such market power on firms. In practice, the most important is large size relative to the market: the situation in which a few large firms account for all or nearly all of the supply. Large size relative to the market is associated with large absolute size of firm. Other reasons, including barriers to the entry of new firms into the market provided by product differentiation and advertising, by patents, by control over scarce raw materials, or by collusive action of existing firms, or by government limitation of competition, are also significant, but they are of less importance than the oligopolistic market structure common in those sectors of the economy that are dominated by large firms.

In manufacturing, nearly two-thirds of the identifiable markets, accounting for about 60 per cent of the value of manufacturing output, showed significant elements of oligopoly; they were especially important in the durable-goods and capital-equipment fields. In mining, the proportion of identifiable markets with oligopolistic structures was much higher, but since the largest mining industry — bituminous coal — is unconcentrated, these accounted for less than 25 per cent of total mineral output. Public utilities, transportation, and finance are all subject to more or less direct government regulation, of more or less effectiveness. But the underlying market structures in these areas are either monopolistic, as in electric and gas utilities and telephone communication, or oligopolistic, as in transportation and finance.[4] Thus, typically, the large corporation in which we are interested operates in a situation in which the constraints imposed by market forces are loose, and the scope for managerial choice is considerable. It is this scope combined with the large relative weight of the giant corporation that defines its economic power; it is substantially on its economic power that other kinds of power depend.

The powerful firm can use its power primarily to increase its profit over what it could earn in a competitive market: the traditional economic view of the drawback of market power has been the achievement of monopoly profit by the restriction of supply. But it need not do so. While the firm in the highly competitive market is constrained to seek after maximum profits, because the alternative is insufficient profit to insure survival, the firm in the less competitive market can choose whether to seek maximum profit or to be satisfied with some "acceptable" return and to seek other goals. Further, the firm in a competitive market must attend more closely to immediate problems, and leave the long future to take care of itself; while the firm with considerable market power necessarily has a longer time-horizon, and takes into account consequences of its decisions reaching further into the future. This in turn increases the range of choice open to it, for the future is uncertain, and no single "correct" reading of it is possible. Many courses of action may be consistent with reasonable expectations of the future course of events. The more dominant the position of any particular firm in a single market, the further into the future will it see the consequences of its own choices as significant, and correspondingly, the wider will be its range of significant choice. The width of choice and the uncertainty of consequences combine to rob the notion of maximum profit of its simplicity; at the minimum of complexity, the firm must be viewed as seeking some combination of anticipated return and possible variation, at the same time perhaps safeguarding itself against too much variation. But even this is too simple. In the absence of the constraints of a competitive market, the firm may seek a variety of goals: "satisfactory" profits, an "adequate" rate of growth, a "safe" share of the market, "good" labor relations, "good" public relations, and so forth, and no particular combination need adequately describe the behavior of all large firms with significant market power.

The large corporations with which we are here concerned characteristically operate many plants and sell and buy in many markets. Their power in some markets can be used to reinforce their power in others; their large absolute size, and the pool of capital at their command, adds something to their power in any particular market which is not explained simply by the structure of that market. In the extreme, the operations of the firm in a particular market can be completely or almost completely insensitive to its economic fortunes in that market, and thus the range of choice of decisions with respect to it may be widened far beyond that possible to any firm confined within its boundaries. Absolute size has to a certain extent the same effect in respect to the operations of any particular short time-period: the impact of likely short-period losses or failures may bulk insufficiently large to form a significant constraint on action.

We have spoken so far of the powers of choice of the corporation and the management interchangeably. By and large, this is justified. Corporate management is typically — in the reaches of business we are examining — an autonomous center of decision, organizing the affairs of the corporation and choosing its own successors. While stockholders are significant as part of the environment in which management operates, they exercise little or no power of choice themselves. The views of stockholders, as reflected in their willingness to hold or their desire to dispose of the corporation's stock, are certainly taken into account by management, but only as one of a number of elements which condition their decisions. The ideology of corporate management which describes them as one among a number of client groups whose interests are the concern of management — labor, consumers, and the "public" forming the others — is in this particular realistic.

How does the giant corporation manifest its power? Most directly, in economic terms, the noteworthy dimensions of choice open to it include prices and price-cost relations, investment, location, research and innovation, and product character and selling effort. Management choice in each of these dimensions has significance for the particular markets in which the firm operates, and with respect to some of them, may have broader significance for the economy as a whole.

Prices and price-cost relations, in turn, show at least four important aspects. First is the classic question of the general level of prices in relation to costs: are profits excessive? Second, and perhaps more important, is the effect of margins on the level of costs themselves. Where the pressure of competition does not force prices down to costs, costs themselves have a tendency to rise: internal managerial checks alone cannot overcome the tendency to be satisfied with costs when the over-all level of profit is satisfactory. Third, there is the problem of interrelations among margins on related products: does the price of Chevrolet bear the same relation to its costs as the price of a Cadillac, or is there a tendency to earn more in the long run on resources converted into the one than into the other? This form of distortion of price-cost relations is common in the multiproduct firm, and can coexist with a modest average profit margin. Finally, there are the interrelations, both directly within a single firm and indirectly through labor and product markets, of prices and wages. Where price increases are the response to wage increases which in turn respond to price increases, the pricing policy of a firm or group of firms can be an inflationary factor of some importance. This has been the case in the steel industry in the postwar period.[5] A related problem is the behavior of prices in the face of declining demand. When a group of firms can raise prices relative to wages although unused capacity is large and increasing, they make a contribution to aggregate instability, in this case in a deflationary rather than an inflationary direction. Here again the steel industry provides a recent example.

The investment decisions of large firms are of primary importance in determining the rates of growth of particular industries, and where the role of these industries in the economy is a strategic one, their impact may be much wider. Again we may point to the steel industry. Overpessimism about expansion in the early postwar period contributed to the continuing bottleneck in steel that was apparent until the 1957 recession. In the twenties, the slowness with which aluminum capacity was expanded led to recurrent shortages in that market. The speed, or slowness, with which investment in nuclear-fueled electric power generation is now going forward, even with the aid of considerable government subsidy, is again the product of the decisions of a relatively small number of major power producers. This is not to argue that the pace chosen is the wrong one, but simply to indicate a choice of possible broad significance, lying in large part in the hands of a few corporate managements.

A particular kind of investment decision, the consequences of which may reach far into the future and beyond the specific firm or industry involved, is the decision about location. Where new plants are placed both in regional terms and in relation to existing centers of population affects the balance of regional development and the character of urban and suburban growth. Characteristically, it is the large multiplant enterprise which has the widest set of alternatives from among which to choose in making this decision; smaller firms are tied closely to their existing geographic centers.

Even more far reaching are the choices of large enterprises in respect to innovation. Decisions as to the technical areas which will be systematically explored by research and development divisions and decisions as to what scientific and technical novelties will be translated into new products and new processes and tried out for economic viability have very deep effects. Ultimately, the whole material fabric of society, the structure of occupations, the geographic distribution of economic activity and population are all profoundly affected by the pattern of technical change. Not all significant technical change springs from the activities of organized research and development departments, but they do appear to be of increasing importance. And the disproportionate share of a few large corporations in this sphere is greater than in any other. Here again, I am not arguing that the decisions now taken on these matters are necessarily inferior to those which would result from some different distribution of decision-making power, but only pointing to the locus of an important power of choice.

It is worth remarking, on a lower level of generality, that the concentration of the power of choice with respect to new products and new models of old products in a few hands has a significance which is enhanced by the large role which producers' initiative plays in determining consumers' choices in our economy. Whether the extent and character of advertising and selling in our economy is something idiosyncratically American, or simply a product of the high average level of income combined with its relatively equal distribution, it is clear that the importance of these institutions adds to the importance of the producers' power of choice in respect to product change and new products. Further, selling and advertising are likewise relatively highly concentrated, and both the pervasiveness of "sales talk" in the media of communication and the relatively large amounts of its income our rich society spends on all kinds of durable goods give decisions in the sphere of product character and selling techniques a wide impact.

The significance of the economic choices that are made by the powerful large firm can be summed up in terms of their effects on the achievement of four basic economic goals: efficiency, stability, progressiveness, and equity. Economic efficiency means producing the most of what consumers want with available supplies of resources. It involves not only the idea of technical efficiency — for example, performing any particular technical operation with the cheapest combination of inputs required for a unit of output — but the more subtle idea of not producing less of any one particular good in relation to others, and conversely, more of another, than consumers' desires indicate. In more concrete terms, whenever one particular good is priced high in relation to its costs, while another one is priced low, then too much of the second and too little of the first tends to be produced in relation to consumers' demands. When the price-cost margin on a product remains high over a period of time, this is an indication of economic inefficiency. So is continued price discrimination, in the sense in which we defined it above. In addition, of course, the lack of competitive pressure on margins may lead to inefficiency in the simpler sense as well: not producing the actual goods with the minimum amount of resources possible. The exercise of market power thus leads frequently to economic inefficiency.

Stability of output and employment at high levels, and, perhaps a little less important, of price levels, is an economic goal which is generally given great weight. The exercise of pricing discretion can contribute to destabilizing forces both in upswings and downswings of activity. As we argued before, there are examples of wage-price spirals in which a significant upward push on wage levels in general, and thus on price levels, is exercised by particular pricing decisions. The maintenance of margins in the face of declining demand is less clear and striking in its effects, but it probably makes a net contribution to further destabilization in comparison with some moderate decline. On the other hand, it is clear that stable prices and wages are far more desirable than continuous declines in both in the face of declining aggregate demand; and thus the choice typically made by the powerful firm may be less than the best but considerably better than the worst possible one.

When we come to test the economic decisions of the large firm against the standard of progressiveness, we find that we can say little that is unequivocal. That large firms spend heavily on research and development is clear. That some industries in which the application of improved techniques and growth of output of new products is spectacular are industries — such as chemicals, oil, electronics — dominated by large firms is also clear. But when we try to look deeper, obscurity replaces clarity. Is the present degree of dominance of large firms a necessary condition of the amount of progress experienced, or even a sufficient condition? Are larger firms more effective, per dollar of expenditures, in producing new ideas and new methods than smaller ones are, and over what size range is this true? Should corporations spend on research and development much more or much less than they now spend? Should the incentives of the market be allowed more or less control than they now have of the whole chain of sequential and interrelated processes from the first observation of a new natural phenomenon or the first conception of a new scientific idea to the introduction into the market of a new product or the application on the production line of a new technology? These are all questions to which well-informed and competent students do not give the same answer, if indeed they give any. However, it is enough for our present purpose to say that there are specific examples of the importance for technical progress of competition, and particularly of the kind of competition represented by new and small firms that are not heavily committed to present products and processes, in sufficient number to cast doubt on the universal correctness of the judgments of powerful dominant firms.[6] While we cannot assert that these judgments are likely to be always wrong, we also cannot say that they need no corrective. When technical change can take the spectacularly wasteful forms that it has achieved recently in the automobile industry, in which new products, introduced at considerable production and marketing expense, are not cheaper to produce, cheaper to operate, nor more durable than those they supplant, and their increase in service-ability, functional efficiency, or even aesthetic appeal is at best debatable, it is hard to deny that "progress" and "free choice in the marketplace" both become phrases of rather dubious content. All the potential gain in productive efficiency in the automobile industry over the last decade, and probably more, has gone into "more" product rather than into cost savings and price reductions. This result is the product of decisions of a small number of managements — perhaps only one — and it underlines the appropriateness of raising the question of whether there is not too much power in the hands of those responsible for the choice.

The standard of equity is at least as slippery as that of progressiveness, although for different reasons. While the importance of equity in the sense of a fair distribution of the income of society as a goal is undeniable, equity itself is not measurable by any economic standard. We have long since abandoned reliance on the notion that the reward of the marketplace is necessarily a "fair" reward, even when the market functions effectively and competitively. Indeed, some of our interferences with the functioning of markets are justified on equity grounds, reflecting our social dissatisfaction with the income distribution resulting from the unchecked operation of the market. But, although little exists in the way of comprehensive standards of equity which command wide acceptance, certain specific judgments are possible. "Excessive" property incomes are suspect: high profits based on monopoly power are widely subject to criticism. Where market power is translated into sustained high profits, the result can be described as inequitable as well as inefficient. Further, where management decision translates a portion of the high profits into high salaries, bonuses, stock options, and generous pension plans for itself, the imputation of unfairness is strengthened. These are recorded as views that command fairly wide agreement, not as economically inevitable conclusions nor necessary moral judgments. It may be that the equally high incomes of crooners and .400 hitters are logically open to as much criticism; in fact, however, they are not so much criticized.

Any discussion of equity moves rapidly from an economic to what is essentially a political view, since equity is ultimately a value problem whose social resolution is of the essence of politics. When we make this move, a new order of equity problems connected with the power of the large firm appears. This is the problem of the relation between the large enterprise and the host of small satellite enterprises which become its dependents. These may be customers bound to it by a variety of contractual relations, such as the service stations bound to the major oil companies who are their suppliers (and frequently their landlords and bankers as well), or the automobile dealers connected with the manufacturers by franchise arrangements. Or they may be customers without explicit contractual ties, yet nonetheless dependent on the maintenance of "customary" relations with large suppliers of their essential raw material, as has been the case with small fabricators of aluminum and steel products, whose business destinies have been controlled by the informal rationing schemes of the primary producers in the frequent shortage periods of the postwar decade. Or they may be small suppliers of large firms: canners packing for the private brands of the large chain grocers, furniture or clothing manufacturers producing for the chain department stores and mail-order houses, subcontractors producing for the major military suppliers. In any case, these small firms are typically wholly dependent on their larger partners. It is worth noting that this dependence may be consistent with a fairly competitive situation in the major product market of the large purchaser, or even the over-all selling market of the large supplier, provided the particular submarket in which the transactions between large and small firm occur is segmented enough to make it costly and risky for the small firm to seek new sources or outlets.

All these relations present a double problem. First, is the treatment which the dependent firms experience "fair" in the concrete: Have there been cancellations of dealers' franchises by major automobile manufacturers for no cause, or, worse, in order to transfer them to firms in which company executives had an interest? Have aluminum companies "favored" their own fabricating operations at the expense of independent fabricators during periods of short supply? [7] Second, and more fundamental, is what might be called the procedural aspect of the problem. Whether unfair treatment by large firms of their small clients abounds, or is so rare as to be written off as the vagary of a few executives, the question of whether it is appropriate for the large firm to possess what amount to life-and-death powers over other business remains.

And the same question arises more broadly than in respect to the patron-client relations of large firms and their dependent small suppliers and customers. All of the areas of decision in which powerful managements have wide scope for choice, with effects reaching far into the economy, that we discussed above raise the same question. Not the concrete consequences of choice measured against the economic standards of efficiency, stability, progressiveness, and equity, but the power and scope of choice itself is the problem. This view of the problem may appear somewhat abstract, and even be dismissed as a piece of academic fussiness: if the outcomes are in themselves not objectionable, why should we concern ourselves with the process of decision which led to them; and, if they are, why not address ourselves to improving them directly? But so to argue ignores the point that choice of economic goals is itself a value choice, and thus a political one; and that direct concern with the loci of power and constraints on its use may legitimately rank in importance as political goals with the attainment of desired economic values. If the regime of competition and the arguments of *laissez-faire* ever commended themselves widely, it has been primarily on political rather than economic grounds. The replacement of the all-too-visible hand of the state by the invisible hand of the marketplace, which guided each to act for the common good while pursuing his own interests and aims without an overt show of constraint, was what attracted gen-

eral ideological support to the liberal cause. The elegance of the
optimum allocation of resources which Walras and Pareto saw in
the ideal competitive economy by contrast has remained a concept of importance only to the most academic economist. When
the invisible hand of the competitive market is, in turn, displaced
to a significant extent by the increasingly visible hand of powerful
corporate management, the question "Quo warranto?" is bound
to arise, whatever decisions are in fact made. And the fact is that
the power of corporate management is, in the political sense, irresponsible power, answerable ultimately only to itself. No matter
how earnestly management strives to "balance" interests in making its decisions — interests of stockholders, of employees, of customers, of the "general public," as well as the institutional interests of the enterprise — it is ultimately its own conception of these
interests and their desirable relations that rules. When the exercise of choice is strongly constrained by competitive forces, and
the power of decision of any particular management is narrow and
proportioned to the immediate economic needs of the enterprise,
the political question of the warrant of management authority
and its proper scope does not arise. When, as we have argued,
the scope of choice is great and the consequences reach widely
into the economy and far into the future, the problem of the authority and responsibility of the choosers is bound to become
pressing.

The market power which large absolute and relative size gives
to the giant corporation is the basis not only of economic power
but also of considerable political and social power of a broader
sort. Some of the political power of large business is of course
the product of group action to defend group interests and, in this
sense, presents no problems peculiar to large business, except
perhaps the problem of the large availability of funds and certain
nonpurchasable resources of specialized talent and prestige in
support of its interest. That we pay, in the form of percentage depletion, an outrageous subsidy to the oil and gas business (which
goes to many small producers as well as to the giant integrated
oil firms) is a phenomenon of no different order than that we
pay nearly equally outrageous ones to farmers. On the other hand,
it is money rather than votes which supports the one, and votes

rather than money which support the other; and the latter situation is, as the former is not, in accord with our professed political morality. More special to the position of the large firm is the power in both domestic and foreign affairs which the large oil companies have by virtue of their special positions as concessionaires — frequently on a monopoly basis in a particular country — in exploiting the oil of the Middle East and the Caribbean. Here the large firms exercise quasi-sovereign powers, have large influence on certain aspects of the foreign policy of the United States and the Atlantic Alliance, and operate in a way which is neither that of public government nor that of private business. While the oil companies are the most spectacular examples of the involvement of strong American companies with weak foreign governments in areas which are important to national policy, they are not the only ones, and other examples could be cited.

Perhaps the most pervasive influence of big business on national politics lies in the tone of the mass media. Both because of the influence of advertising — itself heavily concentrated in the largest firms, and the big-business character of many publishing and broadcasting enterprises, the political tone of the media is far from reflecting even approximately the distribution of attitudes and opinions in the society as a whole. But an influence may be pervasive without thereby being powerful, and the importance of this state of affairs is open to argument.

It is when we step down from the level of national politics to the state and local levels that the political power of the large corporation is seen in truer perspective. The large national-market firm has available to it the promise of locating in a particular area or expanding its operations there, the threat of moving or contracting its operations as potent bargaining points in its dealings with local and even state political leaders. The branch manager of the company whose plant is the largest employer in a town or the vice-president of the firm proposing to build a plant which will become the largest employer in a small state treats with local government not as a citizen but as a quasi-sovereign power. Taxes, zoning laws, roads, and the like become matters of negotiation as much as matters of legislation. Even large industrial states and metropolitan cities may face similar problems: the largest three

employers in Michigan account for probably a quarter of the
state's industrial employment; in Detroit the proportion is more
nearly a third. At this level, the corporation's scope of choice, its
financial staying power, its independence of significant local forces
are all sources of strength in dealing with the characteristically
weak governments at the local and often at the state levels.

The broader social power which the high executives of large
corporations exercise — in part in their own positions, in part in
their representative capacity as "business leaders" — is more difficult to define and certainly less definite than the kind of political
power and economic power discussed above. Yet it is no less important, and to the extent that it is linked to the economic power
of the large firm — a point to which I return immediately below —
no less relevant to our discussion. One aspect of this broad power
to which we have already referred is the position that corporate
management occupies as taste setter or style leader for the society
as a whole. Business influence on taste ranges from the direct
effects through the design of material goods to the indirect and
more subtle effects of the style of language and thought purveyed
through the mass media — the school of style at which all of us
are in attendance every day. Further, these same business leaders
are dominant social models in our society: their achievements
and their values are to a large extent the type of the excellent,
especially for those strata of society from which leaders in most
endeavors are drawn. This, more shortly stated, is the familiar
proposition that we are a business society, and that the giant corporation is the "characteristic," if not the statistically typical, institution of our society, and, in turn, the social role of high executives is that appropriate to leading men in the leading institution.

How much is this kind of social power, as well as the political
power discussed above, connected with the market power of giant
firms? Is it simply a consequence of their economic power, or
does it depend on deeper elements in our social structure? These
are questions to which any firm answer is difficult, in part because they can be interpreted to mean many different things. To
assert that any diminution in the underlying power of large firms
in the markets in which they operate would lead to a corresponding decrease in their social and political power appears unwar-

ranted; so does the assertion that universally competitive markets would end the social and political power of business. But there are important connections. Part of the power of the business leaders comes from the size of the enterprises they operate and the number of people they influence directly as employees, suppliers, customers; absolute size, in turn, is highly correlated with relative size and market power. Freedom in spending money is connected with both absolute size, and the security of income which market power provides. The initiative in the complex processes of taste formation might shift away from smaller and more competitive businesses toward other institutions to a substantial extent; and the ability of firms to spend large resources on shaping demand would be lessened by reductions in their market power. Thus diminution of the economic power of large firms would have a more-than-trivial effect on their power in other spheres, even if we cannot state firmly the law that relates them.

The reasons for concern about the social and political power of business are also worth consideration, since they are not obviously the same as those which the concentrated economic power of large corporations raise. There are two aspects of this question which appear worth distinguishing. The first is the already-mentioned point of the irresponsibility of business power. Its exercise with respect to choices which are themselves far from the matters of meeting the material needs of society that are the primary tasks of business further emphasizes this point. The process of selection of business leaders may be adaptive with respect to their performance of the economic function of business; there is no reason to expect that it should be with respect to the exercise of power in other realms. In short, why should we entrust to the judgment of business leaders decisions of this kind, when we have neither a mechanism for ratifying or rejecting their judgments and them, nor any reason to believe them particularly suited to make these judgments? Second, we can go further than merely to raise the question of whether the training and selection of business leaders qualifies them to make the kinds of decisions and exercise the kinds of power we have discussed. In some quite important respects, it is clear that business values and business attitudes are dysfunctional in meeting our national needs. This is true both with respect to the many problems which we face in our international relations, and with respect to important domestic problems as well. If we look on our economic relations with the underdeveloped nations, especially those of Asia and Africa, as primarily tasks of business firms to be met through the market under the stimulus of market incentives, supported to some extent by special subsidies, it appears unlikely that we will succeed in achieving our political and security goals. If our attitudes toward other governments are heavily colored by ideological evaluations of the kind of economic organization they favor, from the standpoint of our own business ideology, our world problems will be made no easier. And in the domestic sphere, there is a range of problems from education to metropolitan organization and urban renewal which cannot be dealt with adequately if viewed in business perspectives and under business values.

We can sum up these points by saying that the position of big businesses and their leaders contributes significantly to our being a "business society." Do we want to be? Can we afford to be?

These rhetorical questions indicate clearly enough my own view on whether or not we should try to limit or control the power of large corporate enterprise. The crucial question, however, is whether such power can be limited or controlled. Broadly, there are three alternative possibilities. The first is limitation of business power through promoting more competitive markets; the second is broader control of business power by agencies external to business; the third, institutionalization within the firm of responsibility for the exercise of power. Traditionally, we have purported to place major reliance on the first of these alternatives, in the shape of antitrust policy, without in practice pushing very hard any effort to restrict market power to the maximum feasible extent. I have argued elsewhere that it is in fact possible to move much further than we have in this direction, without either significant loss in the over-all effectiveness of business performance or the erection of an elaborate apparatus of control.[8] While this, in my judgment, remains the most desirable path of policy, I do not in fact consider it the one which we will tend to follow. To embark on a determined policy of the reduction of business size and growth in order to limit market power requires a commitment of faith in the desirability of the outcome and the feasibility of the process which I think is not widespread. What I consider more likely is some mixture of the second and third types of control. Business itself has argued vehemently that a corporate revolution is now in process, which has resulted in a redirection of business goals and conscious assumption of responsibility in broad social spheres. This theme has been put forward by academic writers as well.[9] To whatever extent such a "revolution" has taken place, it does not meet the need for the institutionalization of responsibility which the continued exercise of wide power demands. It is not sufficient for the business leaders to announce that they are thinking hard and wrestling earnestly with their wide responsibilities, if, in fact, the power of unreviewed and unchecked decision remains with them, and they remain a small, self-selecting group.[10] Some of the more sophisticated accounts of the revolutionary transformation of business identify business as a "profession" in the honorific sense, and imply that professional standards can be relied on as a sufficient social control over the exercise of business power, as society does rely on them to control the exercise of the considerable powers of doctors and lawyers. This is a ramifying problem which we cannot here explore; it is sufficient to remark that there is, at least as yet, neither visible mechanism of uniform training to inculcate, nor visible organization to maintain and enforce, such standards; and, further, that even if business decisions in the business sphere could be "professionalized" and subject to the control of a guild apparatus, it seems less easy to expect that the same would be true of the exercise of business power in the social and political spheres.

Some likely directions of development of explicit control can be seen in the kinds of actions which now provoke Congressional inquiry, and the suggestions which flow from such inquiries. Concern with the wage-price spiral has led to Congressional investigation of "administered prices" and to suggestions that proposed price and wage changes in certain industries be reviewed by a public body before becoming effective. A combination of the increase of direct regulation of some of the economic choices of powerful firms with an increase in public criticism, and perhaps even institutionalized public discussion of the choices which are not explicitly controlled, appears probable. Such a program will, in effect, do by a formal mechanism and systematically what is currently being done in a somewhat haphazard way by Congressional investigation. On the whole, it is this which has been the active front. The development of mechanisms which will change the internal organization of the corporation, and define more closely and represent more presently the interests to which corporate management should respond and the goals toward which they should strive is yet to begin, if it is to come at all.

6

THE CORPORATION MAN

W. LLOYD WARNER

I. QUESTIONS AND ISSUES

All Americans have been greatly interested in the roles of the managers of the great American corporations, and innumerable scientific inquiries have been made into the subject. Ever since this powerful elite first appeared, stormy debate has raged over its rightful place in our corporate structure and the country's economy and over the proper functions of such positions of prestige in our society. The emphasis of research investigation more often has been on the role rather than the personality of the manager, on the position within the structure of the economy or the society, rather than on the flesh-and-blood individuals. To understand fully what happens in corporate enterprise and the meaning of some of the behavior at managerial levels it is of course necessary to ask who the men themselves are; for what they are as men will greatly determine how they think, act, and feel as managers. Who they are as individuals crucially influences the decisions they make and how and when they will or will not make them. In brief, what a manager is as a person determines how he uses his position, whether he makes the most or the least of its power, the kind of power he uses, and, in the cases of some managers, the kinds of values and beliefs that are encouraged or discouraged in a corporation. To ask what kinds of men are managers raises a number of important questions of fact, theory, and public policy. Let us briefly state two of the more important ones. Broadly speaking, to understand managers as persons we must know the answers to two kinds of questions. What are they as social beings: what has been their social training and what set of social characteristics have they acquired? And what is the nature of the "inner men" that, as it were, lie beneath their managerial skins?

At the level of fact, we must first ask what are the economic and social backgrounds of these men. What did their fathers do for a living? Are they a birth elite, the sons of men of their own kind, or are they mobile men, who have fought their way up from lowly origins? If so, how did they do it? What were the social and economic means they used to climb to the top? And this learned, what do our findings signify? What issues does the evidence raise?

II. WHAT KIND OF MEN ARE MANAGERS?

When we examine the occupational backgrounds of contemporary business leaders [1] to learn who they are we can also discover how much mobility into the higher reaches of management actually exists, and we can use this knowledge to tell us something about the comparative flexibility and rigidity of our occupational and class hierarchies. Over half (52 per cent) of all the major executives of contemporary corporations are the sons of men who have been executives, major or minor, or owners of small or large enterprises. The other 48 per cent is constituted as follows: 15 per cent are sons of laborers, 8 per cent come from white-collar families, 14 per cent are sons of fathers in the professions, and another 9 per cent had fathers who were farmers (all other categories amounted to but 2 per cent). In the adult male population belonging to the different occupational categories in our country, the sons of business men are not found in the same high proportions. But, among the American executives with executive fathers, for every 100 that might be expected by their proportion in the general population, there are 473, or nearly five times more than would be expected by chance alone. Business and the professions (the latter with 350 for every 100 "expected") are the only two occupational categories among the fathers of business leaders that are overrepresented. Those fathers underrepresented are the white-collar men (80 instead of 100), the farmers (73), and the laborers (32), the last obviously well below their proportionate share.[2]

These figures, important as they are, tell us nothing about

what has been happening through the years to the status of the managerial group. Is this pinnacle today more or less accessible than it was a generation ago? Are we now more or less castelike than we were then? In 1928, when Taussig and Joslyn studied the executive leaders of great corporations,[3] they found 967 executives who were the sons of executives, about twice as many as today's 473. There were then 433 sons of professional men, instead of 350. When we examined the numbers of executives who were the sons of fathers in occupations that are now underrepresented, there were only 24 sons of laborers (32 today), 32 instead of 33 sons of farmers, and only 71 sons of white-collar men, compared with 80 today. These figures seem to demonstrate that the status of the business leader in the great corporations for those at the lower social and economic levels is more open to free competition today than it was a generation ago. Moreover, these measurements indicate that it is a much less positive future for men born to families of high position. In brief, the top of the highly esteemed and powerful hierarchy of corporate enterprise has become increasingly a pinnacle to which men of lowly origins can realistically aspire. That the sons of the powerful and high-ranking are at a great advantage today cannot be denied; yet the evidence indicates that the skills, talents, and training of all levels of the society are increasingly being used to provide economic leadership.

Most of us would agree that this democratic tendency which through free competition brings up men from the bottom and thereby increases the likelihood of more men of ability occupying high position is unqualifiedly good and should continue to increase. However, second thoughts raise serious problems. Suppose that the present trend reached a point where the sons of business leaders were at a serious disadvantage numerically in the executive class. Many such men, losing the strong motivations of advancing and securing the family's interests and occupational traditions, might find it difficult to give their best to the job at hand. Moreover, it seems possible that social instability at the higher levels of our society, created by a shifting personnel, would create its own problems for the stability and well-being of the entire society. At issue is the problem of how we can best maintain the kind of leadership that a free society must have and the kinds of values that such men must possess if America is to compete successfully with the rest of the world and realize her own economic and cultural potentialities. The proper proportion of upward to downward movement at the highest occupational levels, in terms of the general well-being of the society, cannot be estimated. We know that today there is still not enough movement from the bottom and probably not enough down from the top. But we should not yield too easily to our Utopian fantasies that it would be impossible to have too much movement from the bottom to the top. Our Communist competitors with their hard-headed realism know better than this. On the other hand, we cannot sit complacently and feel that any movement at all up from the bottom is adequate.

The increase, in the last generation, in the amount of mobility from the bottom, and probably from the top down, as well as indications of more flexibility in our social and economic structure in general, raises the question of why this tendency has appeared. Are there discernible factors in operation, related to this increase in opportunity for those who aspire to corporate leadership? We shall briefly review the evidence for such factors, and then interpret their significance for our problem. Here and there we shall speculate on how these factors might help us to understand our society and to formulate public policies.

III. WHAT DO HIGHER EDUCATION AND THE GROWTH OF LARGE CORPORATIONS SIGNIFY FOR BUSINESS LEADERSHIP?

We have all become aware of the increasing importance of higher education to the society and to the individuals who compete for economic success. How much did higher education contribute to the careers of business leaders and what kind of an education did they get? Do certain kinds of institutions of higher learning, private or public, professional schools or colleges of the liberal arts, make or fail to make their contributions to the important task of training competent as well as wise business leadership? And, these questions answered, what are the meanings and significances of the answers, not only for corporate leadership but for a free society? Moreover, do the answers indicate educational policies that might, if encouraged, provide business and our country with better leadership?

During the generation that has passed since Taussig and Joslyn systematically studied business leaders, there has been an enormous increase in the proportion of executives of big business who attended college, far beyond the increase in college graduates in the general population. Today three fourths of the managers of large corporations have been to college. Of these, some graduated (57 per cent), some did not (19 per cent), and some, usually after receiving a bachelor's degree, advanced to higher degrees (19 per cent), frequently at the better universities. Only 7 per cent of the adult male population as a whole in 1950 were college graduates. Fifty-five per cent had less than a high-school education, in major contrast to the tiny 4 per cent of the business leaders who did not go beyond grammar school.

The relation of education to managerial achievement is most dramatically expressed in comparisons between the last and the present generations of big-business executives. Whereas today six out of ten corporate executives are college graduates, only three were in 1928. Fewer than one in twenty have had less than a high-school education today, but in 1928 approximately three out of ten quit at grammar school (27 per cent). During the intervening period, education has become the principal route for advancement to top positions. Given the facts that the sons of big-business leaders and those of men in the major professions are still disproportionately high among these "corporation men" and are also those most likely to go to college, there is still room for doubt that these figures do in fact represent increased opportunity and realized achievement for the sons of lower occupational levels. But further evidence demonstrates that advantages accrued at all levels. In 1928 only 8 per cent of the sons of unskilled or semiskilled workers graduated from college; today 34 per cent of the managers of corporations who came from this level received at least an A. B. degree, as did 34 per cent of the sons of skilled workers. Forty-eight per cent of those from white-collar origins graduated, as against 20 per cent in the previous generation. When these figures are compared with the 32 per cent for all business leaders who were college graduates in the previous generation, they indicate and probably measure the great importance of higher education as an influence in the increased movement of men from the lower occupational levels into the present top positions of the business elite. There can be little question but that higher education is positively related to the opening of the managerial status to those from below who are sufficiently talented and qualified. This means, of course, that college training is also positively related to an increase in free competition for the more powerful and prestige-bearing positions of authority in industry. Moreover, it implies, I believe, that membership requirements for both our corporate and social hierarchies throughout the country are more flexible and open today than a generation ago.

If highly qualified men are being drawn now more than ever before from all parts of the United States, rural as well as urban, and from all occupational levels, through the power of higher education to positions of leadership in the great corporations, what becomes of, and what must we say about, that curious contemporary epithet, "Organization Man," the corporation robot? It is true that ambitious men and their families move from position to position and, in the process, from community to community. It is also true that most of them center their dominant goals in occupational advancement. Yet if three fourths of these men are college-trained, and sizable proportions are from lowly origins, whence never before could they have attained such heights, it must mean that their capacity for satisfaction in and enjoyment of their roles as corporate men and citizens has greatly increased. They are not robots, slavishly following the iron demands of corporate enterprise, as they have been depicted. Moreover, for many of them positions of corporate leadership mean better and more productive service as citizens of their communities and their country. Since the careers of most, by their own voluntary choice, are not confined to one corporation but extend through several, they are not the organizational automata that the popular journals of the intelligentsia and other superficial analyses allege. The social significance of these men and their families, moving from community to community, must wait for a later section for full explanation. We must now ask what institutions educate them and what kind of an education they get when they go to college.

The colleges and universities attended by these men as undergraduates range through every variety of quality and kind, from the most obscure and scholastically poorest to the most highly esteemed, with the highest academic rank. It should be added that the corporation man is more likely to attend the latter than the former. The first four universities, graduating one fifth of all the managers, were, in the order named, Yale, Harvard, Princeton, and Cornell. The others most often chosen were both public and private, and in every region of the country, and included the Universities of Illinois, Michigan, Chicago, and Minnesota, in the Middle West; Berkeley and Stanford in the Far West; and the Universities of North Carolina and Texas in the South.

But here we must pause, for again such figures might mislead us. We must ask what kind of men went to the great universities? Who were the managers who graduated from the better colleges? Did such institutions contribute their share to the leavening process and train men from the wrong side of the tracks in the skills necessary for competition with those born on Upper Main Street? Or did they educate only the sons of the powerful few? All the managers who went to Yale as undergraduates were sons of business men or men in the higher professions; one half also had grandfathers in the business and professional elites. Three fourths of those who went to Harvard were sons of business elite; one half also had grandfathers in the business and professional elites. Among those attaining managerial rank, not one son of a laborer attended any of the large New England liberal arts colleges.[4] It might be added that no manager who was a laborer's son was present at such places as Princeton, Northwestern, and Stanford, either. But where did these young men go?

The sons of workers were drawn to the larger state and city universities, as well as to some of the technical schools such as M.I.T. and Carnegie Tech. They were also spread through a complete spectrum of small and large denominational, state, and private universities. Although it seems probable that new scholarship programs and recent efforts of the more important colleges and universities to recruit the most able from a wide geographical and economic range are changing the composition of their student bodies, it must be said that the mobile men among today's business leaders were usually trained and prepared for their high and very responsible positions by those institutions least able financially and culturally to perform this important task. Unless more is done by the better-known universities to provide financial assistance, this situation seems likely to continue. However, the efforts of the great foundations, the smaller regional ones, and public and private donors to improve the quality and financing of such institutions obviously should increase not only the percentage of mobile men who use education for their advancement but — perhaps of even greater importance — the quality of the training, technical and cultural, which they receive.

It is at present fashionable for business men, when they strike a statesmanlike pose in their public pronouncements, to declare that what business needs and wants is young men broadly trained in the liberal arts. But despite these noble declarations, it does not take research to predict whether a personnel officer would pick the bright technical-college boy with solid training in business administration and procedure or the lad with a good record in philosophy, history, and literature acquired in a liberal arts college. The recruiters of future business leaders of great corporations spend less time waiting outside the doors of departments of philosophy than on the steps of business administration colleges. If the men who graduate from schools of business and other similar professional schools are to be trained properly in the fundamentals of higher learning, it will be necessary for these schools — as some are now doing — to require a foundation of training in the humanities and the behavioral sciences. When the leaders of the great corporations realize that their own self-interest, and perhaps their very survival and that of their economy, is dependent upon a free society which functions properly, and when they know that they themselves and the quality of their own thinking as managers must be responsible for much of its well-being, it seems probable that an increasing number not only will add to their personal support of higher education but demand that their recruiting officers favor graduates of those schools with a curriculum that embodies technical training well founded on the best of our cultural heritage. Men so trained and the corporations who employ them will have a clear advantage over their competitors.

Although higher education is a demonstrable factor in how and why men from lower levels now rise to the top and are able to compete more successfully than previously for managerial leadership, in itself it is not sufficient explanation for what is happening. It does not tell us why those born to the occupational elites of business and the professions are not now as well represented as previously at the executive level. These men also have gone to college in increasing proportions. College attendance by the sons of major executives who are now themselves executives rose from 52 per cent in 1928 to 74 per cent in 1952. The figures for the professions are, for the same dates, 47 and 73 per cent. Other factors need inspection to help us understand what has been happening.

Research findings demonstrate that during the last generation the huge billion-dollar corporations have increased enormously in size, in the number employed, and in the amount of business done. They are often attacked as undemocratic, and their effect on our equalitarian values is sometimes judged as bad. The truth or falsehood of these criticisms it is not our present purpose to argue. But the increase in the great corporations is directly related to the decrease in the proportion of present executives whose fathers were in the business elite. In the study of today's executives,[5] the great corporations of all varieties were graded according to size, being placed in five categories according to their gross annual income. The proportion of executives who were sons of executives and that of those who were not were determined for each level, and the results demonstrated that the smaller the corporation, the larger the proportion of sons of business executives; the larger the corporation, the smaller the proportion of such men present. Step by step, as one moved from the smaller to the larger corporations, the proportion of sons of executives decreased. More specifically, whereas only 20 per cent of the executives of large corporations were sons of executives, the figure in the smallest corporation was 29 per cent.

In 1928 the story was quite different. Thirty-two per cent

of the leaders of the great corporations were sons of executives (20 per cent are today), and only 25 per cent of those in the smallest corporations came from this occupational level (29 per cent now do). It appears that the increase in the number and importance of the giant corporations is directly related to the advance of men from the lower levels to top positions in management. When men from the bottom are able to prepare themselves for advancement, the more competent among all men are most likely to be selected. This means of course that under these conditions success on the basis of merit is possible to men from any level. The personnel officers of the great corporations now are more likely to select on the basis of ability, whereas in the smaller corporations (many of them family enterprises), it appears that the sons of executives and their friends have greater opportunity. In brief, social and economic status seems to carry less weight in the giant national and international American corporations. It must be remembered, however, that sizable proportions of both the sons of executives and those who are not are among the managers of all corporate categories.

The expansion of higher education explains a substantial part of the increase in upward and downward mobility among the business elite. But it does not tell the whole story. Other influences can be understood only by viewing the process in wider perspective. The following two sections are devoted to this task.

IV. THE WIVES THEY MARRY

In too many inquiries into the kinds of men who are corporate managers, the structural influence of the American family on them as men and on their careers has not been sufficiently emphasized. The connection between family relationships and corporate enterprise is perhaps of more importance than any other single fact as an indicator of the well-being of a free and open society. At stake, I believe, are some of the fundamental values of this democracy and, in all probability, of its continuing economic and social progress. Despite the continuing importance of inheritance, elite positions, as we have seen, are increasingly open to free competition by properly prepared members of the society and not closed by family claims to all but a succession from fathers to sons.

But corporate executives not only have sons; they also frequently have wives! What kind of wives do they marry and who were their mothers? Since marriage is still the principal route of economic and social mobility for women, the informal rules and values which govern the selection of mates by business leaders can and do have very important effects on the character of our society. If they and their fathers marry women only from their own economic class, such marriages tighten and close the status structure, emphasize aristrocratic values in the training of the offspring, and thus contribute to a system of closed corporate and social rank; if they marry above or below themselves the class order is more likely to be open, and women and men from the lower ranks can compete for mates of higher status.

There can be no doubt that the managers of the great corporations more often marry women from their own class origins than from any other occupational group. This is true not only of men whose fathers were big-business executives but also of those who were the sons of laborers: over a third of the former (35 per cent) married daughters of big-business leaders, and some 42 per cent of the latter married daughters of laborers. Despite this tendency toward endogamy, a closer inspection demonstrates that while class values operate in the choice of mates, their marriages were nevertheless quite widely dispersed throughout all occupational categories. Thus the men who came from the laboring class more often married women of their own level of origin, but they also married daughters of big-business leaders (7 per cent) and daughters of professional men (9 per cent), and a still larger proportion married the daughters of farmers, small-business men, and white-collar workers. Managers who were the sons of big-business executives also married throughout the occupational hierarchy. The men whose fathers were in the white-collar class were less likely to marry into their own level than were those from any other category.

One of the principal relationships in the family, marriage seems (from these figures) to be relatively unconstrained by class barriers, for marriages among the top, bottom, and intermediate levels occur in sufficiently high proportions to demonstrate high flexibility in the family structure and rather high autonomy in the individual choice of a mate. These marriages also demonstrate the principle of women's mobility by marriage. Marriage assists the family in maintaining that more flexible system, which we have seen developing, where the sons of executives are less likely to inherit the father's position. The apparent decrease in endogamy and increase in marriages outside the occupational class may be related to the rise in numbers of persons obtaining higher education. Since a higher proportion of children of all occupational groups goes to college, there now are more opportunities for men and women with diverse backgrounds to meet and become acquainted. When they go to college they leave the more rigid class controls of their local communities, where they are more likely to marry women of their own levels. The statistics for the correlation of level of education with in-laws' status between marriage partners provide substantial evidence for this hypothesis. For example, 21 out of every 100 executives who were the sons of white-collar workers and who graduated from college married daughters of the business elite, compared with 12 of every 100 with less than high-school education. Similar ratios between the amount of education and marriage into a higher occupational class prevail for all other occupations. However, education seems to operate in much the same way for the sons of business leaders; 37 out of every 100 college graduates of this group marry women of similar background, and only 23 who did not go beyond grade school marry at their own level. Higher education tends to increase the number of marriages to mates of higher levels and to decrease the likelihood of those born to the gold-lettered door marrying "beneath themselves."

V. INDIVIDUAL AUTONOMY AND THE EMERGENCE OF THE GREAT SOCIETY

The whole meaning and significance of the social and psychological characteristics of the managers of great corporations and, for that matter, any understanding of the corporations themselves must be seen in larger perspective. The dynamics of change in America and the form they take are quite unlike most of what has been discussed in the literature of such disciplines as social anthropology, and not to be made clear by the usual explanations. I have called the type of change that is characteristic of America "emergent." The meaning and significance of emergence is of particular importance for our present purposes. During the several phases of development the emergent American society and others like it originate characteristics that more often come from within as part of the nature of the structure itself than as influences from the outside. Change is built into the very life of such a society; to be what it is the American society must always be in a constant state of becoming something else.

The efficient factors for change are integral parts of this emergent system. This means that the continuing available past, used and modified, comes forth into new ways as the future emerges. More concretely and specifically, the society moves in the direction of increasing heterogeneity, but to maintain cohesion in the expanding division of labor there is increasing need for coordination and unification. Along with increasing control over the natural and human environments, there has been an enormous increase in the power exercised by those at the top of the social, political, and economic hierarchies. There has also been an acceleration of social, economic, and scientific experimentation, as well as the development of a great national society.

The local communities remain, although they have been reduced in their scope, but increasingly the lives of their members are being woven into a great primary community which is national (not to say international) in its unity and breadth. Every day primary face-to-face interaction takes place among men from every part of the country as a regular and necessary part of their jobs. The society develops new political, social, and economic structures, which expand and relate the diversified life in the several regions into a unified whole. Meanwhile, new forms emerge and new characteristics must be domesticated and integrated into functioning and useful parts of our traditional way of life.

The very nature of corporate competition places many if not most executives at the most advanced positions of this frontier; here technological achievements and scientific experiment are incorporated into the activities of most corporations. Competitive advantage now demands that technology and science be a prime concern of the managers. Here they are not only corporate agents bent on competitive advantage but cultural mediators of the present as it moves from the past into the future. They are in the dilemma of holding to the structured past while making decisions that necessarily move them and their worlds into an unstructured and, as yet, imperfectly formed future. Not all men are emotionally and mentally capable, and not necessarily for lack of intelligence, to act adaptively and continuously for themselves and the corporations they lead in such ambiguous, conflict-filled situations. Yet many do with great success and brilliance. What kinds of men are they?

Perhaps the most outstanding characteristic of their personalities is what we shall call autonomy. An autonomous person (in Piaget's terms) is one who has internalized the group's rules and values sufficiently to act not slavishly as their creature but creatively as an individual. In an emergent society, those who lead must almost by necessity be autonomous; they must be free to make decisions in the poorly defined situations that are a natural part of an economy and a society that must be in continual change to realize its potentialities. The values controlling our family life also emphasize autonomy; for most individuals, the family nuclei in which they are born and the nuclei formed by marriage tend to be separate and free and not merged and under one control as they are in most societies. Families with such values are likely to train and produce individuals with personalities that are autonomous, capable of making decisions on their own, and to embody the spirit and values of competitive enterprise and democratic action.[6]

A close inspection of the private worlds of the more successful executives — no more than a thumbnail sketch can be given here — reveals more about these men.[7] Perhaps their most dominant psychic characteristic is a feeling that they are on their own and capable of independent action. More deeply stated, their emotional identifications with their parents have been sufficiently loosened for them to be free and act in the present in terms of the immediate future. This does not mean hostility to either parent but, rather, freedom to make decisions on their own without reference to a past whose control might not be adaptive. They have left home not only in fact; they have left home also in spirit. Such men easily relate to their early superiors and later, as they move upward to higher command, just as easily disengage themselves from them as once again they relate to other authoritative figures in the organizations over which they assume direction. Moreover, their views of the immediate and distant worlds around them (as displayed in projective tests of their emotional and mental organization) are very instructive in terms of how they relate social reality to their psychic organization. They quickly structure what they see; events are not isolated and separate, but viewed as patterned and meaningful in terms of the decisions immediately present. Their personalities are such that they are capable of putting together the changing parts of their society and the flow of events within their economic life to form them into a world of meaning and significance for action. Such men can make decisions without being overcome by the anxiety of those who see too many alternatives of equal worth or equal ambiguity to permit action. Everyone knows that the staffs and other fact-finding agencies of great corporations pour a constant stream of information of the greatest variety across the desks of managers.

Even so, the unknown and the unverifiable are often the most important and crucial data for the decisions that must be made. It is in this world that the manager must create order out of a future that for others may seem chaotic. It is here he must act, frequently and well, if he is to succeed and his corporation prosper. The mental and emotional life of the manager, his total intelligence, here operates adaptively for him and his part of our emergent culture.

These and a number of other characteristics are important parts of the psychic make-up of most successful executives. Their personalities are products, and often adaptive ones, of our emergent society and of the autonomous families which train and rear these men. It has not been my intention to demonstrate a neat fit between society and individual or to say that the successful manager is self-contained and unlike the rest of society. Rather,

I have tried to indicate what the private worlds of many successful executives look like to the investigator in order to show what their larger roles are in this emergent society and to say something about how such men have been produced.

Our society continues to grow and develop. Corporate men, academicians, churchmen, politicians, and those from other great organizations are all part of the necessary organizational expansion. In this sense all of us are "organizational men"; in this sense the managers of corporations and all of us are engaged in the highly important and perhaps fateful task of creating a new society, one perhaps which will be more democratic and more capable of developing and distributing its material and spiritual rewards to our people.

7

THE CORPORATION AND THE TRADE UNION

NEIL CHAMBERLAIN

The old symbolism of "capital" and "labor" as two giants engaged in a struggle from which one would emerge as master and the other as servant has become as dusty as the lace valentine. But the notion of management and the unions as rivals in a continuing and irrepressible contest which frequently becomes bitter still persists. This latter view is only partially correct, however. It will be argued here that the contest has become largely a sporting one, for prizes which are as symbolic as the kewpie doll at a carnival sideshow, and that the reminder provided by the parties and the textbooks that management and the unions are engaged in inevitable conflict has the same uninteresting truth and half-truth as the equally frequent reminder that they have interests in common.

The arenas within which management and unions come to grips are first, the business firm, typically the corporation, and second, society at large in its political aspects. The prize for victory in the first arena consists of — or at least takes the form of — immediate economic and psychological satisfactions and a leg up on further rewards of the same kind in the future. The prize for victory in the second arena, society at large, consists of subtler satisfactions in the form of freedom to reconstruct the social structure in the shape of one's own prejudices.

The prize ring which now occupies most of management's attention is the first one: the business firm, the corporation. This is not at all surprising. For one thing, it carries the trophies which management most enjoys — power over economic resources, enabling it to build hard realities in contrast to ideological intangibles — real plants, real products, real organizations. On these its very considerable constructive imagination can be lavished.

Even to open a corner grocery store takes a degree of belief in one's organizing abilities which most people lack. To direct the fortunes of a large corporation takes peculiar and unusual combinations of creativeness, self-esteem, daring, and drive, and the very use of these qualities in the business firm creates the conditions which keep them fully utilized.

But equally important in explaining management's greater occupation with the business arena is the fact that it is operating within an ideological framework which it and its predecessors largely created. Business no longer has an ideological initiative, because present institutions still largely reflect a fashioning by its hand — government, schools, churches, civic societies, and the producing units themselves. These have been somewhat altered away from their original conception within the last quarter century, it is true, but management's reaction has been one of holding the line against further inroads rather than of creating for itself new conceptions of a society it would like to see installed. It lives with the premise that no society can possibly be any better than the recent past, hence to espouse something new is to betray what is (or was) the best and finest. This dictates a holding or, at worst, a retreating action, since the objective is to retain as much of this ideal as is feasible.

The result is that management as a functional group exercises little social *initiative*. The prize which it seeks in the social contest is only a draw, a tie, which will leave things as they are, or — even better but not very hopefully — as they were. The disillusion with so-called "Eisenhower liberalism" which spread through the business community following his re-election was indicative of this desire to stand pat, although the degree of the president's "liberal" tendencies was modesty itself.

Obviously, generalizations such as these are necessarily inaccurate in detail, but broad-brush treatment sometimes helps to achieve perspective. Probably the above outline would draw sharp criticism only from members of the group depicted, however. The picture as drawn contains nothing new. Indicative of the persistence of the old perception of the capital-labor struggle, however, is the fact that probably few except students of the labor movement would recognize that a fair amount of management's complacency with the social framework may likewise be imputed to the unions.

Despite all its agitation for "getting out the vote" and despite management's sharp criticism of labor's political activity, the unions have offered their members and the public at large nothing different or special to vote for once the votes have been gotten out. The labor movement in the U. S. has taken pride in the fact that it is nonideological. It has reveled in its bread-and-butter or pork-chop personality. The unions, like management, have chosen the firm, the corporation, as the preferred tourney field in which to joust. They have made their objective the quick payoff, since their membership demands full value for dues paid, on an annual basis.

The fact that the extra money in the pay envelope which may result from (or, more accurately, coincide with) such negotiations no longer constitutes a badly needed increment to a subsistence wage has not changed the symbolism. The union feels it must continue to play an importunate role to satisfy its members that they are getting their "fair" share.

If union officials are driven to spend their best effort to win the prize in the corporate arena, this does not imply that none of their number has social objectives as well, which can only be won in the larger, political ring. For the most part, however, these are objectives which are quite compatible with the present system — more public-supported housing, federal school subsidies, higher minimum wage, improved social security. None of these objectives, if achieved, would upset any social order or cause many businessmen a sleepless night. There are among union leaders today few who shelter revolutionary or radical designs. The accusing finger is always pointed at one man, Walter Reuther, largely because he has shown himself to be both intellectual and articulate, but Reuther is not only a lonely man among his fellow union leaders but has had little success in selling his ideas to his own membership.

American unionism can hardly be regarded as a labor *movement*, since it betrays no sense of direction and is content to drift. If management provides no initiative in the social field, neither do the unions. If one were to look for political leadership in the

United States, the labor movement would be about the last place one would expect to find it. The eyes of the union, no less than management's, are directed to the contest in the corporation — to the struggle over a little more money, a little more job security.

For many years irritated corporate officials have complained that the unions, with their continued importunacy, with their readiness to enlarge the scope of their demands, were gradually taking over management's functions. Some argued that the inevitable consequence would be socialism. In the broader context, however, it is evident how little ground for fear actually exists. The alleged radicalism of the unions was only the mark of their conservatism. The fact that their demands were addressed to management's decisions in the corporation was only evidence of their willingness to join with management in keeping the main contest out of the political gymnasium.

How little political steam there is in the unions' boilers was clearly indicated — if indeed there had been any question about it — during the recession of 1957–1958. With unemployment rising to the 7 per cent level, the unions offered nothing but token resistance to the administration's decision that potential inflation deserved more consideration than actual joblessness.

To avoid misinterpretation in an age of suspicion, let it be clear that the point being emphasized is not that the unions *should* engage in political activity for social ends, but simply that they do not, and that their unwillingness to do so has had the effect of confining their energies to the corporate theater. In effect, they have accepted the battleground chosen by management. Satisfied with the social framework within which they operate, they are content to provide an obbligato to management's lead. The unions' "challenge" to management control is more apparent than real. It is probable that never before has there existed a labor movement which has voluntarily so well integrated itself with its society. And indeed, where the worker-driven Chevrolet has become almost indistinguishable from the employer-driven Cadillac, why should the worker feel himself divided from a superior class?

The consequences of this confinement of the labor contest to the business field are several. For one thing, it spares the United States from the more divisive political contests encountered in those countries where unionism is allied to socialism or to other blocs with an ideological orientation. If the reduction of social pressures is a desirable objective (as even radicals would have to admit, at least as an ultimate objective), then the absence of any significant ideological struggle from the American scene contributes to the desired end.

But other consequences too follow from the unique characteristics of this country's labor movement, some less desirable. The question of leadership in the unions is likely to become more and more difficult of solution. One possible source of future union leaders might be the young politically-oriented individuals who see the unions as a vehicle for their political ambitions. But if unions abstain from any significant independent political activity, they cannot offer attractive futures to ambitious young political careerists. What magnetism does a nonpolitical labor movement hold for the politically sensitive? In other societies, the labor movement has traditionally attracted the political nonconformist: it could look to "radicals" for leadership. But how can conservative unionism expect to attract — or to offer ladders to high position to — the free thinkers and radicals? Here one potential pool of leadership talent, on which the American labor movement drew in the past, offers no future promise. If fresh political leadership is important in order for a society not to stagnate, what institutions will nourish the young nonconformist in the United States? In some countries, the labor unions have traditionally performed that function.

Or can it be expected that the economic plight of the working mass will draw to the unions, as it did in previous decades, idealists who seek some personal part in efforts to better the sorry lot of society's population base? Only to ask the question is to answer it. What idealist can be challenged now by the "plight" of workers struggling to secure an increase in pay so that they may purchase a color television set, a better car, a more up-to-date kitchen appliance?

If the political aspirant, the social reformer, and the young idealist cease to be sources of union leadership, what types can we expect in the future to rise to office in unions whose focus is on the award in the business prize ring? Undoubtedly a number of types could be suggested, but two deserve special mention.

First, there is the individual who would have risen in the business hierarchy itself if he had had the ability or the opportunity. This would include those of potential administrative or leadership caliber who had been unable to secure a college degree, something which has now become almost indispensable to success, at least in the large corporation. Union leadership may yet come to be the mark of success of the formally uneducated man. At the present time it includes those, too, who were victims of the Great Depression of the thirties, when corporations were doing little recruiting of young executive talent. It seems unlikely, however, that future depressions will have the duration that would make them promising nurseries of union leadership.

For those in this first category, union office comes as a substitute for a management position which quite likely would have been preferred. It can be expected that union leaders of this type will exhibit most of the same middle-class standards of morality and ambition that characterize their more fortunate business counterparts. Lacking formal education, at least to the same degree, they may not show quite the same polished public image as does the businessman, but beneath the rougher exterior there will be the same desire for respectability and acceptance. No applecarts will be upset by these officials, for whom the act of upsetting an applecart could cause only great social embarrassment. Although they will not frequent the social circles dominated by businessmen, they will be members of the same service clubs and will sometimes be cited by businessmen's organizations for their contribution to industrial harmony.

If the United States is fortunate, its unions will be officered by men like these. From them management can expect some hard fighting, but only in the business field, so that no serious advantage will be forfeited even if management occasionally or even frequently loses a joust. But there is a second type of union leader, of whom this country has lately become more conscious, whose numbers are likely to increase by virtue of the fact that the industrial encounters in this country are confined to the business area, where the rewards in this affluent society are no longer literally the bread and butter or pork chops which some Robin Hood of a union leader sought to secure for his people, but cash, which, if diverted to some buccaneer's pocket, will harm no one else. Unions now offer prizes of power and money to those who are ruthless or shrewd enough to seize them for themselves. Thus a second class of people from whom unions, in the circumstances they now find themselves, are likely to draw their leaders is the class of adventurers.

Some of these adventurers may be pirates outside the law, carving out their own racket dominion within a gangster empire. Others may seek to stay this side of the law, or at least within some shady area where legal censure is uncertain. Probably most of such adventuring will simply take the form of internal political manipulation for personal advantage. In whatever form, it may be expected to occur principally in industries populated by small businesses rather than in the large corporations, but there is no basis for assuming that this will always be the case. At the same time, it would be unwarranted to expect the class of union buccaneers to overshadow the labor movement as a whole. While piracy will probably increase in importance, middle-class aspirations can be expected to predominate.

This is not to say that all unions will be led by men of one or the other of these types. All that is here argued is that if present characteristics of the American labor movement persist, these are two types which are likely to become numerically more significant.

Recent Congressional hearings have indeed awakened public consciousness to the existence of the more colorful of these two strata of union leadership. As one unsavory story followed another on the front pages of the daily newspapers, the association between unionism and corruption in our business society seemed more and more confirmed — corruption in the forms of racketeering, gangsterism, and monopoly position secured by strong-arm methods. But even more interestingly, in marked contrast to the state of affairs preceding World War II, there has been growing acceptance of the view propagated by the public press that unions — under whatever kind of leadership — have gained such strength in the American economy that even the managements of large corporations must knuckle under to them. The attitude has become more generalized that managements have been forced to make major concessions to the insatiable unions and that here lies the principal cause of rising prices. In the new impressionistic abstraction, even General Motors and United States Steel figure as the beleaguered victims, puny figures cringing or dancing before a whip-lashing, grinning monster labeled "Labor." How different from the cartoon versions of even a quarter century ago, in which the giant figure carried dollar signs over his vest and smoked a fat cigar while trampling with pleasure the little men who vainly tried to escape his iron heel!

If unions have been acquiescent in battling with management in the latter's own chosen ground, the corporate field, has this strategy then been rewarded with greater prizes than if they had forced the conflict into the arena of political action and ideology? Have the unions indeed grown so great in the last quarter century, feeding on the meat of governmental protection and public indifference, that their power is now beyond the ability of management to resist? To answer this question we must undertake a side excursion to examine the basis of their relative bargaining powers.

Of course most unions of today are vastly more powerful than their weakling or nonexistent forebears of the early thirties. There was no automobile union prior to 1933, so technically whatever powers the U.A.W. has since mustered represent an infinite increase. So with many other industrial unions. The A.F.L. craft unions, with a few exceptions, found themselves in 1933 preserving only the forms and panoply of unionism, shadows without substance. The accretions of power since then have thus been — relatively — great. But the ratio in which we are interested is not that of today's union power relative to union power in 1933, but today's union power vis-à-vis today's management power compared with that same power relationship in 1933. For if unions have grown in that time, so may have the corporations.

Indeed, it is not even the comparison of present with past union power relative to management power which occupies us now as much as the question of whether union power relative to management power today — whatever it may have been in the past — is overwhelming. Perhaps the most direct way of approaching that question is by inquiring what restraints, if any, are there on the union's power to bargain concessions from management.

First let us assume we are dealing with pecuniary issues — wages, pensions, holidays, vacations. Obviously there must be some ceiling on the amount which unions can win. No union is likely to be granted a 100 per cent wage increase, for example, and when we ask why not, we are asking at the same time why it may also be unable to obtain a 10 per cent increase.

Suppose the wage bill in a company runs to a million dollars. A 10 per cent increase would require the management to find somewhere an extra $100,000. In some circumstances this may not seem an impossible task. New machinery or improved organization may mean that fewer employees will be needed, so that the sum required is actually less than $100,000. Or sales may have been exceptionally good, so that at the new (and probably more efficient) level of output, the higher wage bill can be tolerated and still permit a higher earnings rate. Or demand for the company's product may be so brisk as to suggest that a slight price increase, perhaps coupled with some change in product design, is warranted. Under the circumstances, management might well prefer to grant a 10 per cent wage advance if it was convinced that the alternative would be a shutdown of its operations. If the union were asking a 25 per cent increase, however, and was serious about it, management's calculation of the effect on its income statement of an added $250,000 charge might be somewhat different.

At other times management's assessment of the consequences of a 10 per cent wage increase might run in other terms. The capital costs of new equipment to raise productivity might constitute a sharp drain on income, so that finding an additional $100,000 for employees would cause trouble. New competitors in one's own line of products, or sharper competition from old rivals, or new product lines which reduce consumer interest in one's own offerings are constant threats to even the large corporation, and the assumption of added costs may seem unthinkable at a time when the struggle is simply to keep up present levels of output, since any decline in production decreases income more than it does costs. Moreover, in such competitive circumstances one hesitates to worsen his market position by increasing the prices of his product line. The net effect of these considerations may be that management refuses the increase demanded by the union, offering some lesser sum instead. And if the union appreciates the firmness of management's position and considers that it may have to ask its members to take a long strike if they are to get more than management offers, and may then not get anything more but only endanger certain of their jobs, the strike call will not be made lightheartedly. Indeed, many leaders of local unions will testify that in such situations it is management that holds all the bargaining cards.

It has frequently been argued that pattern bargaining reduces management's power in these latter situations. National unions press on "follower" firms the same settlement that has been wrested from the larger and more affluent firms. To some extent this argument has validity, but the extent is less than is often imagined. In industries like steel and automobiles, the major firms have formed into *de facto* bargaining associations, in which it is usually the hardship of a given settlement on the least affluent member of the junta which controls what offer will be made by them. In other industries, the ability of a national union to force some pattern on follower firms is limited by the same considerations we have already noted.

The belief is unwarranted that national unions have large treasuries out of which strike benefits can be paid, so that workers feel freer to strike because they will suffer no economic loss. Union treasuries would be quickly bankrupted if they were drawn on so irresponsibly. They must be reserved to provide for the needs of the neediest strikers in relatively few strike situations if they are to be effective at all.

There are instances, to be sure, where national union representatives have pushed local unions into strikes in support of some wage pattern against the will of local union members, and these can always be cited in support of the thesis that national unions can harass small firms almost at will. But the number of such instances is small indeed relative to the total number of bargaining situations, and represents for the most part simply mistakes of judgment, where the union underestimated the cost to a company of paying the increase sought, rather than any malevolent, ruthless, or piratical act.

Finally, the notion that business rivals will pose less of an objection to a wage demand if they all pay equally, since their competitive situation will remain the same, is one which we need not consider here. This view has a close kinship with the belief that union-bargained wage increases are largely responsible for a cost-push inflation, a matter still subject to debate among professional economists. But to the extent that this view is justified, we may ignore it in the context of the present argument, since the union under the circumstances imposes no special hardships on the firms with which it bargains, even if it does on the economy: the producer recoups his position at the expense of the consumer. To the extent this view is unjustified, and the associated employers cannot recover added wage costs from the buyers of their products, we may expect resistance to union wage demands for the reasons already indicated.

The conclusion which emerges from this sketchy analysis is that unions do not possess some irresistible power to extract increases which their greedy and irresponsible leaders dictate to management. Their leaders may be as greedy or irresponsible as other elements in our economy, but the corporate managements facing them across the bargaining table have their own powers of resistance, which are sometimes effective. That the results of negotiations have in the postwar years usually been wage increases for employees is probably far more a consequence of the prosperity of the American economy than of the strength of unions.

Indeed, most labor economists who have undertaken research to establish whether unions have been able to provide differential rewards for their members over the employees of unorganized establishments have concluded either in the negative or in a very much qualified affirmative. In particular industries or localities the union effect may have been much greater, of course, but the impression one gets from the careful and objective studies which have been made is that, in general, an agnosticism as to union influence on wages is warranted.

This is not to imply that some manifestations of union power are not excessive and undesirable and should not be subjected to public control. It is to suggest, however, that the notion that union power is so monolithic that it sweeps all before it is more supportable by prejudice than by impartial analysis.

Unions have, however, without doubt influenced the forms of remuneration. The numerous fringe benefits — added holidays; longer vacations; sickness, accident, and unemployment supplemental benefits; improved pensions; jury pay; and so on — have been introduced largely in response to union demands and as alternatives to further increases in hourly remuneration. Here the union's bargaining impact has been substantial; at the same time, it seems hardly a matter of moment to management in what form its workers draw their compensation.

Now let us turn to the nonpecuniary concessions which unions have been able to bargain from managements. These include such matters as reliance in whole or in part on seniority for layoffs and promotions, assurances that rates of pay once set will not be changed arbitrarily, guarantees of prior notice in the event of layoffs, compulsory union membership, provisions against discrimination on grounds of race, sex, and color, but, perhaps most importantly, establishment of a jointly administered grievance procedure. This last is designed to permit enforcement by individual employees of any of the provisions of the collective agreement which they interpret in their favor and also to allow protest of unfair disciplinary action by management.

Whatever the unions' effectiveness may be in winning differential wage advantages for their members, there is virtually no dispute that their representation of members in the grievance process provides a major benefit. The helplessness of the individual employee to protect himself from discriminatory actions of a foreman in pre-union days is now generally admitted by management itself. The individual worker has acquired a feeling of independence through the realization that he can protest with impunity a foreman's decision which appears arbitrary and unwarranted, even though he still is obliged to obey that decision while his protest is being heard. If managements — and in particular foremen — sometimes smart under the decree of worker cockiness fostered by the grievance procedure, it is understandable, but from an uninvolved position one may also quite understandably feel pride in an industrial system that permits its most menial member to defend his rights.

The apathetic attitude many members take toward their union has sometimes been regarded by management as expressing a lack of attachment to the organization. In the light of the grievance function, such a conclusion is probably not sustainable. A great many members who never show up at union meetings, never participate in union elections, seldom read the union publication, and feel no emotional loyalties nevertheless regard it as a desirable "insurance policy." Even a respected foreman or supervisor is susceptible to errors of judgment or to decisions based on misinformation or emotion, and sometimes these create hardship. One never expects this to happen to himself, any more than he expects theft or fire, but he has seen it happen to his fellows often enough that protective insurance seems desirable. His union dues buy that insurance. If he is apathetic toward the union, he is probably no more so than he is toward his other insurance policies.

If the above analysis is correct, the union's economic role has been a relatively modest one, but it has played a major role in providing representation of its members' job interests and insurance against arbitrary actions by management. The more spectacular view that unions have an overweaning power to wrest wage increases almost at will from helpless managements appears to have little validity, and the effectiveness of union power seems largely confined to their modest and appealing success in securing equitable treatment for their individual members in shop and office and store.

If this conclusion is sound, however, it raises the question of why all the union-management conflict? If managements have come to accept unions in the grievance procedure — and this is their greatest contribution — why should union members undergo or face the protracted wage negotiations, the costly strikes, the arduous picketing? If these add little to the unions' gains, why should they make these sacrifices? Or alternatively, if these, even when successfully resisted, save management relatively little, why should it fight them at such cost?

There are several possible answers. One argument has it that if wage gains come too easily workers will be restive. There is some emotional satisfaction in believing that one's earnings are what they are because one has driven a good bargain. The story is told of an employer who gave the union the full 10 cent increase which they demanded, without argument, in the first few minutes of negotiations, leaving the union representatives with nothing further to talk about, no reason for pounding the table, no basis for feeling that they had waged a fight on behalf of their constituents. That same union the following year made sure its demands were high enough to evoke employer resistance and a strike, with a resulting settlement that they helped to make.

Dramatizing a factitious worker control over wage settlements is not a very acceptable rationale for collective bargaining, however. A more likely explanation is that, in the area of wage determination no less than in grievance handling, the union is looked on as insurance. It would be hard to convince many workers — and probably hard to convince many economists — that wage increases of the same magnitude would have come so soon without the union. The differential gain may in fact be slight — hardly enough to upset the business firm, whose costs (and returns) are seldom calculated quite so precisely as is sometimes thought. But the average apathetic union member believes firmly that if he had to wait for management to give him an increase he would have to wait an unconscionably lot longer than is the case when his union is on the job. His belief may be in error, the difference in the timing of his wage increase might have been only a matter of months, perhaps at most a year or so, but he has no way of knowing, and the salient consideration to him is that he no longer has to wait for management in its infinite wisdom to make up its mind, since his union has taken the decision on timing out of management's hands.

Economists have often declared themselves in favor of the unions' noneconomic contribution, which, it has been maintained here, is its most important function. At the same time, some have deplored the unions' efforts at wage manipulation. Such an evaluation may be evasive, however. What if the two functions — the economic and the noneconomic — cannot be disentangled? What if the union can remain a viable organization, performing its day-to-day protective functions, only because members believe it also provides them some insurance against "unfair" wage decisions? It then becomes necessary to determine whether the noneconomic function with its favorable effects is sufficiently valuable to more than offset the economic function which is viewed as adverse.

In the light of the above analysis, the answer might well be in the affirmative. But then a more arresting problem intrudes.

Unions have in recent years been allowed to exercise certain legislated privileges and judicial immunities. Picketing has frequently been undisturbed even though it contained more of an element of threat than of persuasion. Restraints on the use of the strike have been approached with caution. The pooling of resources by numerous local labor groups to form a national organization capable of marshaling general support in any threatened location has been pursued even in industries that are substantially local in their operations. Worker violence has sometimes been condoned or blinked at by public officials, even when the law was contravened, on the presumption that when people's emotions are aroused some overflow beyond the confines of peaceful channels is to be expected.

These privileges have been granted or taken on the ground that without them a union's effective power was emasculated. If one believed in unions at all, one was led along to accept the devices by which unions achieved some degree of bargaining power.

But if it can be asserted that the union's chief contribution is in its protective function in the making of shop rules and their application in the grievance process, then this issue is raised: is the bargaining power which unions bring to the grievance process the same bargaining power which they bring to wage negotiations? If the lenient treatment of union excesses is designed to preserve to the unions an effective bargaining power in wage negotiations, but if the unions' role in wage negotiations is at best a modest one, is it then possible to restrict more severely the unions' strong-arm tactics, without thereby endangering their ability to secure individual fair treatment for their members in the grievance process?

We do not yet have the basis for a confident answer to that

question. Although the power contest between union and management is most generally associated with negotiation of the agreement, and the subsequent interpretation of the agreement through the grievance process is often described as judicial in nature (with power absent as an influence), the fact is that the power relationship between the parties is never settled, even temporarily. There are at least two types of situation in which it continues to manifest itself.

Ever since collective bargaining became governmentally enforceable in 1935, the question has been debated as to whether a management's obligations to its union are satisfied by its adherence to the terms of the agreement signed by both parties. Managements have almost uniformly contended that their only duty was to live up to their contract, and conversely that the union's only rights were those spelled out in that same contract. All other powers were reserved to management, for it to exercise in its discretion. Unions, on the other hand, have tended to argue that management could make no decision affecting the interests of its employees without consulting the union.

This debate has gone unresolved, although in recent years it has veered more to the "management's reserved rights" end of the spectrum. The chances are this argument will never be settled, however. It would certainly appear that once an agreement is signed, for its lifetime management has preserved a right of initiative in the conduct of the business, without any necessity of prior consultation with the union. Such right of initiative is the essence of management. At the same time, it appears equally certain that there is a shadowland wherein management's decisions so intimately affect the interests of its workers that the process of collective bargaining, if it has any genuineness, requires a good-faith attempt at reaching an understanding with the union, even if, in the absence of agreement, the union has no right to block management's action. This shadowland exists not simply because of any immaturity in the bargaining process but because, even if the parties wished most earnestly to do so, they could never anticipate all the situations which might arise or the decisions which management might feel it desirable to make under unforeseen circumstances.

The existence of such a shadowland — even if denied by management and given undue substance by the unions — provides an area within which power relations can be exercised even after an agreement has been signed. The struggle over the wage issues or other terms of a contract, at recurrent negotiating sessions, by no means settles even temporarily the relative power positions of the two parties. They remain in a bargaining relation from issue to issue throughout the contract period.

A separate but related postcontractual stage on which the power contest is fought out is the grievance procedure itself, as established by the agreement, in which individuals may charge they have been unfairly treated by management. In principle, decisions in the grievance process are presumed to have a judicial quality, constituting determinations of whether the terms of the agreement have been properly applied by management or of whether disciplinary penalties have been in accord with common-law standards of equity. In practice, however, the process reflects the bargaining power relationship, as the union seeks to widen the area of the agreement by interpretation, or management seeks to narrow it. At times one side may concede on one case in exchange for victory in another. Or the employees in a shop may threaten an avalanche of grievances against their foreman unless he sees things their way on some matter vital to them. Or the company may overlook some union or employee violation either to gain goodwill or invite reciprocity. Or management may make a concession in interpretation in exchange for the union's agreement not to press a particular demand at contract negotiation time. Even the question of how high in the multi-stage appeals process a case should be carried may be a matter of bargaining strategy, in particular the decision as to whether the issue should be taken to arbitration.

But even when we grant that bargaining power plays an important role in union–management relations during the lifetime of an agreement, we cannot thereby conclude that unions require the same degree or kinds of power and privilege as they now enjoy in order to represent their members effectively. The question still remains: if unions are given legal immunities on the assumption that these are needed in negotiating for agreements on wages and other monetary benefits, and if these bargained benefits are relatively slight, the real gain for workers coming through union protection against unfair or discriminatory treatment, then do unions need their present privileges to provide this latter function?

That this question will be argued more and more in the future there can be little doubt. Until recently, it was only the foes of the unions who were anxious to clip their wings. It is truly significant that in the post–World War II years it is also economists who regard themselves as friends of unions who have become increasingly willing to reconsider the basis and need for their power. It is to be underscored, however, that this attitude stems less from a belief that unions have been able adversely to affect the wage structure and wage level with their power, than from a growing conviction that union power has had a remarkably minor effect so that the unions' exercises have been largely uneconomic and perhaps, under the circumstances, somewhat unsocial.

If this view becomes more widespread and if it has the effect of diluting the resistance to restrictive legislation on union activities, however, one consequence is almost certain. The unions will be driven more and more into political activity, where, economists are convinced, they can have a more potent influence than at the bargaining table, through legislation dealing with tax distribution, transfer payments, public expenditures, full employment measures and so on. The interesting fact is, however, that such a turn of events would be largely anathema to the present contingent of labor leaders. It would thrust them onto a stage on which most of them would feel exposed and uncomfortable.

Let us summarize briefly the above argument. Unions and managements come to grips in two fields of action, the business firm and society at large. Management has preferred to fight its battles with labor principally in the corporate arena, with which it has greatest familiarity and over which it is more capable of maintaining control in a social setting generally congenial to it. The unions have been content to follow this pattern. As a result, they have increasingly tended to breed a strain of leadership suitable to the situation and hence susceptible to the rewards of individual power, prestige, and wealth. As in the larger society within which they operate, these individual rewards may generally be secured within the law, but there are those who have yielded to the temptations of larger rewards in the spreading jungle wilderness of illegal (or at least "less llegal") activity.

Within the corporate prize ring, where such individualists most successfully operate, and where they feel most at home, the unions have acquired a reputation for irresistible power. Corporate empires which once brought state and federal governments to heel must now bow before the union bosses, at least in the word pictographs of the popular press. Union members, vassals of their bosses, are content to be ordered to strike or not to strike, at their bosses' pleasure, because of the high wages which such power secures for them. The findings of objective scholars are quite different, however. It appears that union members enjoy little or no differential wage advantages over their unorganized brethren, and that the unions' chief contribution to their members' welfare has been to free them from the tyranny of arbitrary decision or discriminatory action in the work place. This finding has led such observers, disinterested (and sometimes even partisans of unionism) as they are, to wonder whether alternative forms of union–management relations may not be found which would eliminate the worst aspects of collective bargaining (force, violence, and a privacy which may harbor racketeering) without sacrificing its admirable gains.

Whether an alternative will be thrust upon the unions depends largely on whether the foes of unionism seek to clip a power which they fear and whether the friends of unionism acquiesce in an amputation of power which they regard as unnecessary. If this entirely possible event should take place, however, management would be thrown on the other horn of a dilemma which as yet some of their number have not recognized. For, in that event, the unions would be gradually driven to change their battlefield, and a new breed of leader would be precipitated on the scene. The face of a labor movement led in part by a group which sees it as a means of personal enrichment would fade before the quite different mask of a labor movement led by political reformers, whose objective would be a new social context in which the corporation must operate. Such a metamorphosis may occur in any case, but at a minimum the period of the transition is likely to be affected.

8

TECHNOLOGICAL PROGRESS
AND THE
MODERN AMERICAN CORPORATION

JACOB SCHMOOKLER

One of Madison Avenue's favorite devices these days is to use a wise and benign-looking man in a laboratory smock to present "the latest research findings." The admen thus capitalize on the public's belief in the ability of science to solve its problems, and help generate the notion that private enterprise wages unceasing battle to make science serve the public good.

How big in fact is the corporate research effort? Is it all socially beneficial, or is much of it social waste? What are the forces that brought corporate research into being? What happened to the independent inventor? Why is American private enterprise more research-minded than European enterprise? Is it true that only corporate giants like Dupont and Bell Telephone can bring society technological progress in the future? These are some of the questions this essay will discuss.

For the sake of perspective we shall begin with a survey of the historical background out of which the present situation emerged. We shall see that corporate research in America is a modern expression of the same forces that in an earlier day produced the Yankee inventor. However, considerable doubt exists as to the suitability today of public policies developed to meet conditions of an earlier age.

I

The seeds of industrial revolution spread by England in the early nineteenth century found nowhere as fertile a soil as in America. Sprung from the more adventurous elements of the Old

World, drawn toward material progress by religious conviction and the possibilities of an untapped continent, and endowed with a more open society than any before, Americans demonstrated early the inventiveness which made Yankee ingenuity a watchword the world over.

"The more democratic, enlightened, and free a nation is, the greater will be the number of these interested promoters of scientific genius and the more will discoveries immediately applicable to productive industry confer on their authors gain, fame and even power," Tocqueville wrote in 1840. He recognized early what was later obvious to all. Thus in 1851, in the very citadel of the industrial revolution itself, discussing the Exhibition of All Nations' Industry at the Crystal Palace in London, the London *Times* conceded, "It is beyond all denial that every practical success of the season belongs to the Americans."

By 1851 America had already given the world Franklin's stove and his experiments with electricity, Whitney's cotton gin and his principle of interchangeability of parts for mass production, Fulton's steamboat, the fastest sailing vessels in the world, Henry's discovery of electric induction simultaneous with that of Faraday, Morse's telegraph, Morton's use of ether in anesthesia, Goodyear's vulcanization of rubber, Colt's revolver, and McCormick's reaper. The magnificent products of these independent inventors foreshadowed the flood of inventions to come later, first from the independents and then from the corporations.

In the half century following the Exhibition, hundreds, even thousands, of independent inventors developed the technology which changed America from an agricultural nation to the world's foremost industrial power. Americans in all walks of life, educated and uneducated alike, seized upon the possibilities opened up by the major English inventions — the steam engine, low-cost iron and steel, and rail transportation. Factory methods and standardized products displaced handicraft technique and the craftsman's custom-built product. Water, steam, and, later, other forms of power replaced the muscle-power of man and beast. Narrow localized markets gave way to regional and national ones.

This was America's industrial revolution, and the ingenious ideas of independent inventors were an indispensable, indeed a central, part of it. While some independents, like Edison, made a career of inventing, most were part-time or occasional inventors with only one or two inventions to their credit. Many were entrepreneurs who invented improvements in their own products or methods. The rest were mainly supervisors or skilled workers, making inventions in or out of their own lines of work.

Patent statistics, while only crude indicators at best, help paint the broad outlines of what happened later. After 1900 American patents issued to individuals continued to grow for a time but at a declining rate. The high-water mark of independent invention, in terms of sheer numbers, apparently came in the period 1916–1925 in this country. During that decade, nearly 200,000 different individuals, chiefly independents, took out patents. From then on, the number of patents issued to individuals began to decline until, in recent years, only half as many patents as had been issued forty years before were issued to individuals.

The decline of the independent and the corresponding rise of the hired inventor probably reflect the same forces — the increased complexity of technology, the resulting rise in the scale of enterprise, and the growth of scientific and engineering knowledge.

In the first place, the inventions contributed by the hundreds of thousands of independents created highly complicated industries characterized by extreme division of labor and big factories. The increased division of labor generally deprived all but management and hired technologists — engineers, chemists, and the like — of the opportunity to learn enough of the technology to be able to advance it.

The growth in the scale of business, moreover, fostered the rise of the corporation. Managers and technologists became employees, not owners. Employed to solve technical problems, managers and technologists in a sense automatically become hired inventors. The inventions they make in the course of their work belong to their employers. In consequence, whereas nineteenth-century inventors, when they invented in their line of work, were ordinarily free agents, those who do so today are mainly corporate hired men.

The growth of science and engineering also played a major part in the process: improvements in technology and widening of scientific knowledge made it increasingly possible to solve technical problems by the use of science, and companies began more and more to hire technically trained men for the purpose. Earlier, technical problems were solved by the ingenuity of creative individuals. It was hard to undertake to hire such men, for one did not know in advance who they were. By contrast, today's problem-solvers emerge from colleges and universities graded and labeled, in all sorts and sizes.

Moreover, the vocational preferences of these young men have operated to the same effect. Once upon a time, youngsters interested in science and technology became independent, "woodshed" inventors. Now, after they emerge from institutions of higher learning, they seldom go back to an uncertain existence in the woodshed. The assured income, advancement prospects, diversified experience, and ample facilities offered by large and medium-sized corporations are usually more attractive.

While the advance of science and engineering made corporate inventing easier, independent invention may have become more difficult, not only because industry became so complicated, but also, perhaps, because the fields cultivated by the independents were becoming barren. We do know that when independent invention began declining, total invention began falling off in the fields which independents had created and worked most intensively. These fields, the empirical arts, include such areas as farm implements, the steam engine, traditional fields of textile manufacturing, mechanical elements generally, and consumer goods.

Just why invention slackened in most of the empirical fields is a problem. The lode of invention in any field, scientific or empirical, generally runs out after a time. Such declines may be caused by (a) a decrease in the inherent possibilities for further development in the field, (b) an increased reluctance of industry to innovate, (c) the rise of more attractive fields for inventors to exploit, or (d) some combination of the above.

Did independent invention waste away because of reduced opportunities in the empirical fields? Or did empirical invention dry up because inventive men, finding the scientific fields more interesting, hired themselves out so they could invent in them more easily? We do not know. A decrease in the opportunities for invention in the empirical fields would almost certainly cause a general decrease in independent invention. The opportunities for inventors in these fields could have fallen off because, after a hundred years or more, little was left to invent. Or perhaps the older industries associated with those areas were run by unenterprising managers and therefore offered a poor market for the new and untried. In either case, the opportunities for independent invention would have diminished.

Whatever the answer, inventive minds today generally do find scientific fields more attractive. This kind of creativity, however, usually requires the support of substantial concerns. Inventive men thus may have become employees in order to work in the fields that interest them. (The decline of independent invention may have occurred, therefore, not because of a decrease in the opportunities for woodshed invention but because of an increase in the opportunities for factory invention.)

Whatever its cause, independent invention has declined. But it has not vanished. Even today, about 16,000 United States patents a year are issued to independents. Of these, surprising as it may seem, an estimated 40 or 50 per cent are used commercially (though not necessarily profitably). Thus, at a minimum (since we omit unpatented inventions from our reckoning), each year between 6000 and 8000 new products or processes created by independents are put to use.

Moreover, since hired inventors, as well as college professors, sometimes invent things in their spare time, independents are found in fields as sophisticated as those worked by the Bell Telephone Laboratories. Indeed, a recent and very able study estimated that about half of sixty-one very important inventions appearing since 1900 were made by independents.

Most inventions by independents today, as in the nineteenth century, pertain not to scientific fields but to household goods, recreational gear, and machinery in common use. (Independents, for example, very possibly invent as many "improvements" in the automobile as are made by the hired inventors of the Big Three.) We use daily, as consumers, all sorts of gadgets, with little thought to their contribution to our comfort, and no thought at all to the independent inventors who probably created them. However, though the independent inventor is not extinct, he is no longer the major source of the economy's dynamism. The 16,000 patents independents take out annually now are a far cry from the 32,000 they took out in 1916, and less even than the 23,000 they took out in the early 1900's.

II

The nation's business firms, not the independents, are the principal source of contemporary technological progress. The increasingly greater role of the business firm is suggested by the fact that the number of patents issued to firms roughly doubled in each decade from 1900 to 1930. Such patents exceeded those to independents for the first time in the early 1930's, and no threat to the lead of business in invention has appeared since.

In the preceding section it was suggested that the decline of the independent and the rise of the hired inventor both reflected the same forces — the increased complexity of technology, the rise of large-scale enterprise, and the spread of science and engineering. In a still wider sense, both independent and corporate invention reflect the dominant currents of Western — especially American — civilization. Corporate invention, in large part, merely expresses under modern conditions the same forces that produced the independent inventors. These forces deserve emphasis here if we are to see corporate research in proper perspective. Among the important contributory factors are the frequency of large-scale warfare, the acceptance of competition and private enterprise, the belief in material progress, the open-minded attitude toward natural phenomena, and the diffusion of opportunity which goes with a commitment toward the democratic way of life.

Sponsored research until less than a hundred years ago was entirely under military auspices, except for a brief interlude in seventeenth-century Florence under Medici patronage. The United States Navy, for example, hired inventors in 1789. Similarly, government financing brought about enormous expansion of corporate research for military purposes during the two World Wars, the Korean conflict, and the troubled years that followed. But while any research yielding a military margin over a real or potential enemy may seem justified by the desire of a society to survive or spread, a different test — the test of profitability — is applied in the economic world. For a long time organized research failed that test.

In large part, organized research was unprofitable because the rudimentary state of science and engineering knowledge made it less useful than now and more readily mastered when and if needed. In the early days, invention demanded creative ability more than training and was thus a somewhat uncertain process. Business was content to let the willing independents run the risks.

The simplicity of scientific knowledge was paralleled by a corresponding simplicity of scientific apparatus. Inventors of modest means therefore could ordinarily furnish their own workshops, without assistance from patrons. When they couldn't, private individuals could often be found to back them. These circumstances have been largely reversed by the growth of science and engineering.

One aspect of the underdeveloped state of nineteenth-century science and engineering was the lower likelihood, as compared to the present, that inventive activity would yield results in the field expected. Though even today research often produces surprises, the rules for searching are more reliable. Moreover — and this is also important — because modern firms are bigger, they can diversify more easily when research yields the unexpected.

Organized research by an industrial firm first began under the impact of the discovery of synthetic dyes, by an Englishman, in the chemical industry in Germany, which even then excelled in technical education and organizational ability. By contrast, in the United States organized industrial research, outside the laboratories and workshops of independent inventors, began under government auspices: in 1887, perhaps to calm agrarian unrest, Congress established a number of agricultural experiment stations.

The first American research laboratory in private industry was established by General Electric in 1900. By World War I perhaps a hundred such, chiefly in the new fields of electricity and chemistry, had been created. World War I tripled that number. With the costs of organization already undertaken and with confidence in the value of organized research raised by the success of wartime research, most war-born laboratories continued in peacetime. World War II and the Korean conflict witnessed a repetition of this phenomenon. The significance of war in the growth of organized research, corporate and otherwise, is obviously considerable.

Yet, if wars made organized corporate research increase in spurts, between wars competition between firms made it grow more steadily. Competition between firms with and firms without research programs, and between firms with large and firms with small programs, forced an almost continuous expansion of the total private research effort. Even companies too small to do their own research entered the fray under the pressure of competition. In 1953, 3700 such businesses bought research from independent laboratories and consulting firms. Many small and medium-sized firms were compelled to organize trade association research programs to fight off big invaders from other industries. The cotton textile industry and the synthetic textile firms exemplify this relationship. In other instances small firms secured government research programs to ward off intruders. Some of the research of the Bureau of Mines is in a sense part of the bituminous coal producers' response to the inroads of the big petroleum producers in the fuel business.

The effect of competition on industrial research (and industrial efficiency) is perhaps best demonstrated by the contrast between American and British industry. In most industries, the best British firms equal the best American in efficiency. The real difference between the two nations' industries is in the average firm. The average American firm is usually much closer to the best commercial practice than is the average British firm. This difference, it may be suggested, exists mainly because inefficient firms are more likely to be driven to the wall in America than in Great Britain. In Britain they are often protected by cartel agreements or by the plausible belief that aggressive business behavior is ungentlemanly. In America the prevalence of competitive behavior tends to make industrial research compulsory for all, once it gets a foothold in an industry. In consequence, corporate research is far more common in America.

The greater intensity of the corporate research effort in America has helped build up America's supply of scientists and engineers by providing a market for their services. Thus, in the early 1950's scientists and engineers numbered 5.2 per 1000 population in this country compared to only 3.7 per 1000 in England, a difference of about 40 per cent in favor of the United States. The demand being greater in America, relatively more Americans were encouraged to become scientists and engineers.

Part of this British–American difference in the ratio of scientists and engineers to the total population has another explanation which is also worth noting because it underscores how the ability (as distinct from the desire) of corporations to innovate is conditioned by their culture. Both the costs and aims of education differ in the two countries. Real income per capita has been much higher in America than in England for a long time, so that we have been able to educate a larger proportion of our population. But beyond this, the greater availability of low-cost college education in this country as compared to England also reflects the longer reign of government based on mass suffrage here, making a reality of the public's desire for greater equality of opportunity.

Moreover, the able American college student is likely to prefer science and technology over the humanities, while his English counterpart characteristically doesn't. This difference, which obviously affects the proportion of scientists and engineers in the population, partly reflects the absence of a strong aristocratic tradition in the one country and its presence in the other. It also reflects a higher regard for material progress in America and a greater belief in its potentiality. In turn the stronger belief in the possibility of material progress in America doubtless results from the wider range of opportunities offered the common man here.

Related to the foregoing is still another aspect of American civilization. Valuing material progress, Americans are not bound by custom. They readily shift their trade to sellers with lower prices or better products. More than most countries, therefore, America provides a hospitable environment for the price-cutter and the product-innovator. When alternatives exist for those displaced by innovation, few tears are shed by anyone.

· To sum up, the pre-eminence of corporate research in America today is an outgrowth of the rise of science and engineering and of America's historical experience and institutions. Considerations of national survival in warfare first forced the development of organized research. The growth of science and engineering made organized research profitable for business. A few pioneering firms found this out themselves. The rest learned it the easy way, doing research for the government in wartime, or the hard way, trying to match the lower prices and better products of those who had made an early start in peacetime. Essential to the process was the democratic ethos which, by widening opportunity, made low-cost education available to all, and, by creating the hope of personal advancement, generated a strong interest in material things. Materialism, in turn, predisposed American youth toward technology and developed a consuming public more sensitive than most to lower prices and new products.

One so inclined may lament the decline of the free-ranging independent and his replacement by the captive inventor of the corporate laboratory. Yet in the face of the team research, expensive equipment, and lengthy projects needed to exploit the potentialities of modern science, such a shift was inevitable.

Moreover, the change to corporate invention appears to have brought with it some important but little-noted economic benefits. According to preliminary results of research now under way at the University of Minnesota, the shift to corporate invention probably reduced the lag between the time an invention is made and the time it is put to use. And, according to a study by Barkev Sanders and Joseph Rossman for the Patent, Trade-mark and Copyright Foundation of George Washington University, between 50 and 60 per cent of corporate patented inventions are used commercially, a ratio substantially higher than that for the inventions of independents. These benefits are probably explained primarily by the closer contact of corporate inventors with the needs of industry and the greater confidence their corporate superiors are likely to feel in their ideas.

III

How big are the research and development (which we shall hereafter refer to as RD) programs of private industry? In 1957, according to preliminary estimates, private industry spent $7.3 billion on RD, $4.0 billion of their own and $3.3 billion of government money. The 1957 outlays were roughly double those of 1953, the most recent year for which comprehensive data, derived from a National Science Foundation survey, were available at this writing. In 1953 three out of every five workers in manufacturing worked for companies with their own RD programs. These firms, nearly 14,000, amounted to 11 per cent of all manufacturing companies. Moreover, 1700 nonmanufacturing firms had their own RD programs. And, as noted earlier, about 3700 companies without their own RD facilities paid others to do RD work for them.

Of course the corporate RD effort is only part of society's total organized research undertaking. Moreover, as we have seen, a lot of invention goes on outside the organized programs. It would be wise to see how the organized corporate RD effort fits in the total picture. What proportion of all RD funds comes from corporations? What proportion of RD work is done by corporations? These two questions are not the same. Much of the research performed by private firms, and by universities and other nonprofit institutions, is financed by government. And private firms pay both the government and nonprofit institutions to do research for them.

In very rough terms, from 1952 to 1956 inclusive, private industry supplied on the average 42 per cent of all RD funds, government 56 per cent, and nonprofit institutions 2 per cent. When we turn to where the work was done, however, we see another picture. Private industry performed 72 per cent of all RD work (as measured by money spent), government 19 per cent, and nonprofit institutions 9 per cent.

Lumping research and development together is unfortunately misleading for some purposes, although the practical difficulties of segregating them prevent a reliable separate accounting. The term "research," for the purpose of this essay, denotes the quest for new knowledge. When that quest has no specific technological application in view, we shall call it "basic" research. When the quest is expected to terminate in an outline of a useful application, we shall consider it "applied" research. "Development" then consists in filling in the details of the outline to the point where commercial production can begin. Drawing the line between these activities is very hard in practice. Informed men will disagree in specific cases. Academicians sometimes consider as applied research what business executives regard as basic. And the former are prone to classify as development what businessmen consider applied research. The National Science Foundation, while attempting to collect statistics on basic research separately, did not try in its 1953 survey to separate development from research.

The term "research" deserves a little additional explanation. When one thinks of corporate research, the stereotype that comes to mind is Madison Avenue's laboratory scientist. Not all organized corporate research, however, occurs in the laboratory. Much of it is done with pencil and paper and computing machines in engineering research departments. In 1953 there were, according to one source, only about 4000 industrial research laboratories in the country, but, as noted, there were 15,600 industrial firms carrying on organized RD programs in their own facilities. The industrial laboratories employed only 165,000, but the organized RD programs of these firms gave work to 400,000 (including laboratory workers).

Under the circumstances any breakdown of the nation's organized RD effort into basic research, applied research, and development will be far from accurate. Nonetheless, it is worth attempting simply to get a rough idea of the order of magnitude of these different branches of the nation's scientific and technological effort. Two experts in industrial research have suggested that development typically costs two and a half times as much as research. Using this estimate and assuming that the RD work of nonprofit institutions is entirely research, one would estimate that in 1953 the nation spent $1.7 billion on organized (basic and applied) research and $3.7 billion on development. That is, of the total organized RD effort, about 31 per cent was devoted to research, about 69 per cent to development. These figures, it must be emphasized, are only approximate, and are provided only to give an idea of the order of the magnitudes involved.

In the realm of organized basic research as defined here we are blessed with an independent estimate. In 1953 about $435 millions were spent on basic research. Applying this to the estimate above of a total outlay on organized research of $1.7 billion for all organized research, we arrive at an estimate of $1.3 billion for applied research. This suggests that approximately one out of every four and a half research dollars goes to basic research.

In short, in very rough terms, of the nation's total organized RD outlays, 69 per cent goes to development, 24 per cent to applied research and 7 per cent to basic research.

Of the $1.7 billion spent in 1953 on all organized research, industry alone performed the work represented by $1.1 billion, compared to $.4 billion for nonprofit institutions and $.2 billion for government. In percentage terms, private industry performed about 60 per cent of the organized research, the universities and other nonprofit institutions about 25 per cent, and government about 15 per cent. A breakdown according to sources of funds is not possible with the data at hand.

Of the $435 million spent on organized basic research, industry supplied 40 per cent of the funds and performed 40 per cent of the work, nonprofit institutions supplied 25 per cent of the funds and did 50 per cent of the work, and government provided 35 per cent of the funds and did 10 per cent of the work.

Thus, private industry does approximately 70 per cent of all organized RD work, 60 per cent of all organized research, 75 per cent of all applied research, and 40 per cent of all organized basic research. Roughly 42 per cent of the funds used for all organized RD and 40 per cent of those for basic research come from industry.

The figures on financial support are perhaps misleading. We have seen that from 1952 through 1956 government supplied an average of 56 per cent of all RD funds. However, the great bulk of government funds were for defense purposes (a fact which suggests that roughly half of the nation's organized RD effort during the period was devoted to improving the arts of war, and an equal amount, to the arts of peace). If we could confine our figures to outlays on the peaceful arts, private industry would un-questionably prove to be the most important source of funds by far.

Beyond private industry's contribution to technological prog-ress through its organized programs are the not inconsiderable improvements made by supervisors and scientists and engineers employed in the operating divisions of industry. In 1953, scientists and engineers in the operating divisions of industry outnumbered their RD colleagues by more than two to one. A sample survey in that year found that the former produced about half as many patented inventions as did the latter. Because supervisors, as well as engineers and scientists in the producing, purchasing, and selling departments, are usually immersed in the technical problems of their companies, their inventions will surely continue to be important to the nation.

In light of the preceding, it would be only a slight exaggeration to claim that the RD programs of private industry today are the economy's green growing tip. The contributions of others, of course, are important, the basic research of government and university laboratories particularly so. Beyond these are the independent commercial laboratories, the independent inventors, and the hired inventors in the operating sectors of industry.

Indeed, the tremendous importance of the organized corporate research effort suggests that any major defects in the nation's research undertaking lie elsewhere. Particularly, the question in need of an answer is: can society itself possibly be sponsoring enough basic research if 40 per cent of the total cost of such research is being undertaken for profit? Basic research ordinarily yields far greater dividends to others, and particularly to later generations, than to those who pay for it. There is thus a strong presumption that it should be supported by public funds. That basic research now yields returns so grand that the little a private sponsor can capture is enough to make it profitable implies a great public neglect of basic research opportunities.

This chapter, however, is concerned not with public but with corporate research, and we turn now to a more detailed appraisal of the latter.

IV

Compared with its past, the present volume of corporate RD is certainly impressive. But the appropriate yardstick is not past performance but present need. The more rapid rate of Russian as compared to American economic growth makes urgent the most careful scrutiny of our present RD effort, corporate as well as public. America's power in world affairs will surely decline if the Soviet rate of economic growth continues to exceed ours. Equally certain is the great importance of private industry's RD programs to the future level of our economy.

Two major questions must be asked. (1) Are all corporate RD programs worthwhile? And (2) are firms of large size essential for modern invention and innovation?

Research is ordinarily a social waste if it seeks (a) to make a product worse or (b) to discover what is already known. The first of these requires only brief discussion and we turn to it.

One occasionally hears the claim, for example, that nylon stockings or razor blades are not as durable as they used to be. The inference is then drawn that products are deteriorated to increase sales. At face value, this is a socially objectionable practice, and any research designed to achieve it wastes research talent which could be put to better use. The infrequency of the charge of product deterioration, however, suggests the practice is uncommon, if it exists at all. If this assumption is correct, the implication is that certain social defenses discourage it.

The surest social defense is a competitive economy. Under competition businessmen gain customers when they offer a better product and lose them if they offer an inferior one. Purposeful product deterioration, moreover, runs the danger of violating the antitrust laws. An informed consuming public also discourages the practice.

Finally, strange as it seems, product deterioration is sometimes desirable. A Cadillac is better than a Chevrolet, but if we had only the former it would be worth developing the latter. The loss in quality would be more than offset by the reduction in cost. (Secondly, when a manufacturing process is poorly controlled, the product may vary from outstandingly good to unusable. Improved process control usually has as its object a product of "reasonably good" quality.) A uniform output of "outstanding" quality generally entails a greater cost than consumers would pay. The lucky buyer of one of the rare "outstanding" units of an early batch will naturally be suspicious when he receives only a "reasonably good" unit later. Because consumers probably would not pay what it costs to produce an outstandingly good article, such product deterioration is in the public interest. Over time and under competition, methods and products both improve, and products of good quality tend to be replaced by better ones at the same or lower prices.

The second variety of socially wasteful research, the effort to discover what is already known, is undoubtedly much more important. Research to discover what is actually known may be undertaken intentionally or unintentionally. Few researchers know everything in their own fields. They thus may unknowingly re-create what had been created before. Patent applications are frequently denied because the invention claimed was known; this fate is more likely to befall the independent than the corporate inventor. A corporate inventor usually has at his disposal a substantial technical library. Yet even corporate inventions often duplicate past accomplishments unintentionally. The obvious remedy for such wasted effort is an efficient means for seeking the prior art, and this is one of the biggest needs of industrial research today.

Intentional duplication of effort is an inevitable result of the patent system and industrial secrecy. Companies carry on research to improve their products and processes in order to outdo each other in the competition for the consumer's dollar. If they shared results with rivals, they would lose what they hope to gain. Hence, they tend to keep their results to themselves through patents or secrecy. Few of the best patents are licensed to others. If rivals want to stay in the running, they too have to improve their products or processes. In consequence, much industrial research — just how much cannot be said — is merely devoted to finding another way of doing what can, from a technical standpoint, already be done.

While duplicative inventive activity occasionally turns up something better than the original, usually only a reasonable facsimile of the original is produced. The same effort spent to improve the original method might have added more to society's fund of knowledge. But a rival will not improve another's invention, since use of the improvement would probably entail patent infringment, although he might improve on the original and take out a patent to keep his rival from having it. The patent system and industrial secrecy thus induce much research intended to duplicate rather than to improve existing technology.

Indeed, the patent system assures that much research is based not on the latest technical knowledge but on that of at least seventeen years ago. Except for its novel features, an invention may embody only knowledge already in the public domain (except for more recent knowledge patented by the inventor or his employer). Patented knowledge is closed to the public until the patent right expires, and the term of patents in this country is seventeen years.

A second and perhaps greater waste follows from the first. Patents and industrial secrets, by closing off much of the most advanced technology, limit most firms to making inferior goods with inferior methods. Curiously enough, the Russians, at a cost of twenty-five cents each, buy copies of American patents and use the latest discoveries of American industrial laboratories freely in Russian industry. Yet only patentees and their licensees can lawfully use these discoveries in America.

Responsibility for this situation rests not with private industry but with the public. The patent system, is, after all, a public, not a private, institution.

The arguments over the merits of the patent system have been long, heated, and inconclusive. Its defenders hold that it stimulates invention, disclosure, and innovation; that, the difficulties mentioned above and others as well being granted, because of the invention, disclosure, and innovation it fosters, the technology actually in use at any time is more advanced than would otherwise be the case; and that independent inventors and small business especially need the protection of patent rights.

These arguments carried more conviction when society depended mainly on independents for its technological progress, for independents need something to sell. Corporations, however, can use their inventions themselves.

The patent system, moreover, gives signs of breaking down. Firms expanded their RD activities greatly over the past two decades, but their patenting increased hardly at all. More and more, firms seem to patent only what they have little hope of keeping secret. Thus the objective of disclosure is poorly served. Their research is guided less by the possibility of patents than by the pressures of competition. While they are pleased to have pat-

ents when introducing new products, they usually rely for protection not on them but on beating their rivals to the market. And
more often small firms are kept out of industries by insiders' patents than they are enabled to enter through force of their own.

Impressed by highly publicized disclosures of the abuse of
patent rights to circumvent the antitrust laws, the public through
its elected representatives has contributed to sabotaging the patent system. At least until relatively recently, Congress provided
such poor financial support for the Patent Office that it fell far
behind in its work. The courts, responding to the increasing
disrepute into which the patent system had fallen, have done their
share to sap its vitality. In the past two decades over 60 per cent
of the patents litigated before them were held invalid by the
United States Courts of Appeal. In the Supreme Court a dissent-
ing Justice expressed the fear that the only valid patent in the
future might be one on which that court had not yet passed judgment.

The patent system can be either strengthened (as Congress
has attempted to do in the past three or four years through legislation and larger appropriations), modified in various ways, or
replaced by an entirely different method of achieving its objectives. Which of these alternatives should be pursued is hardly a
question to be answered here. At present the Senate Subcommittee on Patents, Trademarks and Copyrights, and the Patent,
Trade-Mark and Copyright Foundation of George Washington
University are sponsoring numerous studies relating to the patent
system. These should pave the way for a much-needed, large-
scale, coordinated investigation of the patent system as a whole
and its alternatives.

The principal alternatives to the present system are compulsory licensing and the payment by the government of bounties to
inventors or their backers, the inventions thereafter being freely
available to all.

If it could be effectively administered, the bounty scheme is
almost certainly superior to its alternatives. Compulsory licensing
involving payment of "reasonable" royalties would place a burden on the application of the latest technology and therefore discourage its use. The bounty scheme, by contrast, by making new

technology free, would place it in this respect on a par with old technology and not discourage its use. No incentive for inventing around new inventions would remain, and duplication of research effort would be correspondingly reduced. Compulsory licensing, by curtailing inventors' rights below those they now have, would discourage invention and, with respect to such inventions as were made, encourage secrecy. Large enough bounties, on the other hand, might encourage both invention and disclosure well beyond present levels.

Though on a much larger scale, the bounty scheme resembles the suggestion systems employed in private industry and government agencies, through which employers reward employees for valuable suggestions. Whether the public would be willing to pay firms enough to induce them to turn their inventions over to the public is a serious question. Would the $100,000,000 — say — paid each year, under a bounty system, to Dupont or General Electric become a political issue? If the Soviet continues to catch up with the United States, perhaps not.

Another method of eliminating duplication would be to have the government carry on industrial research and turn the results over for industry to apply. However, if private industry also continued to engage in research, duplication would be greater than ever. If the government's program were so extensive as to eliminate private research, then the benefits resulting from the present close proximity of industrial research to industrial operations would be lost.

But beyond that, government research would entail enormous centralization of decision making. All men are fallible, and in the field of choice of suitable research projects, the best men have been amazingly so. James Watt, inventor of the steam engine, discouraged attempts of a subordinate to apply the engine to transportation. The leading experts of the time thought Marconi's long-distance wireless experiments sought to violate the laws of nature. In the early 1930's Robert A. Millikan declared the proof was conclusive that splitting the atom would consume more power than it would produce. The greatest of them all, Ernest B. Rutherford, held a similar view. In the middle 1940's Vannevar Bush contended that intercontinental ballistic missiles were not worth following up. In the late 1940's J. Robert Oppenheimer firmly believed the hydrogen bomb was not feasible.

Charles F. Kettering was fond of saying his researchers made the most progress when they assumed the textbooks were wrong. Many great discoveries are characterized by the extent to which they contradict previous scientific opinion. In this way they open up wholly new territory. Working in terms of existing beliefs tends to yield only improvements, not basic discoveries, either in science or technology. For this reason, putting control of all research in the hands of any single agency, however informed its decision makers, seems bound to insure only pedestrian progress. Decentralization of decision making offers a better chance that all worthwhile avenues will be explored.

In sum, research for the purpose of deteriorating products is probably negligible. Duplication of research effort among firms results from public, not business, policy. Public policy forces firms to find recompense for their research outlays in the market for goods and services. One consequence of patents and industrial secrecy is that many firms are deprived of the right to use the best methods or make the best products. The elimination, or reduction, of these wastes awaits the development of more effective public policies to promote invention, disclosure, and innovation. Such policies are likely to emerge only after a thorough, large-scale investigation of the problems involved. The groundwork for such an investigation is being laid now through a large number of smaller investigations. Public concern over the state of our technology indicates the time has arrived for a definitive-study.

v

Public policy to encourage technological progress must be based on, among other things, a sound appraisal of the relation of competition and large-scale enterprise to invention and innovation. J. K. Galbraith and, before him, the late Joseph A. Schumpeter, both of Harvard, popularized the view that modern invention and innovation are substantially dependent on big firms. Only such firms, they held, had necessary resources for modern research and development. Only the large corporations, they further contended, were likely to be sufficiently insulated from imitators to recoup their RD outlays before the gains were disseminated to the public by competition.

Judge Wyzanski, in the United Shoe Machinery case, suggested instead a contrary possibility: "Industrial advance may indeed be in inverse proportion to economic power; for creativity in business as in other areas is best nourished by multiple centers of activity, each following its unique pattern and developing its own esprit de corps to respond to the challenge of competition." T. K. Quinn, former vice-president of General Electric, has argued the same point in less judicial language.

Almost all agree that, to reward invention and innovation under existing conditions, imitators must be stalled for a while. And this in turn means presumably that the innovator must expect to have, for a time, a degree of "monopoly power." But the necessary time is probably short. Most business investments are made with an expected pay-out period of only a few years. Because of this and because imitators usually need time to bring their resources to bear, a head start is the only monopolistic advantage the innovator needs, given the rapid pace of change today. It is very doubtful that the long-term monopoly Americans find repugnant is necessary for the process. In any case, under the patent system, it is the expectation, not the possession, of monopoly power which innovators need as incentive. .

Yet, if quasi-permanent monopoly power is unnecessary for research and development, is large-scale enterprise essential? Is it only the big firms whose pocketbooks are deep enough for modern research? In 1953, according to the National Science Foundation, of 15,600 companies engaged in research and development on their own premises, 9600 firms employed fewer than 100 employees each, and another 3700 firms employed between 100 and 499. In other words, 85 per cent of the companies engaged in RD in 1953 employed fewer than 500 employees. Only 2.4 per cent of the firms engaged in RD had 5000 or more employees. Even in the industries in which research is most commonly associated with large-scale firms, the same picture prevails. In chemicals and allied products, 80 per cent of the companies doing research, in petroleum 72 per cent, and in electrical equipment 61 per cent, employed less than 100 workers. If these figures mean anything, they mean that some modern research and development can be done by far smaller firms than some would have believed.

On the other hand, big firms are more likely than small firms to engage in RD. Only 4 per cent of the firms in the nations employing under 500 workers had their own RD program, compared to nearly 80 per cent for firms with 5000 or more employees. Moreover, partly because big companies are more likely than small to engage in RD work, they do relatively more research and development than would be suggested by their share in total employment. Thus, in 1953, manufacturing companies with over 5000 employees performed 72 per cent (in money terms) of all organized industrial RD, but employed only about 40 per cent of all manufacturing workers. Much of this difference, however, is explained simply by the greater share of large companies in government-financed research in 1953.

Actually, once a firm is engaged in research and development, the firm's size seems to have little influence on the relative scope of its RD program. If we disregard the government-financed portion of private RD, then small firms engaged in RD do relatively at least as much as big firms. Expenditures for research and development from the companies' own funds in 1953 amounted to 0.9 per cent of sales both for companies employing between 1000 and 4999 workers and for those employing 5000 or more. These outlays amounted to 0.7 and 0.8 per cent of total assets respectively for the companies in these two size groups, a difference in favor of the larger firms.

While data for firms employing below 1000 workers is unavailable for industry as a whole, we have such information for 1953 for six important industries: food and kindred products, chemicals and allied products, fabricated metal products and ordnance, machinery, electrical equipment, and professional and scientific instruments. *In three of these industries — chemicals and allied products, machinery, and electrical equipment — firms engaged in RD employing between 50 and 499 workers spent more on RD as a percentage of their total assets than did bigger firms doing RD.* In professional and scientific instruments, the ratio is largest for firms employing between 500 and 999 employees (the ratio

for firms with between 50 and 499 workers was second largest).
No data are available for firms employing 50 to 499 workers in
the food and kindred products or in the fabricated metal products
and ordnance industries. Only in the food and kindred products
industry was the ratio of RD expenditures to total assets largest
for the largest firms.

If instead of the ratio of RD outlays to assets we use the ratio
of RD to sales, the picture changes somewhat, but it is not reversed. The biggest firms in chemicals and machinery spent on
research a larger fraction of the sales dollars than the smaller firms
did. On the other hand, firms engaged in RD in electrical equipment with between 50 and 499 employees spent more of their
sales dollars on research than did larger firms. On the same basis,
firms with between 500 and 999 workers did relatively more
research than did bigger firms in both the metal products and instrument industries. In food and kindred products, the firms spending the largest fraction of the sales dollar on research were those
with between 1000 and 4999 workers, the middle-sized companies.

While many questions can be raised about the interpretation
of these data, they provide no support whatever for the notion
that only big firms are research-minded or can afford research.
True, big firms are much more likely than small ones to do research, but, as we have just seen, a small firm that does research
spends proportionally as much as a big firm and often more.

The ability of small and medium-sized firms to support research is fortunate. It helps assure the continued existence of
competitive enterprise; the big fish will not be able to eat up the
little ones. Moreover, it increases the likelihood that both the nation's inventive talent and the full range of opportunities presented by the state of knowledge will be exploited. Those blessed
with genius sometimes lack the patience or sense of humor needed
to accommodate themselves to the miles of red tape of large-scale
organizations. The existence of a large number of potential employers reduces the risk that such men will lead lives of continual
frustration and enhances the possibility that their potential contributions will be realized. At the same time the number of centers
of technological initiative will remain large and probably grow
as the quality of management in industry improves.

The foregoing does not mean that the large firm lacks advantages of any sort in the RD field. On the contrary, many fields of research are fenced off to all but the largest firms, and some of these fields are vital to the national defense. Again, since basic research pays off, if ever, only in the dim future, only a firm with great versatility and an enormous life-expectancy can sensibly undertake it. Ordinarily, this will mean only a very big firm. Moreover, many research projects demand an effort so costly as to bar all but the biggest corporations. Dupont, for example, spent $27 million between 1928 and 1940 to develop nylon before it sold the first pound made in a commercial producing unit. One large concern in the atomic energy field expects to lose money in it until 1980.

However, even the capacity to finance research does not guarantee the will to do so. Research conducted in laboratories of large firms is sometimes channeled to avoid encroaching on the interests of large rival firms. Large American companies have on occasion agreed with foreign rivals not to do research in specified fields of technology. Because of such an agreement between Standard Oil of New Jersey and I. G. Farbenindustrie of Germany, the United States lacked a much-needed synthetic rubber technology until after Pearl Harbor. The leading petroleum companies, whether by agreement or not, for a long time failed to exploit the chemical potentials of their own raw materials, apparently out of respect for the large chemical firms. The birth of the new and now rapidly expanding petrochemical industry was thus probably delayed beyond its time.[1]

Moreover, some large firms — many of those in the railroad industry, for example, — have done little or no research of any sort, probably because their large size and apparently protected position made research seem unnecessary. Unfortunately for them, firms in other industries proved more enterprising. In the face of the resulting competition from the goods and services produced by the latter, the Maginot-Line mentality of the former is crumbling. By 1953, 94 per cent of all manufacturing companies with 5000 or more employees were conducting research on their own premises. It is doubtful that in the future any significant number of large firms will be found without substantial RD programs.

Even the railroad firms have begun to support research despite, or because of, declining revenues.

And so, in a sense, we come full swing. As in an earlier day, so today the vitality of America's technology arises largely from the urge of its people for material progress and their consequent eagerness to buy better goods or to pay less for the same goods. The economy's dynamism arises likewise from the pressure of competition generated by a high degree of equality of opportunity.

Partly because the corporation, not the woodshed or base-ment, has become the major seedbed where new ideas sprout, new and unsolved problems of public policy have arisen. But beneath the changes and the problems they have brought, the historic forces of American society continue at work. Major faults in Amer-ica's present scientific and technological organization, if faults there be, lie not in the private sector but in the realm of public policy. This survey suggests that the problems concern the patent system and the scope and character of *public* support for scien-tific and technological research. The major defects in the private sector's technological performance — that is, the duplication of research effort entailed by the withholding of advanced technol-ogy from rivals — results not from private malfeasance but from public policy. The remedy thus will be distilled from changes in public policy.

Yet, if major deficiencies exist in the public, not the private, sector, this too doubtless reflects the dominant character of Amer-ican institutions. Precisely because we have directed our energies toward maximizing the opportunities open to the individual, we have tended only belatedly to recognize important areas of public policy only indirectly related to that goal. Nonetheless, such rec-ognition has usually come, however tardily. Signs point to a grow-ing recognition of the need for improved public policy toward science and technology. These signs need not be spelled out here. The newspapers are full of them. Improved public policy in this sphere unquestionably will permit a more efficient use of the great volume of private as well as public research resources.

9

THE FINANCING OF CORPORATIONS*

JOHN LINTNER

I. BACKGROUNDS AND ISSUES

Nonfinancial corporations at the end of 1957 may be estimated to have held assets with book values of approximately $500 billion. In order to hold a dollar of assets, corporations must have obtained and still be using a dollar of financing. These figures on assets held consequently represent the net amount of financing that has been needed and obtained to support and pay for the plant and equipment, inventories, and other assets owned and used by these institutions. This $500 billion of net previous financing now being used by corporations is approximately twice as large as the present total of the federal debt held outside government trust funds, over three times the volume of currency and demand deposits, and somewhat larger than the *total* assets, until very recently, of all so-called financial intermediaries — a general category which includes *all* insurance companies, banks, savings institutions, mutual investment funds, public and private pension funds, and government lending institutions (of all types in each case), as well as the $50 billion of assets held by personal-trust departments of banks.

Approximately $48 billion of the funds used by nonfinancial corporations on an unconsolidated basis was provided by other corporations in the form of trade credit. After allowing for this degree of financing provided within the corporate sector itself, we still find corporations to be currently using over $450 billion

* This paper is a by-product of research in the general area of Profits and the Functioning of the Economy which the author has been conducting under a grant to the Harvard Graduate School of Business Administration from the Rockefeller Foundation, with particular attention to corporate dividend, financial, and investment policies.

of funds supplied by individuals, financial institutions, and others
in the economy.

The magnitude of these figures naturally reflects the major
role of nonfinancial corporations in the business activity of the
country. In recent years, for instance, over 70 per cent of the
total "value added" of all private business firms in the economy
has represented the values added in corporate business units.
The financial requirements of corporations are further increased
by the fact that — because of their well-known advantages in
attracting capital from many different sources — corporations predominate in those industries such as utilities, railroads, and heavy
manufacturing, which require relatively large amounts of plant
and equipment and other real capital in relation to current output.

The important place currently held by nonfinancial corporations in the economic and financial structure of the economy is
of course not a new development. It is the product of a long,
evolutionary, and complex process of mutual adaptation and
interaction — a process that has involved progressive, and in many
respects fundamental, changes in the character and size of these
corporate enterprises themselves, in the organization and operation of their productive and nonfinancial business activities as
well as in their financial dealings with outsiders. Any attempt to
trace out each of the important individual threads in this intricate
evolutionary process would be far beyond the scope of a single
essay, even if attention were confined to those strands of the
comprehensive skein which most directly involved and affected
the volume and pattern of corporate financing. In keeping with
the context of the present volume, this essay will give particular
attention to a limited number of trends in the position of nonfinancial corporations in the economy and in the patterns of their
financing and financial behavior over the last four or five decades
which have the most direct bearing on several broad but fundamental questions which have been raised, especially in the last
quarter century, concerning the impact of the modern nonfinancial
corporation on the structure and functioning of the economy.

The classic statement of most of these issues is, of course, the
study of "The Modern Corporation and Private Property" pre-

pared by A. A. Berle, Jr., and Gardiner C. Means.[1] On the basis of the evidence then available, Berle and Means advanced the fundamental thesis that economic and financial power was becoming progressively more concentrated in the hands of a limited number of management groups controlling nonfinancial corporations without significant ownership interest and essentially free of the classical constraints which in earlier days had presumably ensured the best possible allocation of resources in the economy and the best possible satisfaction of the owners' legitimate rights and interests.

This result was traced to several different historical developments and trends. It reflected the increasing share of all business being conducted by corporations. More importantly, it reflected the markedly and progressively increasing concentration in a limited number of large corporations of the total assets, employment, income, and product of the entire corporate sector of the economy. Still more importantly, it resulted from the marked centralization of the effective control over the tremendous assets of the large corporations themselves, and of the financial decisions of these corporations, in the hands of small largely self-perpetuating groups of professional managers with very small if not insignificant personal ownership of the assets under their control.

In many ways the centralization of authority in a management separated from ownership was the most fundamental. However inevitable this development may have been, it had fundamentally altered historically important property rights of owners and thereby weakened and in some respects severed the traditional *legal* constraints on management discretion. It had attenuated the classical, and presumably effective, *economic* controls by which each owner's actions taken in his own self-interest would interact in freely competitive markets to ensure the greatest composite social good — Adam Smith's famous "invisible hand." And at the same time, it had placed management in a position where stockholders' rightful interests in dividends could be disregarded. The consequent increasing and excessive use of retained earnings to finance growth directly served to increase concentration, and thereby it ominously magnified the power of large nonfinancial corporations (and the small management groups in control of them) in other dimensions, including product markets. In addition, this greater growth of the largest companies through retained earnings was compounded by more extensive issuance of new securities — securities which, by implication at least, would generally not have been issued if stockholders themselves had really controlled the decisions on expansion and financing in these largest companies. More spectacularly but less significantly,[2] concentration was increased by mergers between large firms — mergers which were greatly facilitated by the centralized authority of managements on both sides of the union. The separation of ownership and control thus impaired the shareholders' position, increased concentration among nonfinancial corporations, gave nonfinancial corporations an increasingly dominant position in the whole financial and economic structure, and led to major (and presumably undesirable) changes in corporate behavior because of increasing freedom from traditional economic constraints and pressures.

In his more recent (1954) study, *The Twentieth Century Capitalist Revolution*,[3] Berle re-emphasizes, sharpens, and extends his position of twenty-five years ago regarding the central and crucially important role of the changed legal and economic position of the stockholder, and of the manner in which large corporations are financed, in the evolution and continuing dominant power position of the large nonfinancial corporation and its restricted management group in the economic structure of the entire economy. There were, however, major differences in the position taken in other respects, which may be briefly noted.

The first important change was that twenty-five years ago, the centralized power of large corporations would distort economic results and increase concentration in considerable part because of the disproportionately heavy use of outside capital — such companies not only saved and retained more internal funds, they sopped up excessive amounts of the savings generated in the rest of the economy, to the distress of other worthy firms and the impairment of their growth and competitive potential. In the fifties, the position is rather that large corporations simply do not use the capital markets because they manage (through retained earnings) not to need to — instead of being distorted, the primary allocation functions of the capital markets are simply bypassed and thus made ineffective.[4]

One would have expected the implications to be ominous indeed. Moderate distortions in the basic mechanisms by which savings are directed to their more desired uses surely is less serious than outright elimination of the mechanism, so far as large corporations, which account for the bulk of all business investments in the economy, are concerned. But it is not so. Berle, like Lilienthal and other disciples of modern "managerialism," has had his vision somewhere on the road to Damascus, and now regards the concentrated authority of the nucleus of corporate management as being not merely inevitable but positively beneficent in important ways. It has probably enhanced the rate of industrial progress, and has stimulated pioneering and fundamental research which such corporations alone can do.[5] And as for spiritual aspects, Berle holds out that the very concentration of authority in modern corporate capitalism may yet produce "the city of God" as managers become statesmen and exercise their power in conformity with the evolving social conscience of the people.

Finally, Berle no longer argued that the share of industrial assets in the hands of large corporations is increasing — he accepted the results of Adelman's study [6] showing that the share held by these companies had been stable at around 45 per cent between 1931 and 1947. He agreed that the level of concentration was "a static condition varying slightly from year to year but increasing or decreasing, if at all, 'at the pace of a glacial drift.' . . . Accepting this, it is still a sufficiently impressive fact on the American landscape" — as it surely is.[7]

In summary, the Berle and Means thesis asserted and elaborated essentially three basic propositions. The first affirmed increasing concentration in the economic and financial structure of the American economy. The second emphasized progressive separation of control from ownership in nonfinancial corporations and the resulting centralization of economic and financial power within these corporations in the hands of small management groups increasingly free from shareholders' influence and classical market constraints. The third, on the basis of this centralization of power and freedom from constraint, asserted major changes in corporate behavior and performance.

As Berle has recognized, assets and employment are little if any more concentrated in large manufacturing concerns than they were nearly three decades ago, and, we may add, they are less concentrated among all nonfinancial corporations in the economy as a whole. But if concentration of assets and economic power within the nonfinancial corporate structure has not on balance increased over the last twenty-five years, what of the asserted trends in the relative position of nonfinancial corporations as a whole in the structure of the economy? Judgments on these larger questions had to be largely conjectural at the time of the early Berle and Means study twenty-five years ago because of the absence of good data. If the relatively well-defined trends toward increasing concentration *within* the nonfinancial corporate sector prior to 1930 have been broken off, or at least flattened out, over the last twenty-five years, perhaps the much more conjectural trends posited regarding the increasing fraction of all economic life and economic power held by nonfinancial corporations may have been similarly modified in the interim. Any such change in these latter trends could affect very significantly the broader implications of the changes which have been occurring with respect to management control within the large corporations in the corporate sector itself. Fortunately we are now in a position for the first time to remove much of the conjecture regarding these latter trends for the period prior to 1930, as well as to identify the resulting movements since that time. The evidence is summarized in Section II.

The Berle and Means study remains a standard reference [8] on the unquestioned fact of the very substantial separation of effective control from the bulk of ownership. But again major questions remain whether these corporations and their management are — or more precisely *whether they act as if they were* — increasingly free from shareholders' influence and of classical market constraints. Major changes in corporate financial behavior were confidently asserted and forecast. In Section III, we will examine the major changes which have occurred in the sources of funds used and the important balance-sheet ratios for nonfinancial corporations over the last half century to determine to what extent corporations in major industry groups, and large corporations in particular, have in fact divorced themselves from the capital markets. In doing so we will look separately at the evidence on such important subsidiary questions as the following: what trends have there been in the use of debt financing? in outside equity financing? What have been the changes in the use of internal funds to finance expansion — in relation to profits earned, in relation to volume of investment being done, in relation to total assets? We will consider whether the changes observed in different periods reflect basic changes in dividend and other financial policies over the years, as ownership has been progressively atomized and spread among an increasing number of shareholders, or whether they reflect reaction to different conditions under substantially the same patterns of behavior and policies. And we will examine what these patterns of financing, whether shifting or stable, imply for the broader issues raised by the basic Berle and Means thesis with respect to the relative effectiveness of the constraints imposed by the capital markets on managements' decisions regarding the amounts and types of internal investment and expansion, and the efficiency with which the economy's savings are allocated to the most desirable and profitable uses anywhere in the economy.

Finally, in Section IV we will review changes in the financial relationship between nonfinancial corporations and financial intermediaries. The rapid growth of these intermediaries has had an important bearing on patterns of corporate financing which needs to be considered in relation to the issues noted above and to broader questions of concentration of corporate control.

The question whether managements have in fact been retaining earnings that the shareholders would prefer to have had distributed in dividends, as is urged in the Berle and Means thesis, raises many technical issues and had best be dealt with elsewhere. I will simply state that my own extensive research on this issue indicates quite clearly that, at least judging by market price fluctuations, most large companies at most times have indeed paid smaller dividends than stockholders would have preferred.[9] As a broad generalization, subject to important exceptions, this basic inference of the Berle and Means thesis is confirmed.

One other important proposition may also be treated summarily, since an analysis of the available evidence has already been published. The Berle and Means position that large nonfinancial corporations grow more rapidly because they retain a larger fraction of their earnings does not stand up if one separates profitable and unprofitable companies. Among profitable companies — which are the ones which would be doing the growing — in every year since 1931, retained earnings have been a regularly and markedly smaller fraction of net profits, the larger the size of the company.[10]

II. THE RELATIVE POSITION OF NONFINANCIAL CORPORATIONS
IN THE OVER-ALL ECONOMY

Data depicting various important trends and the relative position of nonfinancial corporations in the economic and financial structure of the economy since the turn of the century may be brought together and summarized briefly.[11]

Share of Tangible Assets. The tangible assets of these corporations — largely buildings, equipment, inventory, and land — represented only a little over one fifth of all the tangible property in the economy at the turn of the century. After increasing to about one fourth during the 1920's, this fraction receded during the Depression, war, and early postwar years, and increased following the Korean attack to a level of 26.5 per cent — up roughly five percentage points in fifty-five years and just a little higher than during the 1920's.[12]

Share of National Wealth. The total tangible assets of the country, adjusted for net foreign claims, represent the national wealth. Because of the relative smallness of net foreign claims, the general trends in relation to national wealth are very much the same as those shown for total assets.

Share of Total Assets. Since holding intangible assets means holding the obligations of other economic units, and hence the power to enforce repayment of these claims and in many cases to restrain the debtors' activities during the period of the obligation, comparisons which include intangible as well as tangible assets are in many contexts even more relevant than those confined to shares of tangible assets and real property. Nonfinancial corporations held a little less than one fifth of all the tangible and intangible assets in the economy at the turn of the century, and this ratio was virtually unchanged on through the 1920's. After falling to approximately one seventh during the 1930's and 1940's, the fraction rose again in the early 1950's, but the level in 1955 was still *below* its levels of three and five decades earlier.

Assets of Nonfinancial Corporations and Financial Intermediaries. The rough stability or small decline in the nonfinancial corporation's share of all tangible and intangible assets, in contrast to a five-point increase in their share of tangible assets alone, is of course a reflection of the relatively more rapid growth of financial intermediaries in the economy. Since the turn of the century the total assets and liabilities of nonfinancial corporations have increased about eighteen-fold, but the financial intermediaries have increased nearly forty-fold — from $14.1 billion to $545 billion. The assets of nonfinancial corporations were 70 per cent larger than those of all financial intermediaries at the turn of the century, but their growth progressively fell behind the financial intermediaries until by the end of the 1930's, and again in 1949, nonfinancial corporations held only two-thirds as many assets as the financial intermediaries. In the very recent years, this trend has been reversed and the value of all the assets held by nonfinancial corporations has been growing more rapidly than financial intermediaries. By 1955 the total assets at market values of all nonfinancial corporations were slightly larger than those of financial intermediaries ($571 as against $545 billion),[13] but the ratio of the assets of nonfinancial corporations is still substantially lower in relation to those of all financial intermediaries than that at any time in the 1920's and only two-thirds that at the turn of the century.

Share of Financial Claims Held. The ratio of the intangible assets held by nonfinancial corporations to the total volume of all debts outstanding in the economy has progressively declined from over 17 per cent at the turn of the century to less than half this level through the 1940's and was down to a level just over 7 per cent in 1955.

Equities in Nonfinancial Corporations. The pattern over the last half century in the ratio of the total equities of all nonfinancial corporations in all their assets to the total equity interests in the economy follows a pattern very similar to that of their ratio of tangible assets, although, quite significantly, it has been consistently at a much lower level. The equities of nonfinancial corporations represented about one sixth of all equities at the turn of the century, and the fraction rose somewhat during the 1920's and declined during the Depression. By 1955 it had risen again, but only to a level of less than 21 per cent. Virtually 80 per cent of all equities in the American economy *are not* equity interests in corporations, and the one fifth which consists of corporate equities is substantially lower than the fraction of tangible assets in the economy held by these corporations.[14]

Share of Total Debts. At the turn of the century these nonfinancial corporations were obligated for no less than 37 per cent of all the loans, long-term debt, and mortgages outstanding in the economy. Their share of all these debts outstanding declined moderately to 31 per cent following the federal deficits of World War I, and was then stable at this level through the 1920's. Their share of total debt declined again in the 1930's, due largely to the growing debts of governments and liquidation of private debt during the Depression, and it then fell drastically to 11 per cent by 1949 as a result of the tremendous increase in federal debt during World War II and the high levels of liquidity resulting from the war. Even if all public and governmental debts are retained in the comparison, however, it is noteworthy that the fraction accounted for by nonfinancial corporations had been rising rapidly during the 1950's, and by 1955 stood at 18 per cent.

Since the debts of governmental units bulk so large and have been so greatly affected by wars, depressions, and other special influences, more meaningful comparisons can be obtained if attention is focused on shares of total *private* borrowing. Over the first quarter of the century, nonfinancial corporations accounted for between 43 and 44 per cent of all private debts, and in 1929 their share was 40 per cent. The fraction declined during the liquidations of the 1930's, and the exceptional liquidity following the war brought it down to 30 per cent in 1949. But the ratio increased sharply thereafter in spite of surging totals of consumer installment credit and residential mortgage debt. By 1955 non-financial corporations were accounting for 41 per cent of all private borrowing, and the ratio probably increased further in the following years. The 1955 share is somewhat higher than in 1929, and it is substantially greater than the 31 per cent of all *privately held* tangible assets owned by these corporations.

Among nongovernmental borrowers, consequently, it can hardly be said that nonfinancial business corporations are disproportionately light users of credit and the money market for debts and loans, or that they have withdrawn from the money markets and are financially self-sufficient. Nonfinancial business corporations now account for as large a fraction of all the private debts outstanding in the economy as was characteristic of the first three decades of the century. And instead of falling between the prosperous twenties and the mid-fifties, as would have been expected on the Berle and Means thesis, the ratio has at least been maintained.

Summary. The share of nonfinancial corporations in all the tangible assets and all the equities of the country has increased moderately but irregularly since the turn of the century, with most of the increase in the relative holdings of tangible assets coming in the first quarter of the century (the increase has been only 1 per cent since the mid-twenties). Looking at it the other way round, well into the second half of the twentieth century and the Era of Corporations and Mass Production, nearly three quarters of all tangible assets are *not* owned by nonfinancial corporations, and nearly four fifths of all equities are *not* equities in nonfinancial corporations. Similarly these nonfinancial corporations currently hold only one fifth of all tangible and intangible assets — just about the same as a half century ago. The one notably larger share held by nonfinancial corporations — and one particularly noteworthy in view of their alleged capacity to "roll their own" and be free of the capital markets — is their share of all private debts outstanding, which is over *two* fifths. This ratio is substantially the same as it was a quarter of a century ago; and it continues to be substantially higher than their proportionate holding of all privately-held tangible assets, which remains under one third.

Under the Berle and Means thesis, in either its original or its more recent version, the centralized power of the management in large nonfinancial corporations was especially portentous because exercising this power would lead these corporations to increasing dominance of all non financial corporations, and the entire nonfinancial sector would increasingly rule the economic and financial structure of the economy. Some important perspective is provided by noting that neither effect has occurred. This relative stability in proportionate terms of course reflects numerous and partially offsetting developments elsewhere. Of particular relevance, it can reflect either that the power was not as great as alleged or that use of it has been more benign than was contemplated. Looking more specifically to the financial aspects of these questions, we now turn to changes in financial relationships and in the patterns of financing of these corporations themselves.

III. TRENDS IN FINANCING

In view of the predominant emphasis in the broad Berle and Means thesis regarding the great, and potentially very momentous, changes in the patterns of control of nonfinancial corporations, we would expect to find major changes in the extent to which outside liabilities were used to finance operations, in the extent to which internally available funds were relied on to finance capital expansion, and in other similar over-all relationships. But once again, when one looks at the data, one is impressed by the rather extraordinary stability in the broad patterns of financing used and in the patterns of decision-making behavior which are found.[15]

Reliance on External Obligations: Balance-Sheet Ratios. The ratio of the total liabilities to total assets is significant because it shows at any time the degree to which all the funds currently being used to hold assets and finance operations represent obligations to outsiders other than owners. Goldsmith's data indicate that this ratio for all nonfinancial corporations was remarkably stable at a level of 40 to 42 per cent in each benchmark year during the first quarter of the century.

Brill's more detailed tabulations [16] show that for all corporations there was a moderate decline (from 41 to 37 per cent) in the late 1920's, as retained earnings were high and the unusual opportunities to float equity issues at extraordinarily low costs in booming stock markets were used. The ratio subsequently fluctuates between these limits over the next two decades of Depression, war, and early postwar prosperity. What is particularly notable is that the ratio rises rapidly after 1949, and from 1952 through 1955 has held at the highest levels (44 per cent in the three decades covered. If accrued expenses and tax liabilities are excluded, the debt ratios in the prosperous years of the mid-1950's are very much the same as those found in the mid-1920's.

The long-run stability in these ratios for all nonfinancial corporations of course may reflect changes in the relative importance of different major industries and fluctuations in their use of outside funds. If accrued tax liabilities are included with other debts, however, we once again find a picture of rather extraordinary stability in the ratio of debts to total assets in major industry groups over the last three decades. For manufacturing concerns alone the pattern has been very much the same, although, of course, at a somewhat lower level throughout. There was a marked decline in the debt-to-asset ratio in the late 1920's, which held through the 1930's. If accrued expenses and tax liabilities are not considered, there was a further sharp drop in the ratio during the war years, but it has since been rising to levels which are recently just about the same as those of the mid-1920's. With accrued expenses and tax liabilities included, the ratio is substantially higher than that which characterized the previous boom years.[17]

The relative movements of the debt ratio in trade are again in broad terms very similar to those described for manufacturing and for all corporations, but it is perhaps notable that the absolute levels of debt ratios have consistently been higher in trade than in manufacturing and for all corporations generally. It may be remarked that this is in spite of the extensive tendency of these firms to rent real estate, which reduces capital requirements. The transportation and communication industries, on the other hand, have had some decline in their ratio of debt to total assets, as railroads have had relatively low capital requirements and have sought to pay down their historically burdensome debts, while communications, notably the Bell Telephone System and American Telephone and Telegraph, have relied heavily on new outside equity by way of convertible debentures offered to current shareholders on privileged subscription. Even so, debt still accounts for 45 per cent of total financing being used to support the assets on the balance sheet — a ratio only five percentage points below the level of the late 1920's. In public utilities, once again, the ratio has fluctuated within a narrow range around 50 per cent, except for a wartime decline, which was rather quickly restored.

Among large manufacturing concerns, there is similar evidence that the ratio of outside liabilities to the total amount of financing has also been secularly stable, with an upward long-term drift, if anything. The available evidence indicates that the ratio in the first decade and a half of the century up to World War I was just about the same as that characterizing the early and middle 1920's.[18] After a marked decline in the late twenties and early thirties, we again find that substantially the same fractions of outside liabilities and net worth in total financing were restored before World War II [19] and that the ratio is substantially higher in recent years of high prosperity.[20]

It is also significant to note that both in the late 1930's and in the recent mid-1950's, the dependence on outside liabilities for financing is about the same regardless of the size of firm, for all the firms having assets in excess of $5 million — a universe which includes over 3000 firms in manufacturing alone in recent years.[21]

Reliance on Gross Internal Funds for Current Financing. Since outside equity issues in most years are small relative to the total amount of new outside financing,[22] this broad stability in the ratio of outside liabilities to total assets and financing generally suggests and reflects a similar stability in the sources of the funds currently being obtained and used to finance operations over periods of any substantial length. If there were any major or continuing shifts in the relative reliance on internal financing, it would necessarily have to show up in the balance-sheet ratios just considered. This stability in the relative reliance on internal and external financing over substantial periods through the middle of the century is indeed what we find when we look to the data on the sources and uses of funds of corporations. This finding is directly contrary to the broad Berle and Means thesis, to Berle's more recent position, and to widespread impressions not only among the lay public but among economists and professionals.[23]

Nonfinancial corporations were meeting about 55 per cent of their total current financial needs for funds with retained earnings and depreciation allowances in the first decade of the century, as they were in the mid-1920's,[24] and internal sources were about 60 per cent in both 1913–1922 and 1946–1949. It is noteworthy that in the three years 1951–1953 nonfinancial corporations again used internal funds for less than 60 per cent of their total financing [25] — a ratio within the earlier range. In terms of secular, long-term changes between years of prosperity, it consequently appears that there has been little change over more than a half-century.[26] It is also noteworthy that large manufacturers relied on internal funds for 79 per cent, 91 per cent, and 97 per cent of total financing in the three intervals 1921–1924, 1924–1927, and 1926–1929, while the corresponding figures for 1946–1949, 1949–1954, and 1948–1953 are 68 per cent, 66 per cent, and 67 per cent.[27] If there has been any significant change for large manufacturing corporations, it has been a reduction in reliance on internal funds — not the increase predicted by the Berle and Means thesis.

Retained Earnings as a Source of Funds for Expansion. The comparisons given so far relate the total of internally available funds to the total uses of funds of corporations. But a large volume of the plant and equipment expenditures — always a major use of funds for corporations — simply represents replacements of worn-out equipment the continued use of which would be uneconomical. Similarly, funds charged to depreciation and depletion, which are accounting estimates of the reduced value of capital stock due to production in any given period of time, have been included as a "source" of funds. If we eliminate such accruals on both counts, we can relate the retained profits of corporations to the *net* amount of funds used to expand assets in each period, and this comparison is more directly relevant to our present issues.

Even on this more refined basis, retained earnings show a remarkable constancy as a source of funds for asset expansion of all nonfinancial corporations. According to Goldsmith's data, they accounted for 32 per cent of funds used for such expansion in the period 1901–1912, and for 27 per cent in the years 1923–1929, while comparable estimates show that retained earnings accounted for no more than 33 per cent of net funds used to increase total assets in the good years 1951–1953 and again in 1955–1957.[28]

The conclusion seems inescapable that there has been no secular net change in the relative dependence on internal funds to expand assets among all nonfinancial corporations over this broad sweep of time. And, once again, the dependence of large manufacturing corporations on internal funds to finance expansion has been reduced, if anything, over the last three decades. In the three periods of the prosperous 1920's, retained earnings accounted for 62 per cent, 84 per cent, and 94 per cent of the expansion in total assets of large manufacturing corporations. The comparable postwar ratios are 57 per cent, 51 per cent, and 53 per cent.[29] The evidence available simply does not support any inference that there has been a significant or substantial long-term upswing in the use of retained earnings instead of external sources to finance expansion. The relative position of stockholders vis-à-vis management may or may not have become more dependent with the passage of time, but the major effect predicted from such increased freedom and power in management's hands are not discernible in the record.

Response to Changing Financial Needs. The Berle and Means thesis not only predicted increasing secular reliance on internal financing; it clearly implied that the growing separation of ownership from management would substantially alter the way in which management responded to changing capital requirements. So long as any external funds are going to be used, the *mix* of retained earnings and external funds can be expected to vary over a business cycle, and moreover to reflect the strength of the cycle — more change in the mix would be expected in a major cyclical swing in business activity than in a small one. We would consequently expect to find considerable fluctuations of a roughly cyclical character around the stable or declining long-term trends in the net internal–external funds mix we have previously pointed out — and these fluctuations about the trend have, in fact, been very substantial. But it is *changes in the pattern* of such fluctuations in the financing mix over long periods of time that concerns the Berle and Means thesis so long as any outside funds are being used, not the fact of such fluctuations. The thesis clearly implies that relatively greater use of internal funds (and hence diminishing use of all outside funds together) will have been made in more recent years under comparably large increases in the amount of capital required.

But once again the evidence disappoints the Berle and Means expectation: the fluctuations in the internal–external funds mix maintain a quite stable pattern, relative to the cyclical position of business conditions and rates of asset expansion, over the near half century for which we have data.[30] And this stable pattern has a very sensible rationale: when output is expanding rapidly, profits usually increase more than in proportion as the result of the "leverage" provided by heavy fixed charges, and dividend payments are increased by only a rather definite and small fraction of the increased earnings, so that retained earnings increase still more than in proportion to output and assets. At the same time receivables and inventory requirements which need to be financed will expand in an amount that depends upon the increase in output and sales. In view of the relative stability of these relationships, the net demands corporations have for outside financing will depend heavily on the volume of their plant and equipment expenditures — in short, upon how relatively rapidly they are trying to expand their fixed assets. (The extent of demands will also depend, of course, on the average level of output and profitability over the cycle.) Without going through the argument, it will be clear that substantially the reverse occurs during periods of marked contraction.

Turning now to the record, we find the relatively sharp and short-lived expansion in assets incident to World War I required an extraordinarily heavy demand on outside funds, while the early postwar contraction led to a marked reduction in their use.

Demands for such funds were less heavy during most of the twenties while profit rates were high and asset expansion rates modest, and reliance on outside funds dried up during the depressed years of the earlier 1930's. But in the late 1930's, when the assets of large manufacturing corporations were expanding as rapidly as they had in the late 1920's, the reliance on external financing was just as large as it had been in the previous period.[31] And substantially the same pattern continues over the recent postwar cycles. Dependence on outside funds in the early postwar period to 1949 was relatively moderate as the extraordinarily large wartime accumulation of liquid assets were used to finance outlays on plant and equipment and increased inventories. But in the period 1948–1953 (or 1949–1954) and that of 1953–1957, reliance on outside funds increased greatly, for both all nonfinancial corporations and (notably) for the 200 largest manufacturing companies, where funds from outsiders provided as substantial a fraction of all financing as in 1914–1919 — the last period when the rate of growth of assets had been comparably large.[32] These latter data refer specifically and exclusively to the financing patterns of less than 200 *largest* manufacturing corporations — precisely the group out of all the hundreds of thousands of such companies in which "management control" is greatest and the perverse effects should be most glaring if they are to appear anywhere. And among utilities and communications, where giants predominate, dependence on outside funds has at least been sustained over the years.[33] If the Berle and Means expectation of an increasing propensity to "provide their own" by an increasingly independent management group had been borne out, nothing of the sort would have happened. After all, four decades offer abundant time for the forces they relied on to work themselves out, and so far as relative reliance on internal and on total external funds is concerned — given the rate of asset growth which is surely a good index of the need for capital — the net change has been small at best.[34]

Dividend Policies. Similarly, the Berle and Means thesis expected substantial changes in the dividend policies of corporations as managements became more secure in their control position. Our research specifically on the dividend policies of large listed industrial corporations has been reported elsewhere.[35] These policies typically take the form of a relatively fixed pattern of adjusting existing dividend payments more or less gradually to bring them in line with a stated *target* payout ratio, with the result (as noted above) that only a rather small fraction of current changes in profits will be absorbed in dividends. More directly germane to the Berle and Means thesis is the fact that, once set, these policies or patterns of reaction to changed earnings have proved to be remarkably stable over long periods of time, not only in most individual companies, but for all together — so much so that a "statistical fit" reflecting policy and behavior in the period from 1918–1940 can be used to predict dividend payments in the last decade and a half (given the profits in these years), with an average error of 2 per cent! Of all areas of corporate financial behavior, the response of cash dividends to changed earnings should have been most sensitive to changes in the relation of management to ownership, as urged by Berle and Means; the stability actually found in dividend policies is hardly consonant with the expectation.

In sum, the progressive and increasing concentration of management authority divorced from ownership was confidently expected to alter basically dividend policies and increase the reliance of corporations on internally generated funds and thus to make them increasingly free of dependence on outside sources of capital. The fact is it has not done so; dividends respond to changes in income very much as they used to, and the ratio between internal and external funds has been secularly stable. Similarly, the divorce of ownership from management was confidently expected to change the pattern of reaction to changing capital needs. Again, on the record, it has not done so. The relative shifts in the reliance on internal or external funds as the level of business activity, profits, and total financial requirements change have been remarkably stable over a full half century, and the ratio of internal to external funds has been approximately the same in years of comparable level and rate of change of activity.

Dependence on Capital Markets. The thesis of Berle and Means in its later versions, however, emphasized not only increasing reliance by nonfinancial corporations on internal funds but freedom from dependence on outside capital markets. Although the stability we have found in their dividend policies and in their relative reliance on internal and total external funds under comparable conditions refutes the former claim, the latter must be examined separately, since this over-all stability may be consistent with important changes in the mix of outside funds used. In particular, this over-all stability does not require unchanging dependence on the "new issue" capital markets. And here the thesis is on somewhat sounder grounds. While there has been no decrease in the relative reliance on new security issues to finance the heavy capital-using utility and communications industries, where giants predominate,[36] there has been a rather marked decline in the relative importance of security issues (including common stock, bonds, mortgages, and term loans) to total financing and also to total external financing, among manufacturing concerns and consequently among all nonfinancial corporations as a whole.[37] Probably the major reason has been the high level of corporate tax rates — as operating profits go up, accrued tax liabilities (which are interest-free funds) automatically increase.[38] There has also been some notable increase in current obligations exclusive of tax liabilities in recent years, in manufacturing at least.[39]

In short, along with constant relative reliance on total external funds under comparable conditions, there has been a reduced relative reliance on total private external funds in response to higher levels of public external funds (accrued tax liabilities); and increased reliance on relatively more attractive shorter-term types and sources of funds has further reduced dependence on the new-issue market in particular. But while the relative reliance on the traditional private capital markets has been somewhat diminished for these reasons, perspective must be maintained: these markets continue to be major sources of capital to finance business expansion, and any assertion that corporations are no longer dependent upon them for an important part of such financing is sheer exaggeration.

Response to Capital Market Forces. "Freedom from the constraints of the capital market" has another very significant dimension. The Berle and Means thesis not only argued that firms would to an increasing degree free themselves of the need to go to the capital markets for funds, but that they also would become much more independent of the usual market constraint in the *way* they used these sources. In the usual economic analysis, the efficiency with which market mechanisms insure that available supplies of scarce resources will be put to their socially preferred uses depends heavily upon the extent to which the decision makers on both the supply and demand sides of the market respond to economic incentives — the extent to which suppliers will in fact transfer scarce resources from less to more remunerative outlets, and the extent to which those on the demand side will seek out and use the relatively less expensive sources of supply (quality and other factors being the same). The Berle and Means argument was that as managers became increasingly free of the pressure from stockholders they would not need to use the cheapest supplies of outside funds, and indeed would probably not do so.

In this context it is consequently pertinent to note that during the period from the turn of the century through the end of World War II the relative volume of new stock and bond financing through the capital markets closely conformed to changes in the relative costs of these two forms of outside capital — just as would be expected to happen if managers were under strong constraint to respond to market forces.[40] During the phases of cyclical fluctuations when stock was becoming relatively more expensive, the mix in outside financing would quite consistently shift in favor of bonds; and in periods when stock prices were rising and the costs of outside equity were falling in relation to the yields required on bond issues, the amounts of stock financing undertaken would increase both absolutely and in relation to the volume of bond financing.

This same pattern can be readily observed in our postwar experience. During the first five years after the war, bond yields were extraordinarily low by historical standards (and half this low cost would be borne by the government in reduced tax liabilities), while the costs of outside equity were as high as they had been in the early 1920's. As a result, stock issues accounted for only 25 per cent of total outside long-term financing of nonfinancial corporations in 1946–1949 (for comparison, in the 1921–1924 and 1924–1927 cycles, the ratios had been 57 and 44 per cent). But once again, as interest rates rose during the 1950's and the costs of new equity money were reduced in rapidly rising and even booming stock markets, both the absolute and relative volume of stock issues rose substantially to a point where stock issues represented 43 per cent of all long-term financing in the years 1955–1957.

Although we cannot go into the detail here, it is similarly clear that the increased importance of shorter dated obligations (other than accrued tax liabilities) may be readily explained as the normal response of market-sensitive managements to the shifting opportunities available, taking into account relative costs of funds, risks, and other conditions of borrowing. And quite apart from their automatic generation, it should be noted that accrued tax liabilities provide a source of funds which involve no interest costs and carry none of the "restrictive covenants" typical of bond indentures and private placements, nor the surveillance of current operations involved in bank borrowing.

In short, it very generally appears that the observed shifts in the entire mix of external funds used by major groups of firms, in recent years as in previous times, have been substantially those that would be expected if management were under rather effective constraints to respond to the allocative mechanisms of the outside markets for funds. However much the independence and discretionary power of management may have grown vis-à-vis the nominally owning stockholder groups, the evidence thus seems clear that corporations are not only using total external funds relatively as heavily as in earlier periods of comparable growth, but they continue to respond to the relative costs and conditions of the major types of new issues in the securities market in making decisions regarding the types of financing they will use.

Broader Allocative Functions of the Capital Market. The capital markets, however, have a still more fundamental and broadly conceived function which is central to the economist's picture of the proper functioning of the economy and which has important bearing on the fundamental Berle and Means thesis. In an ideally functioning economy, available resources will be distributed to their most desired uses by market forces. New investments will be made in those firms and industries producing products whose supply the economy most wants to have increased. Increased demands for output are expected to increase profits, and the increased profits serve not only to increase the supply of savings available for investment to increase capacity, but also are the magnet which attracts the private savings being made outside the business community in the economy. The clear implication of the Berle and Means thesis is that these broader functions have been seriously and increasingly distorted by the growing independence and discretionary power of management groups controlling large corporations.

We have already seen that there is no trend for increasing reliance on retained earnings over substantial periods of time which indicates that the situation has not worsened in this respect. Nonetheless, since internal funds are used to finance the bulk of all investments and are not subject to direct market allocations, the efficiency of the allocation of all savings to the more desirable investments may have deteriorated seriously. In particular, if companies with large amounts of retained funds have simply used these funds to finance the new investment projects that they happen to have available, it is entirely possible that these corporations have just gone on expanding their own investments and assets (and consequently enhancing their economic power) even though other firms and other industries needed the funds to finance still more profitable investment opportunities — and would have succeeded in attracting the funds if all the savings of the economy were thrown on the capital market and every corporation had to compete in this market for the use of their own large pools of funds against other firms. Fortunately, we do have some useful information on the allocation of all the funds becoming available in relatively short periods of time to finance investments in various cross-sections of firms and industries. And the results, while not surprising, are rather reassuring.

Recent investigations indicate that there has been a definite and generally marked association between the rates of profitability and the rates at which physical assets are expanding (new investments are being made) among different manufacturing industries in each two-, four-, or eight-year period covering the last quarter century.[41] And among different industries and over different time periods, the industries having the greatest expansion in plant and equipment and doing the most investment have quite markedly been those having the greatest growth in profits over the period and earning the highest rates of profit. Moreover, it is quite significant that the associations of investments and profitability in recent years are as good as those found a quarter of a century ago. Since in many of these manufacturing industries, large firms account for a very substantial part of the total assets as well as the total new investments of the entire industry, this association between profitability and volume of investment on an industry-by-industry basis implies that there is a similar association of profitability and investment among the larger firms. But we need not rely simply on inferences. An impressive recent study [42] investigated the factors determining the plant and equipment expenditures of approximately 700 firms in the early postwar period. The study included virtually all the companies, large and small, listed with the Securities and Exchange Commission, in seventeen different manufacturing industries accounting for the bulk of plant and equipment expenditures in all manufacturing. The authors found that the rate of profitability, the level of sales, and the degree of pressure of sales upon current capacity were uniformly the most important factors determining the current rate of investment outlays among these firms — we may add, just as would be expected, if market mechanisms were functioning efficiently. This pattern of results held quite generally regardless of the size of firm. There was a noticeable tendency for large firms (of over $75 million assets) to invest somewhat more closely in accord with capacity requirements and less with reference to the internal availability of funds than for small firms (those having less than $5 million of assets).[43] Other things being the same, the amount of new investment was not only correlated with profitability and increasing sales, but the reliance on the financial markets for outside capital was also closely associated with the rate of growth of the firm.[44]

The substantial body of available evidence seems to indicate that at least the broader and grosser adverse trends anticipated in the Berle and Means thesis have failed to materialize. Not only have nonfinancial corporations failed to encroach substantially upon the rest of the economy, but there has been no long-term trend toward increasing reliance upon internal funds. Nor has there been any clear long-term trend toward lower ratios of debt (obligations to outsiders) to total funds employed. There has been no clear reduction in the responsiveness of corporate managements to the relative costs of broad classes of outside funds, and the observed relative decline in new security issues is readily explained in these terms. Corporations have not become free of the constraints of the capital market. We further find that profitability and the pressure of increasing sales are still the dominant determinants of investment outlays — as they should be in a free-enterprise, market-controlled economy — and that the relative rates of expansion of assets and physical investments among industries as well as among firms is markedly associated with relative rates of profitability in accordance with standard market criteria.[45]

IV.   RELATIONSHIPS TO FINANCIAL INTERMEDIARIES

We have previously pointed out that financial intermediaries have generally been growing very much more rapidly than nonfinancial corporations — more than twice as rapidly on the average during the last five decades as a whole. Financial intermediaries had assets which were only a little more than two-thirds as large as those of nonfinancial corporations at the turn of the century, but by the end of the 1930's and through the 1940's their assets were approximately *half again* as large. Between 1949 and 1955 the assets of financial intermediaries continued to grow rapidly, increasing from a little under $400 billion to $545 billion. Due to the fact that nonfinancial corporations had relatively heavy holdings of tangible assets, and because of the delayed impact of wartime and postwar inflation, the current market value of the assets of nonfinancial corporations is currently a little larger than that of all financial intermediaries. But barring recurrence of major war-induced inflationary pressures, it is probable that previous relative trends will reassert themselves and we should expect financial intermediaries to be growing more rapidly than nonfinancial corporations in the future.

Since the concern of this paper is the financing of nonfinancial corporations, we need not undertake any detailed exploration of the reasons for this markedly more rapid growth of financial intermediaries.[46] Among the more fundamental reasons, however, we may note the continuing desire of the American public for greater liquidity as its income has risen,[47] the secularly growing desire for insurance and other essentially financial provisions for the future in the form of retirement pensions and annuities, and the persistent desire for added safety by way of diversification and professional fund management.

As new needs were recognized, entire new institutions were set up to handle them. New institutions created or coming into prominence since the 1920's — notably mutual investment funds, private pension plans, the Federal Social Security system, and pension plans for government employees — by 1955 had amassed total assets of $79 billion, about 15 per cent of the total assets of all financial intermediaries. But despite and in addition to the growth of these essentially new institutions, the older financial intermediaries continued to grow and to hold an increasingly important fraction of the public's entire wealth. Even if these newer institutions are omitted, the share of the total assets of American households held by the other financial intermediaries was higher in recent years than in 1929.[48]

All told, financial intermediaries increased their share of the entire assets of American households from about one tenth at the turn of the century to well over one quarter in recent years. The increasing tendency of individuals, at least until quite recently, to do their savings through financial intermediaries is even more vividly indicated by the fraction of their current saving which is placed with these institutions. Before World War I these institutions absorbed approximately two fifths of individuals' current saving, while in the years just after World War II the fraction was over four fifths [49] and has remained high in still more recent years.

The very much more rapid growth of financial intermediaries than of nonfinancial corporations naturally resulted in these intermediaries becoming increasingly important sources and suppliers of the outside funds being used by nonfinancial corporations. Before World War I, financial intermediaries were supplying a little over one third of all the external financing (debt and equity) of nonfinancial corporations; during the 1920's they furnished a little over two fifths, in 1946 to 1949 and during the fifties they have provided over one half of all such financing. The importance of financial intermediaries in long-term debt financing increased even more rapidly — from less than 30 per cent before World War I to well over two thirds after World War II (1946–1949) and nearly 90 per cent since 1950. The share of financial intermediaries in supplying outside equity funds to nonfinancial corporations has also showed a very marked upward trend, but the levels have been very much lower than those for long-term debt financing. Financial intermediaries provided only a little over 5 per cent of all outside equity before World War I and nearly 30 per cent during the 1920's; the fraction generally ranged between 10 and 20 per cent from 1945 through 1952.[50] Within the last five years there has been an extraordinarily marked upswing in the share of new corporate financing provided by financial intermediaries.

Long-Term Debt Financing by Nonfinancial Corporations. The sharp increase in the proportion of long-term debt funds furnished by financial intermediaries to nonfinancial corporations is but the counterpart of a fundamental and apparently continuing change in the basic structure of the entire long-term funds market. Before World War II over one third of all outstanding corporate bonds was owned by individuals and nonfinancial institutions and 21 per cent by personal trust departments of banks. The sharp and continuing increase in personal and corporate income tax rates during and after World War II made such securities (the income from which was fully subject to tax) very much less attractive than they previously had been to such investors, while life insurance companies (whose income taxes are low on the basis of special treatment) and qualified pension funds (whose income is not subject to any federal tax) had large and growing volumes of funds to invest. These latter institutions increasingly bought up the bonds being sold by the wealthy individuals and personal trusts who were shifting to tax exempt securities and other outlets for their funds — and at the same time acquired the vast bulk of new issues coming on the market.[51] By the end of 1957, financial intermediaries (other than personal trusts) held over 80 per cent of outstanding corporate debt, while individual holdings (including personal trusts) were approximately 10 per cent. If personal trusts administered by banks are included with the financial intermediaries, the fractions are over 85 per cent and 5 per cent respectively.

This situation clearly means that nonfinancial corporations must look to financial intermediaries for the bulk of their outside, long-term debt financing. Moreover, the supply of such money for bonds and private placements is in fact dominated by a limited number of the very largest insurance companies and pension funds. Financial intermediaries have always been a more important source of outside debt capital for large nonfinancial corporations than for the smaller borrowing units,[52] and, if anything, the dominance of a limited number of large intermediaries as a source of debt financing for the largest nonfinancial corporations, of particular concern to Berle and Means, is even greater today than in previous decades. In 1947 life insurance companies absorbed 93 per cent of the total amount of corporate bonds and notes privately negotiated and the moderate decline in their share in more recent years is entirely attributable to the increasing participation of noninsured pension funds. The direct placements acquired by the eighteen largest life insurance companies (approximately 3 per cent of all) have been running about 90 per cent of the entire dollar amount of all directly negotiated securities acquired by all companies, and it is known that a few largest noninsured pension plans are equally dominant in the purchases by these funds.[53]

Clearly, the whole situation is quite reminiscent of Galbraith's "countervailing power." [54] Without subscribing to all the glowing beneficence sweepingly ascribed to such situations by Galbraith, in the context of the Berle and Means thesis we must nevertheless note that the financial managers of the nonfinancial corporations are having to bargain for their long-term debt money with sophisticated professionals on the other side of the bargaining table, who are not only adept at using the sharp pencil but have nationwide and varied outlets for their funds and seek out the best net returns for their money. This clearly is not the classical atomistic market dear to the hearts of economists and to the traditions of economic theory, but it may be a not seriously inferior substitute.

Equity Financing of Nonfinancial Corporations. No such sweeping redistribution of holdings has occurred in common stocks as we have noted in the corporate bond market. Individuals (not including personal trusts) continue to hold upwards of three fourths of all common stock outstanding in 1949 and 1952 and 1955, as they did in 1939.[55] Nevertheless, in recent years this market has been affected by two important developments which are significant for the future. First, a still small but rapidly growing fraction of individuals' holdings of common stock represents shares of investment trusts which serve as intermediaries for the reinvestment of the funds in a diversified list of selected issues. As late as 1945 investment companies are estimated to have held only 1.6 per cent of all outstanding common stock.[56] Between 1945 and the end of 1956 their holdings of common stocks of nonfinancial corporations increased by $11 billion to a total of $13 billion, which represented 3.7 per cent of all such stock outstanding. Because of the generally high investment quality of the stocks of the largest nonfinancial corporations of particular concern to Berle and Means, the proportionate holdings by investment companies of the stocks of these concerns are correspondingly greater.

The second major development in the market for corporate common stock which is of special concern to us here has been the very rapid growth and the marked shift in favor of these equities by noninsured corporate pension funds.[57] Following favorable rulings regarding tax status and the legitimacy of employers' pension contributions as subjects for collective bargaining, the assets of private pension plans have increased tremendously during the postwar period. The assets of noninsured plans alone have risen from an estimated $3.3 billion in 1947 to over $12 billion in 1954 and $19.3 billion (at book value) at the end of 1957.[58] Equally notable has been the shift in the investment portfolio of such funds. Their holdings of United States Government Bonds have actually declined since 1951, while total assets have tripled. Corporate bonds have gone from 45 per cent to about 54 per cent of assets. But the most notable change has occurred in their holdings of common stocks. Common stocks represented less than 12 per cent of assets in 1951, and the fraction has increased markedly in each year, until by the end of 1957 common stocks represented virtually 25 per cent of the entire portfolio at book value, and 30 per cent at current market prices.

The impact of the net purchases of noninsured corporate pension plans in the market for the net new common stock issues of nonfinancial corporations is even more dramatic. In the five years 1946–1950, nonfinancial corporations issued new common stock in the amount of $4.0 billion,[59] of which noninsured corporate pension funds absorbed $400 million, or 10 per cent.[60] In the four years 1951–1954, net new common stock issues coming onto the market totaled $5.3 billion, of which noninsured pension funds absorbed $1.7 billion, or 32 per cent — over three times the fraction in the early postwar years. Similarly in the three years 1955–1957, net new issues of common stock amounted to $7.6 billion, of which noninsured investment plans absorbed $2.5 billion, or virtually one third.

The well-sustained and rapidly growing purchases of non-insured investment plans have obviously had an important bearing on the entire character of the market for common stocks in the last half-decade. These funds typically "buy and hold" — making sales to switch into preferred issues during rising markets and predominantly holding through falling markets.[61] It also seems reasonably clear that these growing increments of new funds available for stock purchase through pension funds are not available at the expense of other accumulations which would flow to the stock market.[62] Moreover, both because of their prospective growth and the future actuarial character of their liabilities, liquidity requirements are relatively low in such funds and common stocks are a peculiarly appropriate form of investment for these funds as compared with other institutional investors (save investment trusts). The general desire to provide some investment hedge against further inflationary developments is undoubtedly a further factor in their common stock investments.

Experience over the last five years indicates that although the fraction of new assets (investible funds) going into common stock has been rising markedly, these funds have not been going "all out" in common stock investments. Most funds accounting for the great bulk of such assets appear to be shooting for a "balanced portfolio" with a sustained ratio of common stocks to total assets running in the neighborhood of 35 to 45 per cent. Concern with fiduciary responsibilities is generally very strong, and for this as well as other reasons, common stock investments by these funds have been disproportionately heavy in the "blue-chip" category of stocks representing the equities of the well-established companies and those with the most secure positions [63] — a concentration of buying and preference which they share with the investment trust. This concentration of purchases on a limited number of issues of the highest quality has undoubtedly been a major explanation for the so-called "blue-ribbon leadership" of the entire market in the last five years or so. These characteristics of pension-fund operations may be expected to continue within the foreseeable future, and their implications are both fundamental and far-ranging.

Pension funds are still in a rapidly growing phase of development, far short of any sort of "maturity." About fifteen million employees are now covered in private pension plans, an increase of some six million since 1951, and on the basis of current trends and industrial characteristics the coverage is expected to exceed twenty million by 1965, which would be more than one third of the labor force at that time. It has been responsibly, and perhaps conservatively, estimated that by 1965 the assets of noninsured pension funds alone will exceed $50 billion — two-and-a-half times the present total.[64] If two fifths of such assets were invested in common stocks, the funds in 1965 would be holding equity investments at book value of $20 billion — an increase of $15 billion in eight years.[65] Such purchases would clearly serve to buoy the levels of market prices, reduce yields from the levels they otherwise would have had, and encourage new equity issues by nonfinancial corporations. Because of the relative concentration on the issues considered to be of the highest quality, the yield differentials between the issues of the large well-established "blue-chip" companies and the common generality of corporations will tend to be maintained or widened, thus sustaining if not increasing the previous existing relatively more favorable access which large well-established firms have had to the equity capital markets.

Implications for Control. Berle and others [66] have in recent years been concerned with another possible implication of the investment of pension-fund assets in common stocks — the possibility that pension funds would come to own such a substantial fraction of all of a company's outstanding common stock that effective control would pass to the trustees of the employees' pension funds. In Berle's words,

> As a result of this broad-scale buying of equities the pension trusts are slowly "chewing up" control of these corporations which offer the best means of equity investment. These are voting equities. Thus far no attempt has been made to make use of this except in the case of the Sears-Roebuck pension trust fund which undertook to buy Sears-Roebuck stock and presumably now has a controlling interest in the company. As a result, Sears-Roebuck is socializing itself via its own pension trust fund, and is discovering that it is running into the same difficulty which a socialist or any other form of oligarchic government has — that it has self-contained control, and management is thus responsible to itself. Query: Does it continue to have "legitimacy" when the only mandate it can refer to is its own? [67]

Berle estimates that the pension trusts will perhaps level out at somewhere in the vicinity of $70 to $80 billion, so that "if the pension trusts continue to take the good equities that they have been doing, they may well have the prevailing control-stockholding position and the capacity to make it absolute.[68] They will have, say, 20% to 30% of the good equity stocks and the capacity to increase that to 40% or 50% (45% for practical purposes is a majority at any big stockholders' meeting)." [69]

A clear distinction needs to be drawn between the issue as it affects purchases by pension funds in the stock of the "own company" and as it affects the accumulation of a dominant control position in common stocks in general, even within the blue-chip category. So far as the "own company" control problem is concerned, the issue arises only with respect to a minority of pension funds, and is one that can be readily handled in any one of a number of different ways. At the present time nationally, only 3.3 per cent of the total assets of noninsured pension funds are held in "own company" bonds and only 3 per cent in "own company" stock (including Sears-Roebuck), and only 1.3 per cent in "own company" common stock if this one large company is excluded.[70] In late 1954 the Bank Commissioner of New York State reported that only 10 per cent of the funds held by banks in his jurisdiction (which include the bulk of the funds, especially of the large ones) included *any* ownership of own-company stocks *or* bonds, or any other property used in the business of the employer,[71] and a more recent Senate Report found that 94 per cent of all pension and profit-sharing funds over the nation had no investment of any kind in the employing company and only 2.3 per cent of the funds had more than one fourth of their assets invested in the parent company.[72] In the case of Sears-Roebuck, the pension fund held approximately 26 per cent of the total common stock of the company at the end of 1957.[73] In most other plans permitting investment in the company's own stock, there are either provisions to limit the holding both to a small fraction of the company's stock outstanding and to a small fraction of the total assets of the pension fund. In many of these cases, and especially among the plans which permit somewhat larger investments in the company's own stock, there is provision that the voting right of stock held in the fund shall be exercised by the beneficiaries on the basis of their pro rata holdings. We should also note that at the annual meeting of 1958,the stockholders of Sears- Roebuck approved a management proposal to transfer voting rights to the employee beneficiaries on just such a pro rata basis.

In short, the problem is not likely to rise in the case of plans with independent corporate fiduciaries (usually banks as trustees), which account for about four fifths of the assets in all noninsured plans. If investigation shows that in other situations there is a serious problem of incestuous and oligarchic control positions arising between management and management-appointed trustees, it would seem to be simple enough to pass legislation requiring all plans not under independent corporate trustees to "pass through" voting rights to employee beneficiaries, as many plans with noncorporate trustees have already done, and the balloting should be strictly confidential. The disclosure provisions of the recently enacted Federal Welfare and Pension Plans Disclosure Act should further minimize the risk. If still stronger action is needed, all further increments to the assets of such funds could be required to be subject to general diversification requirements, such as those applicable to investment companies.[74] After an appropriate period to allow for the divestment required in some funds, such provisions (or even tighter ones) could be applied to the entire corpus of the fund, and all other financial transactions, with the employing company proscribed if need be.

So far as the specter of pension trusts assuming a dominant position in blue-chip common stocks in general is concerned, the possibility is perhaps a real one, but still rather remote, if not improbable. In late 1954 there were only 17 companies in which all the pension funds held by New York trust companies together owned more than 3 per cent of the stock of the employing company.[75] In only 3 of the cases were the holdings in excess of 5 per cent,[76] and of the ten stocks in which the largest amounts of funds were invested, in only one case (J. C. Penney) did the fraction exceed 3 per cent and the average including Penney was 1 per cent of these shares outstanding.[77] New York banks held a little over half all noninsured pension fund assets, so that *if* other funds were similarly invested in these stocks the figure may be doubled. Now *if* the same concentration of holdings in these issues were maintained through 1965, and *if* the prices of these securities did not rise in the meantime, and *if* none of these companies issued new common stock in the meantime, then the more than quadrupling from the 1954 base of noninsured pension-fund assets expected by 1965 would still leave pension funds holding less than 10 per cent of the stock of these companies. In point of fact, of course, such buying by the pension funds (assuming favorable business conditions on the whole) would tend to increase the prices of these stocks, and the changing relative yields available in the market under these and other pressures may be expected to widen the diversification of the funds and reduce their relative holding of these securities. Moreover, some of these "favorite" companies may be expected to increase the available supply of their securities in the market by new equity issues in the meantime, which would further reduce the percentage held by pension funds.

But let us continue our hypothetical projection. In 19—, when noninsured pension funds reach the $80 billion asset point, the *same* concentration of holding in these *same* ten issues would still leave pension funds holding 15 per cent of their stock — less than one third the levels contemplated by Berle. While the *capacity* to run up the holdings in a limited number of leading stocks to the 40 or 50 per cent level contemplated in the quotation would doubtless exist (as it does now), the required concentration of buying on a *very* few issues would be so contrary to all of the traditions and standards of respectability among corporate fiduciaries and so contrary to all the canons of sound financial policy, it would surely appear that this possibility of outright control may be ruled out as *de minimis*. But even 15 per cent of the stock of widely-held corporations, voted as a block, would effectively determine the outcome on many issues and constitute practical control: "as goes the 15 per cent, so goes the majority." The 15 per cent would, however, be held by a substantial number of different funds, voted and held by different institutions as trustees; overtly concerted voting is hardly to be expected.

The fact that, by and large, large investment trusts and the institutional trustees of pension funds generally tend to vote their proxies with management undoubtedly serves to strengthen the self-perpetuating central control position of management, but the difference made by a 15 per cent instead of — say — a 3 per cent institutional holding in this regard may easily be exaggerated: the great bulk of individual shareholders in most cases more or less automatically vote with management anyway as long as things are going along reasonably well. And if they aren't, the stock is sold by the institutional investor as it is, usually, by the individual holder.

This problem of pension funds and institutional investors in common stocks generally thus comes down basically to the central one of whether on the one hand the incentives to socially desirable management performance are presently appropriate and sufficient, and on the other, whether the constraints and penalties against undesirable performance are adequate. These incentives and constraints take on many forms. They certainly include the shifting relative evaluation of a company's stock in the market, the pres-

sures of large stockholders' direct representation of their preferences and the small shareholders' more numerous letters to management, the constraints born of managements' very real desires to
avoid expensive and disagreeable, if not personally disastrous,
proxy fights, and other more social pressures — as well as existing
legal standards, institutional machinery, and regulatory arrangements. The prospective growth of pension funds managed by independent institutional trustees is not likely to lead to any weak-
ening in the structure of incentives and constraints surrounding
the management of large nonfinancial corporations, nor is it likely
to make any substantial difference in the basic control position
over these companies which their managements have long held.

1 0

THE CORPORATION, ITS SATELLITES,
AND THE LOCAL COMMUNITY

NORTON E. LONG

The corporation has made possible in many cases what before had been possible only in the rare and exceptional case: the amassing of large aggregates of enterprise under a single centralized direction. While the occasional great family — Ford, Rockefeller, Carnegie, or Harriman — might amass this power and create a personally owned economic empire, in the nature of the case this had to be exceptional. Without the corporation the bulk of enterprise would probably have remained locally owned and locally managed. With it, at least in major segments of the economy, enterprise becomes increasingly characterized by the branch plant and the headquarters office. Major parts of the local community's economy become not just members of a regional or national market but field offices of a far-flung bureaucracy with a new structure of roles, loyalties, and goals.

The large corporation takes its place along with the church and the armed services as an organization that transcends the local territory and cuts across political boundaries, at times even those of the nation and state.

For some of the members at least, the corporation represents a value-laden institution that outranks the local community as a focus of loyalty and a medium for self-realization. It would scarcely be saying too much and perhaps is tritely apparent that people may be more citizens of the corporations for whom they work than of the local communities in which they reside. Those whom Lloyd Fisher and Clark Kerr have dubbed "the plant sociologists," writers such as Elton Mayo, see the corporation as a means to harmonize the conflicting drives of modern man and achieve a happy union of the putative psychological blessings of medieval society with the material blessings of modernity.[1]

Philip Selznik, in his recent book on executive leadership, calls for a kind of Aristotelian statesmanship on the part of top corporate management.[2] The highest duty of the executive he finds to consist in infusing the organization with value and preserving the value so infused — the spirit of the corporate policy — against stasis and decay. Carl Kaysen, writing not so long ago on monopoly, sees the goals of the large corporation as growth and survival rather than profit in the classical sense.[3] These conceptions are more conventionally appropriate to the calculations of statesmen than businessmen. If they are actually those that substantially control the thinking of large-scale corporate managements, they indicate the obsolescence of conventional economics for their description and the increasing relevance of politics. The corporation becomes more like a college, a church, or a state than an economic instrument valued almost solely as a source of income. The famous Hawthorne experiment brought tardy recognition to what socialists like De Man had long contended, that the process of the organization was valued by many as much or more than its product. The corporation provides a complex habitation for managers and men. As greater and greater effort is made to bind its members with a more-than-pecuniary loyalty, it aspires to the status of a social institution competing with church, family, and territorial community for the allegiance of men.

The corporation has profoundly changed the role structure of the local community. Increasingly, it replaces the old families as owner and operator of the most profitable local business. In all except the largest communities, a growing number of enterprises are branch plants run by bureaucratic birds of passage with career lines stretching onward and upward to the magic haven of the head office. The libraries, hospitals, and museums that bear the names of leading local families stand out as monuments of a civic past. The charities of the leading local citizen have been replaced by the corporation's committee on solicitations, whose federal-tax-induced beneficence has replaced the older order. In the lesser communities, the officers charged with the duty of corporate almoner are frequently limited to Community Chest and Red Cross, requiring higher approval for any departures from defined head-office policies on company benefactions.

Branch plant managers in their proconsular role are worlds apart from the leading citizen-owners of the past. As Schulze has pointed out in his study of Ypsilanti, their role as economic dominants does not give them the grip on local social institutions possessed by their predecessors.[4] A recent study of a smaller southern community supports the view that branch plant managers are too sensitive to home-office approval to risk rocking the public-relations boat by decisive action. The phenomenon of absentee ownership, on which Veblen lavished his irony, has developed into the practice of absentee management by non-owners. That this lack of ownership interest has made absentee management by corporate headquarters staffs any less responsible, from the point of view of the local community, is doubtful. In fact the professionalization of corporate managements and their public visibility and newspaper accountability seems to have given them a thinness of skin quite uncharacteristic of the earlier race of absentee owners.

While the local catastrophe pictured by John Barlow Martin in the mine disaster of Centralia Number 5 is a phenomenon of absentee management as well as absentee ownership, it is likely that absentee corporate managers were far more sensitive to newspaper criticism and public opinion than absentee owners.[5] This criticism, flowing along the wires of the press services from the local community, can come to haunt them at their distant executive suites and jar their security and cloud their careers. The mine disaster of Centralia, with its tragedy of well-nigh classic Greek proportions of foredestined doom for the men in the pits, appealing to remote political, business, and union hierarchs to save their lives, dramatizes the general problem of remote control over vital decisions in the local community. In this case absentee corporate control of the mine was paralleled by, and even largely determined, absentee political and union control of decisions that could have saved miners' lives. In the Centralia case there was almost the ideal type of the local community so eviscerated of vital decision-making power that it lacked even the elemental capacity of self-preservation.

Yet absentee corporate control is far different from market control, and, while corporate centralization may not be quite the grave-digger of capitalism that Schumpeter warned us it was, it seems inexorably to socialize a kind of responsibility that approaches the political. The management decision made in New York to close a mill in the Piedmont of North Carolina may provoke repercussions in Washington, labor troubles elsewhere, and an unfavorable piece of publicity in the St. Louis *Post Dispatch*. The size of the giant corporation, which at first sight seems to give self-evident verification to the ascriptions of managerial omnipotence given currency in Marxian, Veblenite, and the C. Wright Mills schools of thought, creates a vulnerability both to external pressure and to internal political weakness. As John Gunther in his *Inside U. S. A.* remarked of the automotive titans of Detroit, they resemble Japanese wrestlers, enormous but flabby, easily set quivering by a public-relations panic. A Harvard professor of government in the troubled days of the thirties was asked by a leading public-relations impresario what to do about a client's employees who had welded shut the doors of the plant in the course of a sit-down strike. The professor somewhat callously suggested the use of an acetylene torch. The gentleman from Madison Avenue, in horrified tones, said that this would never do, it would violate the God-the-Father governmental image.

In a short thirty years we have passed from a corporate order whose managerial style derived from the so-called "robber barons," the divine-right Bayers, and the public-be-damned Vanderbilts, to the business-school-trained, public-relations-conscious professional of the highly specialized complex corporate bureaucracy of today. While the latter-day manager may not be as other-directed as Riesman and William H. Whyte, Jr., suggest as a nonowner and a professional manager, he has a concern for harmony and the avoidance of trouble that sets him apart from his predecessors. His attitude toward striking employees can never quite have the same sense of outraged feudal lordship confronted with a servile revolt that envenoms the Kohler strike.

Nor as a nonowner can he have quite the same view of the corporation as his property to do with as he pleased, by God, as seemed so right and fitting to the self-made Calvinists of American industry's heroic stage.

The company town had an attraction for the older industrialist of the past. The names Lowell, Lawrence, Hershey, Pullman, Kohler sound like so many industrial duchies. The conflict in Marquand's *Sincerely, Willis Wade* illustrates the familiar owner with sentimental and patriarchal concern for employees and local community and the business-school managerialist. A Harcourt finds it hard to close the Harcourt Mills. For Willis Wade it is but a business transaction, albeit one to be treated with finesse, a degree of humanity, and a great deal of public-relations concern. All over the country, the paternalistic company town with mill-supported public service is giving way to a new philosophy that shuns the responsibility and the doubtful glory of conspicuous community dominance. Few corporations today regard it as desirable to have a major portion of the local labor force dependant on their payroll. When business decisions have too visible an effect, management must weigh public relations in the scales with economics, frequently to the disadvantage of the latter. Birch in his study of Glossop, the seat of the Dukes of Norfolk, points out how the Dukes built a branch railroad for the local community, a benefaction it could never expect from the corporations of the present.[6] The modern corporation has found the price of community dominance an inconvenient conspicuousness, that in a day when distant publics are potent, seriously limits corporate freedom of action.

If the corporation no longer views the company town with favor, the same cannot be said of its feelings toward the suburban satellite that enjoys access to a central city labor force but immunity from central city taxes and welfare problems. The literature of corporate location policy, at least latterly, pays homage to the principle of paying the corporate way for its employees' schools and other services. However, the suburb with nothing but the plant and lots zoned for five acres produces a congenial neighborly environment that has its temptations. The move from high-rise, narrow-bay structures to the single story wide-bay modern plant and the tremendous demand for parking space have played a dominant part in the suburbanization of industry. River Rouge, Aliquippa, and other industry suburbs antedate this more recent technologically induced development. Reputedly, the explanation of them resides in company desire to control the local police, avoid central city taxes, and escape responsibility for the relief of their periodically unemployed hands. In one case, anxiety over company control of suburban police is given as a major reason for one of the early failures to secure metropolitan government in the Pittsburgh area.

The strikes that ushered in the great labor-organizing drive of the thirties strained and tested the allegiance of all segments of the local community. The Mohawk Valley Formula, as described by R. R. R. Brooks, successfully pursued, lined up all respectable elements in the community on the side of law and order and against the strikers.[7] Almost as crucial in determining the outcome of the strike as the role of police and militia was the shutting off of credit by the local merchants. In case of a showdown between strikers and mill, whatever their private sentiments, sooner or later the stores and the landlords were bound to side with management.

Perhaps the most important change in the local scene is the growing evidence that this one-sided line-up has shown a dramatic shift. Peter Rossi's studies of Zanesville, Ohio, and Gary, Indiana, show that not only do the local merchants continue to give credit to the strikers, but the whole community, including the police, tends to side with them.[8] While this phenomenon may not be wholly chargeable to the development of absentee corporate control and branch plant management, it seems vitally related to it.

Rossi's data and evidence from other sources point to the effect of the branch plant system on local susceptibilities. Economic dominants who are not, and do not become, part of the local social structure may be as foreign within local communities in the United States as the United Fruit Company in Latin America. The upward-mobile branch plant executive and his associated corporate birds of passage may be as alien as the white plantation manager in the tropics. The phenomenon of colonial nationalism is not irrelevant to the politics and attitudes of local communities in the United States. Southern resentment against "Yankee imperialism" is an old story, but the development of absentee corporate control has given a visibility to alien power in the local community that the impersonality of the market tended to hide. The passing of the regime of the old families has created a gap between positions in the economic and social tables of organization.

A further indication of a new order of local power and prestige is the gradual but increasing local recognition of labor leaders in the Community Chest and the Red Cross. These middle-class-minded organizations have been rather reluctant to admit labor leaders to effective participation in their decision-making process. Inability of corporate executives to insure worker contributions has forced recognition of the changed facts of power.

The corporation, by merging the individual plants in separate local communities, has created the tangential relationship from which the large and industrial union has sprung. It is part of the folklore of the labor movement that a highly centralized industry was far easier to organize than one characterized by a host of small firms. Certainly this was the experience with textiles in New England. No opponent of unionization was quite so bitter as the small marginal owner-operator. The large company with its bureaucratic management was far easier to crack.

The case of union centralization in the United Mine workers that eviscerated local union decision-making in the Centralia disaster is on the extreme end of the labor continum. Local union discretion in the generality of communities is probably much higher than that of local management. Furthermore, continuity in positions of power in the union and lengthy local residence gives the local union hierarchy more identity with the local social structure than is likely to be the case for the more mobile members of a large corporate career structure.

In a curious sense the corporation is more absorbing for the latter-day nonowning managers than for the older generation of owners. Clearly, branch managers have the public opinion of the central office to consider as well as any local opinion. Careers are made in the company rather than the community. Concen-

tration on business and avoiding any involvement in local controversy is the counsel of wisdom. The stakes of local community
action for the branch plant manager are unknown but quite possibly they are serious penalties if he gets in trouble, dubious and
uncertain rewards if he succeeds. The ritual activities of Community Chest and Red Cross, the noncontroversial symbolic
activities, are helpful if they don't take too much time from the
business, but controversy is poison.

The galloping succession of assistant secretaries in the Department of Defense and other Washington agencies under the
Eisenhower Administration indicates not just the unwillingness
of corporation executives to put up with the lower monetary
rewards and the harassments of public life, but a genuine fear
that the world — their corporate world — will pass them by if
they absent themselves too long from the stage of their primary
careers. Others will replace them if they stay away too long.
William H. Whyte, Jr., has reported how reluctant executives are
to take even a month off. The business must go on; someone will
be messing in one's personal files. One might be found out. The
apparent solidity of the corporation conceals an internal political
weakness. *Executive Suite* may be overdrawn, but the rivalries,
insecurities, and anxieties beyond the middle management of the
corporate hierarchy are real.[9]

When a president of the largest bank in a community says,
"We are all hired hands here," of himself and other local corporation executives, he is not echoing the proud humility of *servus
servorum Dei.* Rather he expresses the felt limitation of the paid
professional manager who doesn't own the business. Berle's and
Means's *Modern Corporation and Private Property* documented
a position of management via the proxy mechanism that seemed
to render it as potent as any owners of the earlier period. Indeed,
the doings of the holding-company era supported such a view.
But present managerial behaviors give rise to doubt as to unrestrained managerial power. How management is surrounded
by a network of constraints and fears is as yet an unwritten chapter in industrial sociology. Certainly bureaucratic specialization
and division of labor in the management team has given rise to
internal checks within the corporation that amount to vested

interests in specialized skills and lores. The office of the general counsel of the corporation threatens erring colleagues with the vague menaces of the law — must threaten them, too, if the prestige of the shop is to be maintained. The public-relations vice-president or public-relations consultant must magnify the dangers and importance of the irrational demonic force of public opinion as well as the capacity of his skill group to sell or charm the public Caliban. The personnel department has a vested interest in union perversities and its needed capacity to deal with them. The lobbyist and political fixer, corporate hierarch or consultant, has a like interest in his special capacity to deal with the distant underworld of politics. Each corporate specialty has the same amiable adversary affinity to its subject as the cancer fund to its disease.

The modern large corporation executive likes to think of himself as a professional. Ideally, if not typically, he is the product of a business school. The business schools, *Business Week, Fortune, The Wall Street Journal,* and other media have appointed themselves the task of turning business managers into unimpassioned bureaucrats who worship along with the city manager at the altar of administrative science. In practice this has meant that corporate executives are rather vulnerable to the intellectual fashions that sweep the business schools and the media from which they derive their ideas as to what is currently modish in top-drawer management thinking. This is especially the case with respect to those matters that are remote from the segment of reality that comes under their corporate competence. A St. Louis insurance executive will inveigh against the jurisdictional mess of his metropolitan area in a staff-ghosted speech that repeats uncomprehendingly the clichés of current municipal reform. This activity is good corporate citizenship, the more so as the executive hasn't the foggiest idea as to how the changes he advocates will help his company, though doubtless in all honesty he thinks they will. It is difficult for the corporation executive to avoid a kind of ritualistic do-gooding when he embarks on the unfamiliar role of city father.

Where issues hit home to the corporate profit and loss account, there is a reasonably realistic calculus of appropriate action.

At least the executive confronted with choices as to taxes, off-street parking, highways, and other governmental activities that seem to affect his business directly has a basis for rational action. This action may be as shortsighted, as when downtown stores seek to route an expressway through their basements, but at least the calculus is in principle rational rather than magical.

Top positions in the large corporation form a major segment of the prestige structure of the local community. Occupants of these positions are a natural target for the pressgangs seeking to man the local civic-committee structures. The executive finds the civic committee both a burden and an opportunity. Some activities, such as the Community Chest and the Red Cross, are built into company work loads and are even expected parts of a man's job. Moving up in them is part of a man's career. Good marks in them are functional to a man's favorable evaluation by his superiors. A smashing success in a fund drive may be a more visible mark of personal achievement than any company activity makes possible. In many quarters good corporate citizenship is regarded as a major public-relations value. Top management must personify, if not, as Maitland quipped of the British monarch, parsonify the institution. A president of a lesser corporation will candidly avow that his board of directors thought it not a bad thing for him to serve on a committee that might yield first-name acquaintance with the president of a large insurance company.

Such committees are usually safe vehicles for mixing with the prestigious members of the business community and securing pleasant and even useful publicity as a public-spirited leading citizen who represents the kind of corporation that has a "soul." Corporate executives discussing their roles in publicized civic committees point out that their service impresses and pleases their employees.

There is, however, a modicum of danger in the civic committee or even the assignment to a usually merely honorific post on a public board. Top-level civic committees are in the ordinary run merely required to lend their names to ceremonial occasions, the civic luncheon with its press release, the legitimatizing of some civic staff proposal, or, in the more arduous case, joining a plane-load of their peers in a flight to Washington or New York to plead the cause of the Chamber of Commerce in the wooing of a building. The unpleasant side of this otherwise merely time-consuming and occasionally profitable involvement is the frustration and loss of face when the publicized civic ceremonial fails. Usually failure is hidden from view by a change in the newspaper spotlight or obscurity as to just what the ritual is supposed to accomplish in particular. However from time to time newspapers, politicians, and public turn on the corporate elite as the savages beat their idols when they fail to bring rain. The expectation that the top corporate hierarchy should display some kind of effective leadership is fitful but real. The places of the leading families have to be filled or a kind of lubberland emerges. For a variety of reasons, the politicians cannot in the main attain the prestige of members of the corporate hierarchy. Where, however, the corporate elite fails to replace the old families in the top positions of the social structure, a situation results in which the rest of the local society is inclined to regard the management of the corporation as an alien force — almost, as was stated before, as the colonial representative of a foreign imperialism.

The process of suburbanization has placed many corporate managers, in even quite large head-office cities, in positions not unlike those of branch plant managers in smaller communities. The executive tends to be neither an active citizen in his suburban dormitory, nor more than a chamber-of-commerce ceremonial citizen of the central city where his office lies. The suburban politico and small businessman is likely to look on him as a resident alien and a spokesman for the big-town chamber of commerce, rather than for the local interests. In the central city, lack of residence and vote has a crippling effect on a more than ceremonial or checkwriting role. Beyond these disabilities a major, and often neglected, one is that of the corporate executive's preoccupation with his business. Amazingly enough he is busy, and this simple fact accounts for a good deal of his difficulty in competing with others of lesser status who are full-time professionals. The tired and overworked executive is wheedled and wheeled into place by civic and other staffs to provide the needed trappings of legitimacy to their own activities. The very scarcity value of prestige insures that a small group of top executives must stumble from one civic committee to another, without time for preparation and with exhausting demands on the limited time they can rob from their business, their families, and the daily toll of commuting.

Since prestige can only inhere in a few at the top — to spread the load would pack the "House of Lords" and fatally cheapen the titles — the few must pay the penalty of being both over-worked and used. Their ceremonial roles are too numerous to be self-directed. Their conspicuousness, the fatal result of corporate status, makes them vulnerable to public demands for their servi-ces. These services they can only refuse at the cost of seeming callously aloof from the folk belief in their duties as work givers and civic problem solvers. They must touch for the king's evil whether they will or no. At best they can avoid being had by the numerous band of public and private courtiers who seek to further their own ends through the manipulation of their prestige.

The alienation of the corporate hierarchy from other segments of the local community is the progressive result of the trend toward corporate centralization and the branch plant. Even when top management resides in the headquarters city there is a ten-dency for it to regard its responsibilities as so national in char-acter as to inhibit conspicuous local citizenship activities. Un-charitably viewed, this might appear a mere rationalization to escape a burdensome chore. However, in many cases the dilemma is sincere enough and Rousseau's caustic remark about the phi-losophers, that they loved the world in general in order to escape having to love anyone in particular, does not apply. The contrast between top managers whose status is derived from family and inherited wealth — the Rockefellers, the Fords, and the Mellons — and the nonfamilied is striking. For the man of family and inherited position, conspicuous local leadership has an appear-ance of legitimacy and appropriateness of role that seems lacking in the other case. In a real sense, a Rockefeller twice removed from the robber baron may be as much an acceptable gentry image as an earlier gentry several times removed from its robber-baron predecessors. The security with which some familied men of wealth have been able to appeal for the suffrages of the public at large is in marked contrast to the anxiety and almost wall-

flower-like withdrawal of their associates in the corporate hierarchy from a dance whose steps are beyond them and whose
necessary contacts repel them.

In an earlier day the utilities, requiring public franchises and
deeply dependent on municipal politics, were in the thick of it.
The relationships described by Lincoln Steffens were close and
the major figures in the companies were in intimate and sometimes sordid contact with the world of politics. The satiation of
businesses with the fruits of successful political activity led to a
withdrawal from overt and intense participation in the field of
local politics. The activity of tending the local political fences
became a specialized department in the corporate hierarchy and
was no longer a main concern of top management. The position
in the hierarchy of the man responsible for taking care of the
corporation's local political problems became downgraded and
with the intensified disesteem of politics and politicians, especially at the local level, his post suffered from the bad odor of its
clientele. The courts and a successful lobby with the state legislature permitted a growing neglect if not contempt for local politics. Suburbanization meant a physical unconcern for all but
company-related local services, and the politics of top management's suburban residence represents scarcely anything more
momentous than the politics of the country club. Thus the replacement of robber baron, resident owners, and leading families
by a withdrawn managerial elite has left vacant positions in the
local structure.

The managerial elite has been neither willing nor able to
fill these positions except in a ritualistic fashion that seems trans-
parently the product of company public relations rather than a
personal community commitment and identification. The socially
perceived public responsibilities of the manager's positions in
the local economic hierarchy have differed increasingly from their
own perception of their role as representatives of the company
in the local banana plantation (apologies to Keynes). While their
economic position has made the managers seem to be the appropriate and duty-bound incumbent of top local civic statuses, their
lack of family legitimacy and enduring local residence identification in the community makes them more the representatives of

a foreign power than the rightful chiefs of the local tribe. This alien allegiance on the part of the corporate segment of the local structure is productive of public disaffection from the corporation and a sense of anxiety and alienation in the corporate hierarchy.

A recent statement of General Electric on relocation policy, in which the corporation expresses its alarmed concern with conditions in New England and New York, is illustrative of the type of anxious sense of alienation from the local community expressed in many corporate statements. A paragraph from the General Electric release published in the September-October, 1955, issue of *Industrial Development* is worth quoting at length. Under the title "Community Loyalty," the paragraph proceeds as follows:

We watch to see if the thought leaders and other representatives in the community speak well of the *deserving* employers there or consider them whipping posts. Spokesmen for unions and other organizations, as well as individuals among clergymen, teachers, politicians and publishers can all have a very material effect for good or bad on the *cost of producing goods* and on the *amount and regularity* of the *sale* of those goods. A little noted fact is that public criticism of an employer — to the extent it is believed — tends to cut down jobs for employees. Likewise — understanding, approval and warranted public praise of an employer tend to cut his costs and increase his sales — *and jobs.*

In the earlier portions of this extraordinary statement the corporation is represented as being ready to pick up its dolls and go elsewhere if local public opinion and action prove too unsympathetic. This, be it noted, the company is prepared to do at the cost of millions of dollars of investment that would be wiped out by the move. How oddly the voice of C. Wright Mills' *Power Elite* [10] and Hunter's *Community Power Structures* [11] sounds in this rather querulous appeal for affection and understanding from the local natives who, in the company eyes, seem ready to kill, or at least drive away, the goose that lays the golden eggs.

Company attitude and local attitude are startlingly like that of a Middle East or South American oil company and the native inhabitants in the throes of colonial nationalism and the threats of withdrawal and shutdown on the one hand and expropriation on the other. It is interesting to note that in both cases the company is reduced to the threat of emigration.

Why doesn't the corporation's management have enough acceptance in the local social structure to be able to fight back? With
a case as strong as that presented by General Electric management should be able to secure allies enough to win the fight
rather than run away. Andrew Hacker, in a short study, *Politics
and the Corporation*, gives an important part of the answer.[12]
Hacker finds that the growing class of "middle-middle class" —
executives below the policy level, increasingly in demand by the
large corporation — are typically transients and propertyless.
Without roots in the local community and without the security
property would afford, they have become spectators of politics.
Such interests as they have are so vague and general that they
perceive no ready way for their achievement. This new corporate
middle class is inert and apathetic. To use a union phrase, it is a
free loader on the body politic. Hacker's concern is with the depth
of commitment to democratic values. Corporation executives are
more concerned with the depth of its commitment to the Republican Party and the political activity they believe necessary to
preserve and protect the "enterprise system."

Shocked at the Republican weakness at the polls, corporations such as General Electric have gone out to educate their
middle and lower managements for political action. The revela-
tion of corporate weakness in the local communities has been
startling. The reaction, however, has seemed more like an attempt to buy a political patent medicine or some educational
nostrum to vitalize Republican precinct workers, actual or potential, than a realistic assessment of the situation. Long ago Machia-
velli warned the Prince that if he wanted to rule a captured
province he had better live there. This is a lesson the corporation
would do well to heed if it wants to avoid the ugly effects of
colonial nationalism as local populations turn against even bene-
ficient alien rule.

The reintegration of economic dominants into the local social
structure is one of the main problems of our local civic life. This
is a problem not only for the corporation and its alien caste of
career bureaucrats; it is also to an acute degree a problem of
labor. The president of a large corporation in a relaxed moment
will admit that heads of a national union aren't such bad fellows;

they too abominate wildcat strikes. But that Mulligan who leads the local wildcat strike, he's trying to prove something: his local power to the national union. Local autonomy in capital and labor is difficult to reconcile with effective centralized control. And local territorial loyalties provide a fertile field for those who would stir up resistance to the remote control of outsiders with no local legitimization for their power.

Clearly there are wide ranges of corporations and communities with differences ranging from the twenty-thousand-acre corporate ranch with Mexican peons, through the automobile company with a tough union facing a tough management, to the multi-million-dollar insurance company with its docile world of secretaries and file clerks headed by the million-a-year salesmen.

What the corporation is doing to the local community is an abstraction as dangerous as any Weberian ideal type of construction. Yet as an intuitive impression from a broad but scattered collection of data, there seems reason to suspect that the conflict between the corporation as an institutionalized center of loyalties and the local territorial community is real and important. It seems clear also that the vacuum created in the local social structure by the decline of the old owning families and resident economic dominants has upset the informal structure of political power. Whether the public-relations and educational onslaught on the problem of corporate political decline will succeed seems dubious. Re-establishing a valued legitimate elite structure in the local community is a major and possibly insoluble task. In the divided loyalty between corporation and local community, can one or other be more than synthetic? It would be reassuring to be able to say that a system of centralized corporations and unions is compatible with the reality of vigorous local self-government.

11

THE BODY POLITIC OF THE CORPORATION

EARL LATHAM

One of America's most important political problems is a long-needed and now urgent redefinition of the relation between giant corporations and the commonwealth, for the growth of the corporation has produced a tension of power in which giant enterprises have at points come to rival the sovereignty of the state itself. The great corporations are political systems in which their market, social, and political influence goes far beyond their functional efficiency in the economy. Indeed, in the very culture of the American people, the influence of the larger principalities overflows the banks of their corporate jurisdiction or economic reason. In the name of free enterprise, corporate collectivism has made deep inroads upon the celebrated individualism of the economy, and corporate welfarism has gone an equal distance toward tranquilizing the historic initiative of the individual in a smother of narcotic "togetherness."

It is the purpose of this paper to discuss these corporations as systems of private government.

I. THE CONCEPT OF THE CORPORATION

Although the political influence of the corporation on public affairs is widely appreciated, its political nature as a system of private government is not. It is easy to see it as an economic institution, as a complex of legal rights and duties and even as a social system. But the economic and political natures of the corporation do not dwell apart in a Nestorian separation. To go back no further than Hobbes, we find a clear statement that the elements of the corporate nature are welded in a single body; and that the dominant characteristic is the political. In speaking of the infirmities of the commonwealth, of the diseases from which governments might suffer or perish, Hobbes spoke of "the great number of corporations; which are as it were many lesser commonwealths in the bowels of a greater, like worms in the entrails of a man." [1] Although the physiology may be distracting, the political figure is unexceptionable, for, indeed, corporations were "lesser commonwealths," distinguished from Leviathan, according to Hobbes, only in that they are normally less absolute in their dominion than the state. The identity they share with the state, he said, is their characteristic as *systems*, public systems, and like all public systems they are known as a "body politic." Or, as Arthur Bentley put it twenty-five decades later, "A corporation is government through and through." To be sure, "certain technical methods which political government uses, as, for instance, hanging, are not used by corporations, generally speaking, but that is a detail." [2]

Although the economic aspects of the corporation have received widest notice, the concept of the corporation as a political system is by no means unknown. The work of Walton Hamilton makes free use of the Hobbesian concept that the corporation is a lesser commonwealth, and indeed in some cases not the lesser but the greater. [3] Merriam has spoken of business enterprise as a form of private government and has concluded that sectors of it at times have controlled the public government. [4] C. Wright Mills refers to the corporation as a political institution. [5] A. A. Berle, Jr., also talks of the corporation as a political institution, and thinks that it should be studied as such because this "is the stuff of pure political theory," which stuff is, however, otherwise unidentified. [6] In another flash of fateful precocity, Berle found politics in all manner of organized enterprises besides the corporation, a view he shares with Aristotle and Walton Hamilton. [7]

In the literature on corporations, there are even corporate equivalents of bad German theories of the state. Thus the citizen of the corporate state — the individual stockholder — is made to disappear in the mystic organic unity of the corporate totality in the statement, "It might even be said without much exaggeration that the corporation is really socially and politically a priori whereas the shareholder's position is derivative and exists only in contemplation of law." [8] This is a little like Gierke's belief in the fundamental reality of the Group-person from which so much misfortune has flowed, from concentration camps to the euphoric groupism of the "organization man." [9]

Besides modest recognition of the political concept of the corporation, some small attention has been given to certain institutional aspects of the corporation as a political system. More should be done in this field, since the corporation surrenders a rich yield of political experience and confirmation. Dimock, for example, has said of business firms that they, like governmental organizations, "are inescapably involved in the distribution of power and influence in the society," [10] and his earlier work in the Temporary National Economic Committee did much to demonstrate the essential identity of the problem of bureaucracy in both business enterprises and the public government. [11] A recent work on business leadership in large corporations carries inquiry into the bureaucratic characteristics of the corporation well beyond the point to which the authors of the Temporary National Economic Committee monograph were able to or perhaps cared to carry the analysis. [12]

But the literature lacks full-scale examination of the corporation as a political system, as a lesser commonwealth (to return to Hobbes), and some of the writing that does exist makes faulty analyses. [13] A mature political conception of the corporation must view it as a rationalized system for the accumulation, control, and administration of power. Speculative theories of the corporation, like speculative theories of the state, whether metaphysical or juristic, yield less understanding than do more empirical approaches. The corporation is a body politic which exhibits describable characteristics common to all bodies politic. In a functional view of all such political systems it can be said that there are five essential elements: (1) an authoritative allocation of principal functions; (2) a symbolic system for the ratification of collective decisions; (3) an operating system of command; (4) a system of rewards and punishments; and (5) institutions for the enforcement of the common rules. A system of organized human behavior which contains these elements is a political system, whether one calls it the state or the corporation. And state and corporation are mature political systems to the degree in which they exhibit all the essential characteristics.

II. THE AUTHORITATIVE ALLOCATION OF FUNCTIONS

In the state, the constituent power makes an authoritative allocation of governmental powers and functions through a constitution, whether written or unwritten. In the lesser commonwealth of the corporation, this allocation is made through the corporate charter. The earliest corporations were groups of private adventurers, created as bodies politic in order to fulfill some public purpose. The charters of the early corporations were not only instruments to organize the internal government of the corporation. They created what were, in effect, branches of the public government. The companies of the mercantilist period, for example, were "charged with responsibility for commercial regulations and fiscal administration in particular spheres of foreign trade, and were equipped even with military forces and their own courts." [14]

The use of corporations to fulfill political ends and the exercise by corporations of the functions of the public government are illustrated by the colonial charters in America. The first charter of Virginia in 1606 vested in certain "loving and well-disposed Subjects," Knights, and Gentlemen not only the right to take up part of the royal domain in America for a colony but to exercise in it some of the powers of the Crown, including the creation and management of military forces and the coinage of money.[15] In the Second Charter of Virginia, granted in 1609, the company was given "full and absolute Power and Authority to correct, punish, pardon, govern, and rule" all "such Subjects of Us" as might journey to Virginia and come under the jurisdiction of the local company.[16] At the northern end of the Atlantic seaboard, the First Charter of Massachusetts in 1628 created "one body corporate and politique in fact and name" and gave to the "Governor and Company of the Mattachusetts Bay in Newe England" the authority to exercise powers of the public government.[17]

It is clear that these corporations were created for public purposes, indeed, more specifically, to exercise for the state certain functions of the Crown, such as the regulation of the economy and the spread of empire. This is not to say that there were no more narrowly commercial companies than those that established the colonies, for there were such. But of the thirty-four joint stock companies incorporated in England and Scotland before 1700, fourteen were established to perform some peculiarly public function, and of the rest, the principal aim was to introduce some new line or process of manufacture.[18]

In the nineteenth century, the management of the economy passed largely from the state into the hands of private enterprisers. The charters of the seventeenth century were instruments by which private persons served public purposes; the nineteenth-century charters became instruments by which private groups used the state in the enrichment of private interest.[19] Or rather, it may be said that this was the consequence at the end of the century of a process that started rather slowly. In the early years, "it was not considered justifiable to create corporations for any purpose not clearly public in nature; each application was considered by itself, and if favorably was followed by an act of incorporation."[20] The great change in the basic relation of the state and private interest in the control of the economy came with the abandonment of the special act of incorporation and the adoption of general incorporation laws for special classes of corporations. The climax was reached in some states when permission was accorded in advance for incorporation "for any lawful purpose."[21] At the same time the competition of the states with each other for the privilege of giving away privileges to the corporations produced a great relaxation of the safeguards by which the rights and interests of the public were preserved and protected in the earlier limitations.[22] For example, directors were given the authority to reshape the capital structure of the corporation at will, and only a few states enforce the principle of accountability to the state for the manner in which the corporation exercises its franchise.[23]

This trend made it possible for incorporators, not the state, to define the values both of the corporation and the state, and to fix the allocation of fundamental functions in the corporation. The corporation thus acquired the constituent power from the state, and came to share the sovereignty. For constituent power is the power to make the constitution which fixes the basic distribution of powers, rights, and functions in the society. Those who share the constituent power share the sovereignty.[24] The

corporations have acquired the power to make their own consti-
tutions.

The formal view is that the corporation is a dependency of
the state, owing its existence to the state, and receiving only
those rights and privileges which the state chooses to grant, but
this overlooks the politics of the relation between the corporation
and its legal creator. Can one suppose that the great Dupont empire is a dependent of the state of Delaware, and forced, without
influence, to accept the mandate of state functionaries? Or that
the political power and influence represented by control of the
international oil market, which is in the hands of seven integrated
companies, is of equal weight with and may be countervailed by
bucolic legislators in provincial states? [25]

Having the constituent power which they pre-empted from
the state, the corporations have designed the basic functions and
distributed power within the corporation in a standard structure
which violates the prevailing values of the American democracy.
Corporation charters permit the disenfranchisement of the qualified through manipulation of the voting rights of owners of various classes of stock, they institutionalize minority rule through
the diffusion of stock ownership and the separation of ownership
and control, and they deny the principles of due process in the
adjudication, within the corporation, of relative rights, such, for
example, as those of dealers, minority stockholders, workers, and
consumers. More will be said below of the elements of due
process in corporate adjudication. As William Graham Sumner
said fifty years or more ago, "Industry may be republican; it can
never be democratic." In the exercise of their constituent power,
the corporations have fashioned massive clusters of antidemo-
cratic force and influence. As another writer has put it, management has "substantially absolute power," and the "only real control which guides or limits their economic and social action is
the real, though undefined and tacit, philosophy of the men who
compose them." [26]

III. SYMBOLS AND RATIFICATIONS

Every political system, whether the state or the corporation,
has an apparatus for ratifying and making legitimate the basic
choices of the collectivity. It has a ritual for approval of the

choices of policy, of the fundamental decisions, of the selections among broad alternatives of action — in short, a legislative system. The corporation has its legislature, and, moreover, it has parties and publics which attempt, respectively, to win the legislative power and to influence its course.

Let us first consider the legislative power. The legal constituency of the corporation is the multitude of owners; it is they who are the citizens of the corporate state. They are the lawful electorate. This electorate, like that of the public at large, holds the franchise which chooses the corporate legislature — the board of directors — and gives it legal authority to legislate. But it is only a mockery of the representative principle to say that the owner-constituency of the corporation elects its representatives in the board of directors who then meet to enact legislation that the president and his officialdom carry out. The constituency is either apathetic, or otherwise normally incapable of exercising its franchise. Over a million stockholders of American Telephone and Telegraph cannot possibly get together to wield the formal authority of the ballot on issues they don't understand for candidates they know nothing about. The managerial class of the corporation has come to diminish the role of the owner-constituent-stockholder-citizen who is usually interested only in a pecuniary result. His normal recourse is to withdraw from the corporate state, if he isn't satisfied, and to take up citizenship in another.

The election of the legislature in the corporate political system is practiced every year, however, with farcical solemnity. The annual stockholders' meeting is held, the managers are bright and brisk with the agenda, the newspapers get the usual laugh out of the usual crank who wants to protest, the business of the meeting is conducted with slick efficiency, and the winning slate wins as predictably as it does in a rigged election in a gangster-ridden union.

The meetings of this legislature, once elected and re-elected, are as rigidly ritualized as those of a conclave, a Zuñi ceremony, or a fraternity meeting. Board meetings have a pomp and circumstance appropriate to the occasion and the class. The walnut-paneled rooms, the grey flannel suits, the boned-and-polished shoes, the good cigars, the deep rugs, murmurous acolytes and courtiers — these are some of the appurtenances that legitimize decisions about big money. Crap games have their rituals also, and a special vocabulary, but this is generally a lower-class pursuit favored by soldiers, and the stakes are trifling compared with corporate standards. Imperial decisions are ratified in this regal atmosphere — decisions to divide up the United States, develop Venezuela, support an Arab oligarchy, lengthen cars so that they fit nobody's garage, approve treaties with other satrapies of economic power and influence — in short, *govern* in the name of free enterprise.

This oligarchic regimen is occasionally moderated by the appearance of party factions.[27] In the public government, the party system exists as a regular method by which the government can be changed. It is one of the more important functions of the party that it enables the electorate to line itself up — for and against. Thus the element of party affords the voters the voice that would, unorganized, be a meaningless babble, or mute. But corporation governments can be changed only rarely by the owner-constituencies they presumably represent, because there is no continuous party system to organize their grievances or to test periodically the confidence of the electorate in the corporation government. However, corporate parties do appear often enough to take them out of the statistical limbo of remote contingency. The operation of the party system in the corporate state, as a device for challenging the government of the corporation, is best seen when there is a contest over control of the corporation. In the make-believe democracy of the corporate commonwealth, the stockholders vote by casting ballots, or by giving their proxies to others to cast. This is a refinement of machine politics that no public party organization would dare propose.

Famous fights for control were the successful raid by Robert Young against the management of the New York Central Railroad, and the battles between A. P. Giannini and the Bank of America, Louis Wolfson and Montgomery Ward, and Charles Green and Spyros Skouras in the struggle over 20th Century–Fox. Although the rituals of a democratic contest are practiced and the symbols of democracy are brandished, these struggles are usually contests between adversary political machines. All of the rhetoric of a national campaign is employed — the apostrophes to reason and good sense, the celebration of virtues like honesty and loyalty, the promises to reform, the campaign literature in which party leaders are portrayed in flattering hyperbole by their partisans, while the opposition is seared, crimped, and shrunken by caustic reductives. In the meantime, behind the scenes, professional organizations hired for the purpose solicit the proxies of the sovereign owner-electors, much as a city machine quietly organizes the vote while the candidates fill the air and the press with outrageous declamation.

Then the sovereign owner-elector comes into his brief own. The showdown in the New York Central fight took place in the Tenth Regiment Armory in Albany. Public-relations men, company employees, and some owner-electors wore buttons for the president of the road, bearing the legend "We Want White"; while the insurgent partisans wore buttons with the caption "Young At Heart." Rival slates of candidates were read off, they made speeches, the balloting took place, and Young was declared the winner by 1,067,273 shares, of which 800,000 were contributed by two members of his alliance from Texas.[28] Although these fights are expensive, there are certain opportunities for the winner to recoup. At the annual meeting of the stockholders of the New York Central in 1954, it was voted to reimburse the Allegheny Corporation, of which Mr. Young was again chairman, in the amount of $1,308,737.71, this for the necessary expenses of the campaign by which Mr. Young secured control of the road.

The two-party system in the corporate commonwealth, however, is not a permanent institution. The corporate state normally is a one-party state, in the hands of the managers. But no oligarchy works in a political vacuum, however much it may be dominated by the management. In the making of the broad choices which represent policy, in the decision-making process, both the symbolic and the operative agencies of choice find their autonomy inhibited by various "publics" with which they must contend. These publics may operate as a moderating influence upon the otherwise unchecked power of the managers, even although stockholders may not be able to supply much restraint through the exercise of their franchise.

In the important field of labor relations, for example, the unions have managed to acquire a share of the former autonomous power of the managers to legislate wages, hours, and other working conditions. Here the existence of strong unions constitutes a two-house structure for the making of decisions that affect workers, and legislation is enacted only by the consent of both houses. The bargaining table is the corporate equivalent of Capitol Hill.

Other publics of the corporations also have from time to time limited the power of managers to legislate the rules that affect those publics. The significance of the mass of regulatory legislation that began to grow in the 1880's is that each Act represents a compromise that corporations had to make with disaffected publics — farmers, shippers, customers, competitors, and so on — who were strong enough to influence the public legislatures to establish protective agencies.[29] The weakness of these compromises is that sometimes they do not continue to be operated in favor of the publics that forced them, because these publics do not represent themselves and are not represented within the management structure of the corporation, but are outside it.

Some of the publics with which corporate legislatures have to deal — like the financiers — have come to represent their own interests very skillfully, occupying inside entries of access, and some — like consumers — have rarely learned to represent themselves at all, and don't do it very well when permitted.[30] As to the financiers, when large corporations depended almost exclusively on the market for their capital requirements, the financiers cut themselves in for important slices of control to protect their investments, and to expand their power. Increasingly, however, corporations have been able to free themselves in considerable part from reliance on the market for capital requirements, and this freedom has removed one form of control from the decisional autonomy they have recovered.

The consumer interest, however, has never been satisfactorily structured nor continuously organized to serve as an internal check to the power of corporation governments. Widespread consumer resistance to the vulgarities of automobile design that the manufacturers said the consumer insisted upon having is thought to have had something to do with the recession of 1958. And the commuters on the New Haven Railroad were able to force the resignation of a president when highhanded inefficiency threatened to collapse the service on the line. But these are peasants' revolts; they do not, and did not, achieve anything like a share in the enactment of corporate legislation. Their historical prototype is Wat Tyler, not the barons at Runnymede. *Piers Plowman*, not Magna Carta, is their text.

Although occasionally moderated by parties and publics, the power to legislate, like the constituent power, is almost absolute in the corporate oligarchy. The growth of virtually unchecked corporate power has drawn some speculation about the course of the future, with many answers of varying kinds. The inner circle of the legislative power of the corporation may be a family, a dynasty, a managerial group, or, as C. Wright Mills has lately suggested, in an elite with some class characteristics, but however animated, the power is formidable. Control of this power by a supposed automatic countervailance in the economy is unlikely, for the countervailance is, for the most part, leverage on the seller's side of the market; and it doesn't work in times of inflation, which has been most of the time in the last two decades. It has been suggested that corporations — anthropomorphic corporations, endowed with intelligence, will, personality, and other human attributes — will develop that final testimonial to St. Augustine and Freud, a conscience, the operation of which will curb and control the excesses of corporate power and establish a benevolent regimen: the new "City of God," no less. But one of the lessons of politics is that it is power that checks and controls power and that this is not done automatically and without human hands. The unions show the way, and the consumers are the example of ineptitude. If the legislative power of the corporation is to be curbed and controlled, the checks will have to be bulit into the structure of corporate enterprise, and not just merely laid on from without, nor entrusted to the subjective bias of the hierarchs within.

IV. THE CORPORATE BUREAUCRACY

The third requirement for a political system is an operating structure of command. In the classic definition of bureaucracy, supplied by Max Weber, there must also be added a structure of functions, and methodical provision for the recruitment and replacement of qualified personnel.[31] When these three elements are in conjunction, the resultant organization of the wit and muscle of numbers of people is a bureaucracy; and corporations have bureaucracies, just as does every large rationalized organization, like the Pentagon, the Roman Catholic Church, and United States Steel. Indeed it is hardly necessary to point out that bureaucracy, in this technical meaning,[32] has existed in the business world since long before Frederick Taylor discovered the one best way to do everything; and it was two General Motors executives who wrote books to establish the proposition that the principles of large-scale organization are universal social laws.[33]

There are critics who say that the term "bureaucrat" as applied to the top levels of the business world is as anachronistic, or at least as misleading, as the word "entrepreneur," not because corporations do not exhibit most of the characteristics of large organizations, but because corporate practice violates the third of Weber's qualifications for bureaucracy. C. Wright Mills has said that the "bureaucratic" career in corporations means not only a climb through a hierarchy of offices but "more importantly, it means the setting up of strict and unilateral qualifications for each office occupied." Usually these qualifications involve both specified formal training and qualifying examinations. The bureaucratic career also means that men work for salaried advancement without any expectation of coming to own even a part of the enterprise. But the advancement of corporation executives to the higher levels is "definitely mixed up in a 'political' world of corporate cliques."[34] Choice is in the hands of superiors, "and there are no strict impersonal rules of qualifications or seniority known to all concerned in this process."[35]

Support for this view is provided from an unintended source, the former president of the New Jersey Bell Telephone System, who formulated the functions of the executive in the corporation as three in number: maintaining communications; securing services; and formulating purpose.[36] These were for the most part an arrangement of familiar principles of administration, including the third. But his discussion of informal executive organization, at the time, was fresh. The general method of maintain-

ing an informal executive organization, he wrote, "is so to operate and to select and promote executives that a general condition
of compatibility of personnel is maintained." [37] Those are chosen
who "fit," and fitness includes "education, experience, sex [it is
not clear whether this is compulsory], personal distinctions, prestige, race, nationality, faith, politics, sectional antecedents," and
"manners, speech, personal appearance, etc." [38] This informal executive organization is based upon few if any rules, and represents, according to Barnard, the "political aspects of personal relationship in formal organization."

Bureaucracies are systems for the making of decisions; and
central to the success of decision-making is leadership. Few will
now disagree that the leadership function in corporations has
been transferred from owners to salaried managers.[39] And this
transfer is properly thought to raise important questions concerning the "distribution of powers within the corporation" [40] and the
functioning of the free enterprise economy itself. In the discussion of symbols and ratifications, attention was centered on the
gulf that stretches between the owners and the management, and
the problem was treated *ex hypothesi* as though the board of directors were the effective legislature of the corporate commonwealth. Attention here is centered on the decline of this legislature (just as the legislature in the public government has tended
to decline in the importance it once had) as an "active and independent decision-making body." [41] The legislature in the public
government — the Congress, at least — has developed compensa-
tory institutions for the control of the executive. In this respect,
as in other aspects of governance, the corporation is behind the
public government.

A great deal of the initiative in the making of corporate decisions comes from the lower ranks, as Gordon has demonstrated
and as Barnard earlier stated. The small size of the stockholdings
of professional managers frees them from the impulses that generate decisions oriented toward the maximization of profits, impulses that presumably worked for the owner-entrepreneur. Although profits may not be disregarded, since the directors and
the stockholders regard the corporation as a revenue-producing
agency, the professional managers are free to respond to such

considerations as prestige, power, and social welfare. They become private planners.

The hearings of the Senate Subcommittee on Antitrust and
Monopoly of the Senate Judiciary Committee gave evidence that
much of the administration of General Motors is done through
committees, one of which, the price review committee, receives
price recommendations from the divisions, and then makes recommendations to the operations policy committee, which usually
ratifies the recommendation. In view of the profit of over a billion
a year, after taxes, that General Motors has recently been making, interest was expressed in the method by which prices are
reached. The theory of pricing requires a standard, which has
not changed in twenty years, under which the planned yield is
15 to 20 per cent on the net capital employed. That is to say, the
leaders of General Motors plan their pricing as though the corporation were a public utility; and although the return to General Motors from 1948 to 1955 far exceeded the standard, prices
were not lowered because, it was said, the volume at some time
in the future might decline.[42] In these determinations, which are
largely free of market considerations, the General Motors managers closely resemble the top functionaries of the public bureaucracies, and are almost exactly like the managers of socialist enterprises, the difference being that between the public collectivism of the socialist state and the private collectivism of the corporate state.[43] Price rigidity is not the result of factors external to
the firm but is in part the result of factors internal to the firm.[44]

V. REWARDS AND PUNISHMENTS

The fourth requirement in a political system, whether that of
the corporation or the state, is a system of rewards and punishments. The system is internal — to the ranks under the command
of the corporation — and external — to various publics that threat-
en the security of the corporation. The growth of corporate welfarism and the bureaucratization of benevolence are recent trends
in the development of complex reward systems. The execution
of sanctions against threatening publics external to the corporation has a range from the violence of a Memorial Day massacre

to the Byzantine subtleties of legal sabotage against the antitrust laws.

The bureaucratization of benevolence is a function of the depersonalization of work. Pats on the back by the entrepreneur-owner and an extra day off around the time of the accouchement of the worker's wife were the equivalents of the fringe benefits that are now written with scrupulous and mechanical generosity into union contracts. Bureaucratized benevolence for the lower classes of corporate society is paralleled by the development of corporate welfarism for the middle classes of that society. Millions are bound in a system of tribal dependence through paternalistic personnel policies, conformitarian training programs, tax-deductible expense accounts, an ever-ringing celebration of corporate interest through advertising propaganda, and the growth of the new company towns in suburbia and exurbia. The new middle class of suburban split-level Babbitts, riding the 8:05 into the city and the 5:05 out of it, wearing the status badges that mark their level in the corporate world, more anxious than yearning, looks for solace and safety in the "togetherness" of the corporate collective. For the upper classes of corporate society, bonuses play an important part in the reward system, as do the numerous opportunities for beating the tax laws; and the risk of loss of status is a powerful incentive to conform when the juniors are being looked at closely to see whether they will "fit." For all classes the threat of deprivation of these social sweets is a strong sanction that makes the cruder forms of discipline less necessary.

In the relations between the corporation and its various publics, the political function of crime and punishment is somewhat more difficult to administer because the corporation is unable to control as many of the variables as it does in its internal affairs. An example, however, of the rather full range of sanctions against threatening publics was provided by the Cement Institute, which the Supreme Court held to be in violation of the antitrust laws in 1948.[45] The Institute was a security system for cement producers in which truckers, dealers, customers, domestic rivals, foreign importers, and Federal and state agencies were subjected to discipline. Punitive taxes, for example, were laid in the form of differential charges on customers who wanted delivery to trucks and not to railroads. When this penalty pricing did not work, members of the combination in many instances refused by flat prohibition to allow delivery by truck. Penalties and prohibitions were also used to prevent dealers from competing in the manufacturers' products at prices lower than those that the manufacturer was charging the customer. Efforts of customers to beat the basing-point system by diversion of traffic were met by the use of no-diversion bills of lading, which the railroads were invited to honor. The companies influenced government procurement officers to buy from dealers at a higher price than the companies could have got from the manufacturers direct. When the TVA threatened to make its own cement to avoid the squeeze of noncompetitive prices, the companies complained about coercion, arbitrary government, and ruthless declarations. The appearance of imported cement in the American market brought upon the dealers who handled it attacks that included espionage, encirclement, systematic price undercutting, boycotts, and reprisals.[46]

The courts themselves may become a form of harassment of rivals. Early in 1953, the organized truckers of Pennsylvania sued the eastern railroads in a United States District Court for $250,-000,000 in treble damages. The Pennsylvania Motor Truck Association and thirty-seven trucking firms sought damages because, counsel for this combination said, the railroads had used dishonorable means to restrain commerce illegally. Thirty railroads and the Eastern Railroad Presidents Conference filed a countersuit for $120,000,00 in treble damages. The total damages of $370,000,000 claimed by both sides represented the symbolic stakes in a rivalry that had nothing to do with the damages claimed. The railroad attorney charged that the truckers had filed their suit after the president of the Pennsylvania Railroad had refused to withdraw his objections to the removal of certain truck limitations on the highways. The suit was pressure on the roads, if not reprisal, and the countersuit of the railroads was counter-reprisal.[47]

Although the state has a theoretical monopoly of violence, the corporation has command of forces that commit violence when this ultimate resort seems necessary. The history of labor relations in the steel industry through the 1930's provides many examples of naked warfare and death on both sides. Not unusual are company-maintained detective services, constabularies of guards and security forces, police forces in company towns, and access to the state soldiery through the intervention of compliant public officials. These add up to a body of militia of considerable strength. Bentley's remarks about hanging seem particularly apt at this place.

VI. THE JUDICIAL FUNCTION

The fifth requirement for a political system is a set of institutions for the enforcement of the common rules. We have already seen in the discussion of the previous two sections that corporations have an administrative apparatus and a system of rewards and punishments, and these are part of the machinery for the enforcement of the common rules. But the most mature political systems also provide an objective agency for making judgments about the application of the common rules to individual cases — a judiciary of some kind — and although the judicial function is not as fully developed in the corporation as in the state, it nevertheless exists.

In the hearings on General Motors held in 1956 by the Senate Judiciary Committee Subcommittee on Antitrust and Monopoly, there was evidence that dealers were bound to the company by agreements which gave the company practically unrestricted rights to renew or to cancel.[48] GM lawyers, in the few cases in which dealers sought to enforce their agreements in the courts, argued successfully that the "contracts" were not enforceable. Unenforceable though they were in the public courts, these contracts were nevertheless litigated in a private judiciary maintained by the company. Provision was made for the appeals of dealers from decisions of nonrenewal or termination by division heads, to a court of last resort established in 1939, and staffed with "judges" who were company men. In this corporation court of last resort, over a period of eighteen years, few cases were decided in favor of dealers. The proceedings in this private judiciary lacked the basic elements of due process of law, for only dealers and members of their organizations, without benefit of counsel, were permitted to appeal and appear.[49]

The quality of the justice that was strained through this private judiciary appears in the testimony of a dealer in Lake Orion, Michigan, who had strongly irritated the company officials by provocatively criticizing the company policy that granted to GM employees and executives in his territory the right to buy cars from the manufacturer at the same price he had to pay. The company was competing with one of its dealers. For his protests against the company policy of selling cars at the factory discount in his territory, the dealer was given notice that his franchise would not be renewed. At his hearing before the final court of corporate appeal he was called a "Red" and sneered at by the president of GM, who asked him what Art Summerfield (Postmaster General and a former automobile dealer) was "going to do for [him] now." [50] The dealer was not allowed to take counsel with him, nor was he given a transcript or other record of the proceedings made by General Motors.

Corporations in certain industries like the garment trades made regular use of arbitrators, who comprise a lay court, and the American Arbitration Association is a serviceable private judiciary, from which "judges" may be assigned for specific commercial and labor cases as they arise. Arbitration by private "lay" judges has been a well-known procedure for years in certain areas of labor relation. The procedures used by firms working on government contracts for the discharge of persons thought to be security risks may be scrutinized by the United States courts for compliance with the minimum requirements of due process. It is possible that the public courts may require the private judiciaries within the corporations to conform to the standards of the public judiciary in such cases.

VII. COMMONWEALTHS: GREATER AND LESSER

Hobbes might think that today's corporations were not "lesser commonwealths" embodied in a greater but, in fact, rivals to the formal sovereign both in size and power. The Temporary National Economic Committee reported with awe the existence of billion-dollar corporations. In less than two decades after the TNEC, General Motors produced a billion-dollar profit after taxes. Through the General Motors Acceptance Corporation, GM controls the financing of approximately 50 per cent of total car sales. Although the GMAC and GM were found guilty of violating the antitrust laws in 1939, "nothing was done to separate them so as to deprive General Motors of this competitive advantage." [51] They did pay a fine of $20,000. The yearly budget for advertising in GM is around $100,000,000. Although this corporate prodigy is outstanding, it is by no means unique.

The literature of law and economics has tended to discuss corporations and the concentrates into which many have clustered in terms of the legal rules, like the antitrust laws and courts decisions, optimum size, economic efficiency, and welfare considerations that touch upon the condition of small business. New concepts of function and control must be devised, and these formulations cannot neglect the basically political character of the corporation.

1 2

THE AMERICAN CORPORATION IN

UNDERDEVELOPED AREAS

RAYMOND VERNON

The American corporation today is a prime example of the validity of the proposition that survival and growth are a matter of adjustment. In a hundred years, a kind of continuous interplay between the corporation and its environment has left both the environment and the corporate institution changed beyond recognition. The process will go on, of course. New challenges will engender new adjustments by the corporation to meet them. And of the various challenges, the problems to be encountered and overcome in the underdeveloped areas of the world may well play a significant part.

One characteristic that dominates the operations of the American corporation working in the underdeveloped areas is the extent to which it is hemmed in by governments. Governmental attention comes from three directions: from the ministers of the host governments, anxious not only about the strength of their home economies but also about their own domestic political position; from the Soviet Union and the governments tied to it, ready to use their powers to compete in the underdeveloped areas, both in offers of capital goods and in the sale of products; and from the United States government itself, eager to achieve its foreign-policy goals in these underdeveloped areas.

It is hard to know exactly how the American corporation is likely to adapt itself to its highly exposed role. The likely process of change, however, can be illuminated a little by exploring three questions. One of these involves politics: how the performance of the American corporation in these underdeveloped areas is being reconciled with United States foreign policy and how it is likely to be reconciled in the future. Another — not altogether separable from the first by any means — involves finance: how the American corporation is contributing and how it is likely to contribute to the massive flow of capital which seems an indispensable requisite of added growth in these areas. The third — barely separable from the second — involves impact inside the economies of the underdeveloped areas: how the American corporation is likely to perform in building up the productive capacities of the developing countries by their activities inside those countries. But before we turn to these questions, it will be helpful to take a preliminary look at the way in which the operations of American corporations have been changing in the underdeveloped portions of the globe.

I. THE CHANGING PATTERNS

The current problems of meshing governmental and private activities abroad are not simply new versions of familiar situations. The history of overseas investment by Americans is too recent to have developed much in the way of precedents. Apart from some limited commitments in the Western Hemisphere, investment of this sort goes back barely forty years.

Up to World War II, United States government experience was largely confined to the tactics involved in pushing an open-door policy. There were problems of securing access for American business in the face of discriminatory barriers, such as those which typically existed in the protectorates, colonies, and mandated areas of Africa, the Middle East, and Southeast Asia. And there were problems, as well, of preventing expropriation in Latin America or of exacting some reasonable compensation where expropriation had already occurred. As circumstances demanded, treaties of friendship, commerce, and navigation were negotiated and the Marines were sent to hover on unfriendly shores. In today's perspective, the diplomatic exercises involving our foreign investments before World War II seem extraordinarily — perhaps deceptively — uncomplicated.

There were other aspects of American international investment in the period antedating World War II which distinguish that period from later years. This was the era when a considerable proportion of American investment still took an "indirect" form — the public ownership of foreign stocks and bonds, rather than the direct ownership of overseas branch plants or operating subsidiaries. Such indirect investment grew in the 1920's, propped up by the creditable record of foreign obligations in the untroubled days before the first World War and by the uncritical buying wave of the great bull market. But the drive to fabricate securities and the willingness to fabricate the facts about them led to the creation of some extraordinarily fragile obligations, and the Great Depression put that fragility to the test. As a result, the American public's taste for this kind of investment was almost nil for several decades.

In the past few years, it has become possible once again to sell foreign issues successfully in United States markets; indeed, all the signs of a full-sized boom in such issues seem to be shaping up. But the participation of governments and enterprises from the underdeveloped areas in such a boom is likely to be fairly limited. For one thing, where public offerings are involved, the ground rules of the Federal Securities Act of 1933 require that such securities be offered without too much adornment of the essential facts. For another, the external credit-worthiness of the nationals and governments of the newer underdeveloped countries has still to be built up.

The record and the prospects for *direct* overseas investment present a quite different picture. For some years since World War II, there has been an outward flow of considerable sums from the United States, associated with this type of investment. Much of it has gone to Canada and Western Europe, but a few hundred millions annually have been directed at the underdeveloped areas as well. Lately these figures have begun to show some significant increases, rising as high as $1.234 million in 1957.[1] And if one adds the sums ploughed back into these areas from local earnings, the figure comes to $1.741 million.

Meanwhile, conditions in the underdeveloped areas themselves have changed. It is hard to say whether the changes have improved or worsened the "climate" for foreign direct investment; indeed, the question itself may be too simple for a useful answer. Latin America seems, on the whole, more mature with regard to the acceptance of foreign investment than it has been in some decades; Mexico, Venezuela, Colombia, Brazil, Argentina, and Peru, for instance, now offer a fairly benign political climate.

To be sure, the foreign investor in Latin America is still exposed to occasional excursions and alarums. Though the area has experienced a remarkable development since the end of World War II, the very speed of that growth has stimulated the demand for more development through its effect in raising domestic incomes and increasing consumer appetites. There has been a mounting desire to hurry the pace, a desire which is all the more strident as governments grow more responsive to public wishes. In the period when rotating dictatorships were the rule in Latin American republics, the foreign investor's task was to make his peace with each successive revolutionary, on pain of sudden expulsion and expropriation. Today, the test of "good" performance in Latin America is more demanding on the whole, though the penalties for "failure" may be less summary. Spurred on by the urge to expand, Latin American governments are constantly tempted to supplement private activity with public investment, to elbow the private investors aside, or to engage in competition with them on an unequal basis which some like to call "creeping expropriation." Yet, on the whole, the direct investor's outlook is more hopeful than it was a few decades ago.

Africa, the Middle East, and Southeast Asia offer another sort of atmosphere. Though broadside generalizations of this sort are invariably confounded by cases which do not fit the pattern, the suspicions directed against foreign capital seem stronger here than in Latin America. In many of these countries, experience with colonial investment is more recent and colors political and personal attitudes.

Yet the leaders of the newly created nations of this portion of the world are anxious to develop their respective economies at breakneck speed. Their approach is more disinterested and at times more ingenuous than those of the old-style Latin dictators; Nkrumah and Nehru are a different species from Trujillo and Gomez. Even the new crop of generals who have sprung up to rule some of the underdeveloped countries in Asia and Africa do not seem quite so fixed in their political seats nor quite so in-

sulated from popular aspirations as is the Latin American prototype.

What is more, there is a lively interest throughout the East in
the examples of development offered by the Soviet Union and
Communist China, and there is an intellectual willingness to draw
lessons from those examples. The suppression of personal freedoms and private opportunities is no great problem where neither
freedom nor opportunity as we understand it had really existed.
Even more so than in Latin America, therefore, private investors
in these areas are on trial, and their ability to survive depends in
part on what the governments of the area think of their performance.

The willingness of the area east of Dakar to study the Soviet
model is complemented by a willingness of the Soviets to provide
the necessary instruction. We now have a dozen well-documented
accounts of the Soviet capacity to provide steel mills, cement
plants, oil refineries, and the like where an advantage is to be
gained in supplying them. In general, the financial terms are
generous and the ability to deliver and install is adequate. If
private investors are unwilling to finance and build a steel mill in
India, the Soviet Union is; and if American oil companies will
not explore Morocco's hinterland and refine its oil on "acceptable"
terms, Soviet or satellite technicians and equipment offer a possible alternative.

The Soviet bloc enters the development field with one re-
sounding advantage over the United States — namely, the fact
that all its capital and all its technology are effectively at the government's command. What is more, as matters now stand, the
Soviet bloc is in a position to ship investment goods and technicians abroad with an indifference to profits and to recruitment
difficulties which no private investor can match.

So far, of course, actual deliveries of investment goods have
been quite modest, on the order of $100 million annually. No one
knows for sure to what extent shipments of this sort squeeze the
Soviet economy. There is a respectable body of opinion which
takes the view that the Soviet Union could not make very much
enlarged shipments of capital goods and technical skills without
beginning to take into account the cost to its own development

plans and to those of Communist China. Valid though this view may be, the fact remains that the present practices of the Soviet Union and the United States give the former a considerable edge in maneuverability. However, the comparative position of the Soviet bloc and the United States has to be weighed not in terms of the existing practices of the latter but in terms of how those practices may be changed.

In summary, then, the pattern of international investment is changing. A major quadrant of the world outside the Soviet bloc desperately wants foreign capital from any source, yet places private investment on constant trial and is slow to offer the rights and guarantees which might speed the flow of such investment. For decades or longer, a widespread suspicion of private investment will linger. Suspicious or not, the underdeveloped areas will experiment in public investment and public control, seeking to push their development pace beyond the rate at which private investment is bringing it about. Confronted with this operating fact, the problem of the United States government and of American overseas investors is to find that combination of efforts which responds best to United States foreign policy interests.

II. THE PERFORMANCE OF EXISTING INVESTORS

We turn now to the first of the three questions with which this essay began: the question of reconciling the performance of United States investors abroad with United States government interests. As matters stand, Americans already have upwards of $13 billions in direct investments in foreign countries outside of Canada and Western Europe. Most of this large stake, to be sure, is in just a few countries and the bulk of it is in only a few extractive industries. Yet, all told, the sum represents a considerable economic force in the underdeveloped areas.

To begin with, most of the activities of American corporations abroad present no problem of "reconciliation" because they raise no sectors of conflict. Investing in plants, applying technical skills, making and selling goods, these entities simply operate like any other in the local economy. To the extent that cognizance is taken of their foreign origin, as we shall point out in the sections that follow, the political reaction they invoke is more likely to be helpful to the United States than otherwise. There are a few situations, however, in which the very magnitude of the investments, relative to the national economies in which they have been made, elevates them above the level of ordinary business in the eyes of the host countries. Aramco in Saudi Arabia, Creole in Venezuela, Firestone in Liberia, and United Fruit in three or four banana republics just are not ordinary business ventures to their hosts, much as the American firms would have it so. For the distinction between the policy of a giant United States national in a foreign economy and the policy of the United States government in that economy is not one to which foreign governments would be especially sensitive. Even where the distinction is recognized, foreign governments often find it hard to believe — indeed, American nationals also find it hard to believe — how slight the influence of the United States government ordinarily is in the making of private business policies overseas.

So far, the problems posed by this identification of the United States government with its nationals in underdeveloped areas have not been overwhelmingly difficult. The modern-day American corporation in underdeveloped areas is typically quite conscious of the critical role it has to play, and plays it well. Yet there are times when such corporations, willy-nilly, shape the country's foreign relations without benefit of government portfolio. The negotiation and renegotiation of major oil concessions, involving political issues of tremendous moment, are settled in the last analysis by the companies involved, on the basis of such considerations as the companies think relevant. The handling of labor relations inside the country — a ticklish problem with heavy political overtones — is also undisputedly in the private province. The same is true of marketing policies: what is produced is sold through channels and to destinations of the company's own choosing, even where United States political interests may be involved.

Yet, though such policies may affect vital United States interests, there are strong reasons for approaching the problem with a major presumption of noninterference. For reasons which we shall shortly discuss, the policy of the United States government is to encourage overseas investment, not to inhibit it; and excessive interference will almost certainly put a damper on investment activity. Besides, interference by government involves the familiar dilemma of the nation devoted to personal freedom: how far it is justified in modifying that freedom in order to ensure its continued existence.

Faced with this dilemma, there have been times nevertheless when the United States government has elected to interfere. In the last few years, the "independent" oil companies would have had much greater difficulty cracking the solid phalanx presented by the four "majors" in the Middle East if the United States government's blessing had not been so much in evidence. A decade ago American businessmen might have made somewhat earlier contacts with the provisional government in Indonesia if the United States government had not so obviously expressed its displeasure. There have been cases, too, in which United States government intervention has been more formal. In screening Export-Import Bank loans and in considering guaranties against expropriation and devaluation for companies investing abroad, government agencies sometimes take into account the marketing arrangements of prospective recipient companies and sometimes refuse aid when such arrangements seem inimical to the competitive objective. There are even times when United States law is invoked to prevent business actions by American corporations abroad, as when the Ford subsidiary in Canada was prevented from shipping trucks to the Soviet bloc.

Some mechanisms already exist, therefore, for the evaluation and control of United States nationals' overseas operations. And it is quite possible that the problem may be diminishing, rather than increasing, with time. For as private direct investment has grown, the number of investors has grown, too. At the same time, some of the economies in which the investments are made have been growing as fast, sometimes much faster. The behavior of any given investor, as a result, has tended to become less prominent and less closely identified with United States government policy as a whole.

Though the risks of error by United States corporations abroad are probably declining, the penalties of error are growing greater. This is the fact which may well push the United States government in the direction of maintaining closer contact with the policies of its nationals abroad. Whether the coordination of critical policies will be achieved through a purely voluntary program is hard to predict. There have been numerous cases in which the United States government has asked the voluntary cooperation of overseas investors in modifying their policies and has achieved the necessary response. However, this is scarcely a universally effective approach. Besides, it is sometimes unfair to those who respond to such an appeal, since those who do not are in a position of inequitable advantage. Once we leave the field of voluntary adherence, there is a range of possibilities: the withholding of flag protection, for whatever meaning that may have; the withholding of rights in the foreign country, established under treaties of friendship, commerce, and navigation; the withdrawal of tax forgiveness, granted under double taxation conventions or United States law; and so on.

Today, none of these latter tools exists for ensuring compatible policies by overseas investors. This paper scarcely lays the basis for demonstrating that such tools are either essential or inevitable. Yet the odds seem very high that they will be examined more than once in the decades ahead.

III. THE FLOW OF CAPITAL

Our second question is different in tone and more important in substance than the first. To what extent will the United States corporation contribute to the massive flow of capital that seems called for in underdeveloped areas? Before exploring the question, it is important to sharpen some concepts.

The question contains a very large assumption: that a greatly enlarged outflow of fresh funds must be brought into the underdeveloped areas if these economies are to attain their needed rate of growth. The word "needed" in this context has no absolute scientific meaning, of course. It develops a meaning only as one defines some explicit goals and calculates the resources needed to achieve those goals. One way in which the goal can be defined is the expansion of production sufficiently to allow for modest annual increases in living standards in the underdeveloped areas; and this goal, in turn, demands the eventual achievement of domestic savings large enough to generate the incremental investment needed for such growth. Whenever a serious attempt has been made to frame such goals in hard quantities and to place a dollar sign on the added flow of foreign resources needed by the underdeveloped areas to achieve them, the estimates have been on the order of one or more billions of dollars annually for a sustained period.

Of course, estimates of this sort are shots in the dark. The fact is that once a foreigner invests his funds in another country, he sets in train a stream of events whose complexity defies measurement. The first visible effect is on the country's supply of funds available for purchase abroad. But then foreign purchases are made; domestic resources are mobilized; domestic production is stimulated; exports may grow; imports, too, may rise; incomes in the country will shift; prices and wages in the country are altered; some profits are taken home by the foreign investor; some are ploughed back in more investment; skills are irrevocably expanded — in short, the country is never the same again. To stop at any point in the complex process and to attribute so much change but no more to the initial investment always involves some distortion, sometimes serious distortion. For all that, there is a fairly general conviction among those who have tried to cut through the complexities of the problem that the net fresh capital needs of the underdeveloped areas are exceedingly large — to put it another way, that much more foreign capital is needed even after taking account of the indirect effects of such capital in increasing net exports and adding to domestic capital formation.

As long as the underdeveloped areas regard this formulation of their needs as accurate, they are bound to look to other sources to supplement the activities of private direct investors. One reason is that a large proportion of their needs entailing foreign expenditure is of the sort from which direct investors are excluded — building and operating the public roads, for instance, or providing public power. Another reason is that such investors tend to concentrate their underdeveloped-area investments heavily in just a few countries. For example, of the $1,234 million which American direct investors sent to countries outside of Canada and Western Europe in 1957, about 65 per cent went to Venezuela and another 18 per cent to four other countries in Latin America; the rest of the underdeveloped world received only $222 million. And almost the same degree of concentration occurred in 1956.

The flow of direct overseas investment outside of Canada and Western Europe was concentrated in still another way. In 1957, some 83 per cent of such investment was directed to mining and petroleum ventures; only $205 million went to manufacturing and other activities. Because some unusually large petroleum transactions occurred in that year, the typical figure for mining and petroleum investments is rather lower, perhaps in the neighborhood of 60 or 70 per cent, but the general pattern of concentration is still there.

From the viewpoint of underdeveloped countries, this kind of concentration has drawbacks. For one thing, foreign investment in the extraction of exhaustible resources presents a touchy political problem in such areas, just as it does in the United States. The sale of these exhaustible resources, once developed, is sometimes seen as the liquidation of a natural asset rather than as the generation of income. Besides, some of these countries are uneasy about placing too heavy reliance on earnings achieved through the export of raw materials, since the demand and the price of these products are sufficiently variable that their contributions to the foreign reserves and to the national product of the host countries are liable to be highly erratic. If governments could be persuaded to think through the whole causal chain, of course, their reactions might be quite different. They might well see — indeed, some of them already do see — that the initial exploitation of their raw materials could provide a base for broader industrialization of their economies. Yet, there is a certain uneasiness accompanying these investments, an uneasiness which some economists share. The fear is always present that the activities carried on in the exploitation and processing of raw materials will remain largely insulated from the rest of the nation's economy, imparting little in the way of skills and capital to other activities.

Apart from the spottiness of direct investment, the underdeveloped countries see still another limitation on the role of private direct investors as the conduit for large net capital flows.

Not unreasonably, investors expect to receive a return on their investment in repatriated profits and dividends. Eventually, perhaps much too soon for the development process, the counterflow of profits and dividends can exceed the current flow of investment to the underdeveloped areas. A little experimenting with various hypothetical patterns of investment flow will readily indicate that this possibility is not unfounded. Indeed, even though American direct investors sent record amounts of added funds in 1957 to enterprises located in areas outside of Canada and western Europe, the record inflows did not quite match the earnings repatriated in that year on prior investments.

The balance-of-payment implications of any foreign private investment do not stop here. Nor do we intend to abandon the analysis at this point. But it is fair to say that private direct investment is not a reliable mechanism for effecting a massive net transfer of foreign capital in the early stages of development. Nor can the future be expected to look much different from the past in all these respects. Dollar investment must compete with investment opportunities in the United States, Canada, and western Europe, where the risks of expropriation or devaluation are slight or irrelevant. With a few interesting exceptions, the large American corporation of today is not attuned to unusual risks for unusual profits. Decision by committee does not allow as readily for daring flights of the Harvey Firestone sort, nor do the SEC's proxy and disclosure rules contribute to management's spirit of derring-do.

As a result, direct dollar investment in the underdeveloped areas during the next decade or so will continue to be largely — though, of course, not exclusively — of two kinds. Producers of raw material will continue to provide developmental expenditures for cocoa and rubber plantations, copper mines, and oil wells. This type of development requires a dollar grubstake, especially in its initial stages; and if the long-run views of the Paley Commission are still valid, such expenditure may even expand somewhat. But there is no reason to expect a large diffused dollar flow to develop out of the grubstaking process.

Another category of direct overseas investment which could grow is that provided by the erstwhile exporter who finds it necessary to manufacture abroad in order to retain his foreign market. Whenever some country embarks on a new program of domestic protection, it touches off a certain amount of investment of this sort. The introduction of preferential trading systems among a group of countries is also commonly a stimulus for such investment. The expansion of the Imperial preference system in 1932 set off such a wave by United States firms in the British Commonwealth countries, especially Canada. The OEEC trade-liberalization system contributed to another wave in the years immediately after World War II, with the United Kingdom and the Netherlands numbered among the principal beneficiaries. And the European Common Market promises to enlarge that trend. The underdeveloped areas may yet benefit from such a tendency, especially if they should begin to develop preferential trading arrangements among themselves. But the constricted size of the markets these underdeveloped areas have to offer, compared with such areas as the British Commonwealth or western Europe, will limit the dollar flow responsive to stimuli of that sort.

If economists are right in supposing that a massive increase of foreign capital is required in order for underdeveloped countries to achieve a satisfactory rate of development, the problem remains of finding the means. This is ground well worked over. Various lines of action have been proposed, including the expansion of the existing guaranty program and the provision of tax relief in one form or another. Imaginative use of such facilities as the United States Export-Import Bank and the Development Loan Fund could also add to the flow, as well as aggressive activity by the American-supported foreign development banks of other countries. Beyond that, some expanded activity by existing international institutions, notably the World Bank and its satellites, could add a little more to the flow. All of these deserve consideration and very little basis for a choice among them can be established within the limits of this paper. Yet there is a strong presumption that when everything has been done on these lines that can reasonably be done, a major residual role will exist for government-to-government transfers of foreign capital.

IV. UPGRADING THE DOMESTIC ECONOMY

We observed earlier that the total effects of any investment could not be gauged by cutting off the process at any point and summing up the effects to that point. To rely solely on the measures we have so far discussed is to risk a major misunderstanding of the effects of American direct investment abroad. Once made, these investments have contributed in various ways which escape the yardsticks we have used so far. The contribution is found within the economies of those countries: in the ability of the direct investors to put idle resources to work in the under-developed areas, producing both for export and for domestic consumption; in their capacity to train and upgrade labor; in their impact on the production, marketing, and labor practices of local businessmen; and in their propensity for distributing a considerable part of their profits on lines which stimulate further growth.

One manifestation of this performance is the heavy exports which such investors have managed to generate out of their host countries. In their 1955 operations in Latin America, for instance — a time and place for which exhaustive data have been prepared by the United States Department of Commerce — American direct investors developed exports of $2,092 million and they found it necessary to import only $703 million of goods. To be sure, most of these exports, once again, were in petroleum and minerals, on which their hosts place a certain discount. Moreover, such exports, even after being netted against the enterprises' imports, cannot simply be counted as net gains to the foreign exchange position of the economies concerned: various foreign exchange costs may be involved, through the stimulation of low-priority consumption imports and through the occasional pre-emption of local productive factors which otherwise might have been used in another useful way. But the benign effect of these exports cannot be seriously questioned.

More reliable, perhaps, an index of the direct investors' contribution to the host countries are data on the uses to which they put their sale proceeds. In 1955, sales of $4.901 billion by American direct investors operating in Latin America are associated with local tax payments of $1.098 billion with plant and equipment expenditures of $424 million and with increases in other local assets of $255 million. If the extractive industries are eliminated from these totals, the pattern looks just as benign for development, with modest profits relative to sales, substantial tax payments, and a heavy plough-back of profits and depreciation allowances into increased assets. If the local production factors used for these operations would otherwise have been idle, the gain to the economies involved speaks for itself. If the factors involved would have been used by others in the countries concerned, the appraisal grows more complex. But one need make only a limited obeisance to the latter possibility.

The record seems to suggest, therefore, that the development process would be hastened by the presence of American enterprises in underdeveloped areas, a fact which contributes to the diligent efforts of the United States government to gain their admission in such areas on reasonable terms. But as we indicated earlier, the odds are fairly high that no large wave of investment will develop in such areas, given the alternative opportunities of American business at home and in the more advanced portions of the world; more precisely, no large wave of investment will develop if it entails a large grubstake in dollar terms. What, then, of an alternative possibility — the possibility that American enterprises may go abroad in increasing numbers, contributing their technical information and business methods rather than their dollars in underdeveloped areas, in return for some form of compensation?

To begin with, such a flow already exists in modest proportions. The W. R. Grace interests in Latin America, operating through a network of manufacturing subsidiaries, are old hands in the export of technology to underdeveloped areas. A score or more of major American firms, such as Westinghouse and RCA, also have operated such programs. And the flow seems to be increasing.

Apart from the firms which export technology to the underdeveloped areas as a part of their interest in making and selling goods, others have lately appeared whose chief preoccupation is the sale of technology alone. With the increased specialization of

American enterprise, engineering firms have developed in a number of industries whose primary interest is the design and installation of plants, and whose activities include the training of local personnel and the maintenance of such plants. Power stations, oil refineries, steel mills, cement plants, milk pasteurizing and bottling works, and many other types of installation can be developed on this basis.

What is more, the United States government and international agencies are learning to work in harness with such firms in coordinated programs — programs in which the governmental source provides the funds and the private source provides the technical skill. Numerous World Bank loans and various private contractor arrangements financed by United States foreign aid programs are patterned on these lines.

Yet there is a major gap in these arrangements. Unlike the government of the Soviet Union, which has direct access to all the skills and technology which its industry possesses, the United States government has no easy access to its nationals' skills and technology whenever such nationals prefer not to sell or donate those resources. Nor should this area of inaccessible skills and technology be minimized. If one could quantify the range of productive processes and managerial skills to which access is effectively barred, they would cover a formidable part of the total range of production and distribution.

In general, American firms are extraordinarily openhanded about such matters. The published reports of the Anglo-American productivity teams which visited the United States in the early 1950's marvel repeatedly at the willingness of American business managers to open their doors to competitors and outside visitors, a sharp contrast to traditional European methods of doing business. But the sale or gift of privately-held technology usually involves much more than opening one's doors to visitors for a day or two. It typically requires the contracting firm to detail a management team abroad. And such an arrangement can be costly and disruptive to the firm. Despite cases like W. R. Grace and despite the overseas activities of two or three scores of other firms, most American manufacturers are primarily absorbed with exploiting the domestic market.

This preoccupation with domestic markets is especially true of industry whose technology would be important in the early stages of overseas development. While American firms in industries with comparatively advanced technology have commonly been exposed in some degree to foreign investment and foreign trade, those using a comparatively simple technology have not. The comparative advantage of the United States is such that it either does not trade at all in goods based on a simple technology or is on an import basis with respect to such goods. As a result, American firms in a position to provide firsthand technical information of the beer-footwear-paper-bricks sort usually have little interest in the international market.

The difficulty in finding American technicians for overseas assignments is enhanced by another problem. The sort of men who can carry out the task of installing and running a branch plant on their own, with minimum supervision from the headquarters office, are usually a scarce ingredient in growing American enterprises. Even when they can be spared, such men are usually loath to stray too far from headquarters. When stars are being distributed, it has often been observed, colonels in the field fare rather less well than those at headquarters. And an assignment in Medellin is more remote from headquarters than one in Des Moines.

In addition, there is already some appreciation among American management that industrial experience in a highly developed economy may not be so readily transferable to underdeveloped areas. The literature is replete with cases in which efforts to apply the technology of advanced countries to backward areas without suitable adaptation were disastrous. American enterprise is accustomed to operating in an environment where freight transportation is comparatively reliable and inventories accordingly can be low, where power is dependable and failures are rare, where spare parts are on easy call and replacement is simple, and where labor's adaptability to factory discipline is taken for granted. In addition, American planning proceeds half automatically on certain familiar assumptions about the relative costs of labor, power, and machinery — assumptions sometimes violently at variance with conditions in underdeveloped areas. Sophisticated American management therefore appreciates that in many cases considerable effort may be involved in adapting its skills and its personnel to the conditions of underdeveloped areas.

The prospect of engaging in technical assistance in Africa and the Middle East presents a special difficulty to some American firms. Prior to World War II, patent and process interchange agreements between American firms, on the one hand, and Western European or Japanese firms, on the other, typically recognized the paramount interest of the Europeans and Japanese in these export markets. This recognition commonly led United States firms to grant exclusive licenses in these areas to their foreign colleagues, often in return for exclusive licenses from the latter to Western Hemisphere markets. Some of these arrangements have survived and, once the postwar reshuffling of markets settles down, more are likely to develop. Where such arrangements are in force or in contemplation, an active development program in the Eastern Hemisphere would run counter to the pattern, with marketing implications well beyond those of the particular underdeveloped country concerned.

Indeed, what seems like a local development proposal often involves implications beyond the local market. Development proposals, for instance, may involve the use of unpatented processes. But such processes are not easily protected, and when they are transmitted outside the firm it is wise to place them in safe hands. Otherwise, the risk exists that the local firm will use the information to invade third-country markets or the United States market itself; or, worse still, that the local firm will pass on the information to more mature and more formidable competitors, with similar disastrous results. This concert of fears by American firms appears repeatedly in accounts of overseas operations.

How can obstacles of this sort be overcome? To begin with, how can one deal with the fact that so many American corporations and so much of American management are oriented to the domestic market? Part of the problem might conceivably be met by the development of joint industry-wide vehicles created in appropriate American industries, staffed for the long run with men committed to overseas operations and empowered to draw on the technology of the industry's members for sale abroad.

There are attractions in the approach, but there are also difficulties. Firms comprising such groups, for instance, might be reluctant in some cases to confide their unprotected technology to an organization in which their domestic competitors participated. Besides, for products in which American corporations had overseas interests, such industry-wide vehicles could easily become a device for apportioning overseas investment and sales among their members and could run afoul of the antitrust laws.

It may be, therefore, that such efforts would have to be supplemented by other means. It seems promising, for instance, to think in terms of some independent third party — either a non-producing private entity with "chosen instrument" overtones, operating under contract with the government, or else a government staff itself — to act as the conduit for unprotected information abroad. On the other hand, the necessary interest and the necessary technical personnel to man the "chosen instrument" or the United States government staff will not develop on any large scale until it is evident that the United States government is in the business of assisting the transmission of technology for the long pull. The basic difficulty of our present technical-assistance programs — the difficulty that participants have no normal expectation of a career with the program but live instead on a string of short-term commitments — would have to be overcome. And the terms offered to private contractors or governmentally-employed technicians would have to be sufficiently attractive to compete with opportunities in the United States. Until these conditions are met, we shall not have begun to match the Soviet Union's coercive capacity to rally its home talent for overseas assignments.

But such steps would not deal with the whole problem. Even if American firms felt no fear of disclosure or unauthorized use of technical information by their domestic competitors, there would still be the difficulty in some cases of risking unauthorized use abroad, as well as the threat to existing licensing structures and marketing arrangements. Some of the problems cut across international borders, involving private contracts with foreign nationals. The precedents for dealing with such situations are scarce. Only some wartime arrangements involving British,

Canadian, and American nationals and some postwar situations under the bilateral military aid programs seem relevant. In these situations, governments have performed various roles; special forms of compensation for unprotected technology have sometimes been arranged; the adjustment of conflicting agreements has sometimes been mediated; and the possible exercise of *force majeure* has at times been considered. There are grounds for feeling that the possibilities are sufficiently rich in this field that one need not despair of overcoming the difficulties.

V. THE ROLES OF GOVERNMENT AND ENTERPRISE

Without knowing for sure how the corporate entity will respond to the challenges outlined in these pages, one is reasonably safe in predicting that a response will occur. There will be improvisation in unfamiliar areas and tinkering with settled institutions and with ways of doing business. And from all the signs, the change will involve closer collaboration between governmental and private institutions.

Given our long-run stake in maintaining the largest possible field for enterprise, it is worthwhile considering what such collaboration is likely to lead to in the end. The need to explore the implications for the underdeveloped economies is much greater, on the whole, than the need to explore the effects in the United States. For all its election-time pyrotechnics, the political economy of the United States is quite stable — quite capable of expanding or contracting its governmental activity as circumstances demand, without either paralyzing the government function or hogtying private enterprise. The risks presented externally by the Soviet bloc seem a great deal more real today than the risks presented internally by enlarging government's role.

In the underdeveloped and ideologically uncertain areas, it is another story. Here twigs are being bent; a shift in position today can have considerable portent for the long term. Accordingly, if one could only read some simple lesson from history — if one could find support, for instance, for the proposition that the easiest way to enlarge the relative and absolute role of private enterprise in developing countries was to hold down the relative and absolute role of government — one might have some obvious guidelines to a course of action. But the course of development, history suggests, is much too complex for so simple a rule of thumb.

In some cases, it is evident, government's failure to invest in public capital has hampered private investment. Developers of raw materials abroad, taking on governmental functions in default of governmental action, have sometimes been obliged to concern themselves with schools, hospitals, water supply, sewage, roads, and communications. In each case, the hope and aim of the companies concerned have been to shed these duties as fast as they could be competently assumed by government. If government had been prepared to assume these duties in the first place, the enterprises on the spot would no doubt have heaved the corporate equivalent of a sigh of relief and concentrated upon the business in which they are specialists. More important still, other enterprises — enterprises whose incentive for investment was not so great that they were willing to take on these governmental burdens — might have decided to enter the country if the necessary governmental services had been functioning.

There have been occasional cases, of course, in which the government in underdeveloped areas has stepped beyond its usual role and has been the catalyst in the development process. Even in such instances, the long-run role of private enterprise has not inevitably been hurt. The classic case is Japan, where the initiative for the planning and financing of much of early industry lay with government, but where ownership eventually came to rest largely in private hands. We have yet to see if the newest crop of governments of Asia and Africa will ultimately draw back from some of their enterprise operations at an appropriate stage, but there is no reason for despair on this issue.

One reason why there has been a widespread disposition to be pessimistic about the eventual role of productive private enterprise in underdeveloped areas is that the motivations and reactions of the people of those areas so often differ from those of the West. It is one thing to recognize the point, however, and another to be paralyzed by it. The counteremphasis offered by men like P. T. Bauer is also worth stressing — that for all the social and cultural differences of the inhabitants of underdeveloped areas, a critical segment commonly behaves like economic men when there is reason and opportunity for it to behave in that manner. In order for private enterprise to secure a foothold in an underdeveloped area and to expand that foothold as development occurs, it is not essential that most of the area's inhabitants should promptly adopt the whole system of economic values which goes with private enterprise. All that is needed is for some critical segment of the economy to seize its economic opportunities as they arise.

Another reason why there has been a tendency to despair about the underdeveloped areas' eventual allegiance to private enterprise is the near-universal preference of their intellectuals for socialism in one form or another. But here, too, one must not leap to premature conclusions. One reason for that preference is that intellectuals in most of these countries have no outlet for their training and ambition other than in government service; the possibility of rising with the growth of indigenous enterprise is largely barred to them. Accordingly, the drives of this group are centered on increasing the scope and power of the institutions through which their ambitions may be realized. But once growing private enterprises were available as an outlet, the drives of the trained and literate groups in these areas would be much more complex.

It is altogether possible, therefore, that the strength of the instincts for private acquisition and for workmanship, though restrained by communal habits and social values, may have been underrated as a long-run force in underdeveloped areas. The recent history of Mexico, India, Pakistan, Turkey, and Brazil offers grounds for optimism that increased governmental investment may stimulate private enterprise in underdeveloped areas. Manufacturing activities and specialized agriculture have commonly appeared in the wake of heavy social investment in roads and education. As a result, some of the easy generalities that these underdeveloped areas were wedded to socialist enterprise or that their private initiative would be limited to trade and real estate speculation, have had to be reconsidered.

To be sure, the risk of the governmental omnivore is not altogether fanciful; the cases of the Soviet bloc and of Communist

China illustrate the threat much too pointedly to be disregarded. But thus far, the kind of tyranny associated with economic totalitarianism has arisen out of economic stagnation or outside conquest more commonly than it has arisen out of government-induced growth. One has to search hard to find the case of an underdeveloped nation which, while enjoying some measure of economic growth, has evolved into an advanced state of totalitarianism. This is not to suggest that it may never occur; history rarely offers up its lessons quite so neatly. But if history is being read correctly in these pages, there is no real basis for a doctrine of the slippery slide when appraising the role of government in the development process.

This is the sort of reasoning which permits one, while cherishing the advantages of private initiative, to accept the possibility of added governmental participation in the process. Some forms of governmental participation can be more constructive than others and some can be downright harmful. But, for the moment, the principle is what is important — that the enlargement of the governmental role in the development process would not necessarily be hostile to enterprise, American or indigenous, and might well enlarge their opportunities, absolutely and relatively, in underdeveloped areas.

13

THE PRIVATE AND PUBLIC CORPORATION
IN GREAT BRITAIN

C. A. R. CROSLAND

It is not possible, in a single essay, to present a comprehensive study of the corporation in Great Britain. One can only select and summarize a few essential facts, so that readers of the preceding essays may roughly compare the position in Britain with that in the United States. It will probably be found that, despite the greater extent of both public ownership and state control in Britain, the similarities are more marked than the differences, and furthermore that despite the immanent presence of a strong socialist party in Britain, future changes are not likely to be in a very dissimilar direction.

II

In the private sector of British industry, the 100 largest companies (as measured by net assets) were responsible in 1953 for 31 per cent of total industrial profits.[1] Some 3000 companies, consisting of all industrial companies quoted on the stock exchange, together with the largest foreign-owned subsidiaries, were responsible in 1951 for 46 per cent of employment and 56 per cent of gross output in manufacturing industry.[2]

We cannot assert definitely that the relative importance of the largest firms has increased over the last twenty-five or fifty years; for the evidence as to changes in the degree of concentration over long periods of time is extremely tenuous. Of the two best-known studies, the first suggests tentatively that within the quoted company sector, business concentration (in the sense of the proportion of total assets controlled by the largest firms) increased in the period from 1885 to 1939 and decreased from 1939 to 1950; but the authors state that "changes in business concentration in the economy as a whole over the past half century may not be very great." [3] The second study, an industry-by-industry survey based on Census of Production data, comes to an even more negative conclusion: "We cannot tell you whether concentration in British industry has changed since 1935." [4]

There appears, however, to be clear evidence that both the 100 largest companies and the 3000 "quoted" companies, the former more especially, have increased their share of industrial profits over the last decade.[5] If one bears in mind also that nationalization has entailed a process of forcible concentration in several important industries, it seems probable that the large corporation, taking public and private together, has increased its relative dominance in the British economy during the postwar period.

Some people believe that the private corporation wields "excessive" power in Britain, others that its area of free decision is sufficiently circumscribed by external influences. The most important limiting influences are competition, labor, public opinion, and government; these will be discussed in turn.

Monopoly situations undoubtedly exist in Britain; at the other extreme, perhaps one fifth of industrial employment is in trades where market conditions "are likely to bear some essential resemblance to conditions of perfect competition." [6] The most prevalent situation, however, is one of imperfect oligopoly. But competition, although often taking forms other than price-competition, appears to be real and effective in most oligopolistic industries. In addition, the large firm is of course also threatened both by the development of new products and (increasingly) by new competition from established firms in other industries. It is also arguable that competition is more widespread than it was before the war, owing to the effect of government legislation against restrictive practices, a more rapid rate of technical innovation and development of new substitutes, a higher level of profits available for use in new directions, and the gradual crumbling of resale price maintenance. At any rate, it seems safe to say that, as in other modern mixed economies, the large corporation in Britain is subject to a substantial degree of actual and/or potential competition.

The second limiting influence is the power of labor. This has naturally been greatly increased by the fact of full employment and a seller's market for labor, though it has also been enhanced by changes in the political and social climate. Trade-union influence now extends well beyond the traditional wages sphere. The British unions have not, it is true, invaded management prerogatives on the same scale as some of their counterparts in the United States. Nevertheless, they have steadily extended the scope of collective bargaining both horizontally, to embrace a wider range of subjects, and vertically, to include continuous day-to-day negotiation in the plant. They now exert a strong influence on (for example) dismissals, plant discipline, the size of the labor force, promotion policy, hours, the organization of work, changes of machinery, the number of apprentices, and so on. Few managements today would take an important decision likely to affect labor relations without prior discussion with the unions. Thus over a wide range of decisions affecting the day-to-day life of the worker, the unions impose a significant check on the policies of management.

Third, public opinion, which in Britain (as elsewhere) exerts a definite influence on business decisions, has altered markedly in the last hundred — and even twenty — years. The area of what is socially permissible has been sharply circumscribed, and the result is a pronounced tightening of the accepted rules of business behavior. The large corporation tends to be especially sensitive to this change in the social climate, and its business policies — for example, its behavior toward competitors, dealers, or suppliers — show little of the traditional capitalist ruthlessness.

This sensitivity is reinforced by the severely practical consideration that a Labour Government is always in the offing. The combined effects of this political anxiety and the change in public opinion are sometimes remarkable. One example may be quoted. The steel industry — in Marxist folklore "the strongest bastion of capitalist power" — based its recent campaign against renationalization not, as might have been expected, on a defiant appeal to the principles of free enterprise, but on the claim that it was already subject to so high a degree of public control that nationalization would make little difference.[7] This is indeed a far cry from the days of "the public be damned."

The last and most important restraint on business freedom is the actual or potential intervention of the state. Governments in Britain now exercise a far more pervasive control over business decisions than they did before the war. This is due primarily to the explicit acceptance, enforced by a major shift in electoral opinion, of government responsibility for the level of employment, the rate of accumulation, the state of the foreign balance, the degree of monopoly, the distribution of incomes, the location of industry, and generally the correction of glaring discrepancies between private and social cost.

The most conspicuous form of government intervention is the use of "global" weapons (nondiscriminatory fiscal or monetary policies) to achieve "global" ends (in particular to determine the total level of demand and the broad division of output among consumption, investment, exports, and social expenditure). But governments also constantly intervene in a selective and discriminatory manner: that is, in such a way as to influence or determine the price, production, and investment policies of particular firms or industries. This they do partly through a wide range of positive and negative indirect taxes (especially purchase-tax), partly through legislative action (for example, on restrictive agreements on the location of industry), partly through selective physical or hire-purchase controls, partly through their influence as a final buyer of goods on an enormous scale, and partly by pressure and persuasion. This last alone needs comment, being a much more potent weapon than is generally realized, especially in Britain where the "Old-Boy net" operates strongly between industry and Whitehall. Without any recourse to formal legislation, the government frequently imposes its will by threatening (as with the steel industry, which under the threat of nationalization accepted an astonishingly close degree of public control), or by bullying (as when Sir Stafford Cripps virtually bullied the motor industry into exporting a higher proportion of its output), or by cajoling (as occurred after 1945 in respect of new oil-refineries), or by bribing (as when the offer of government money, or at least the underwriting of the risk, has persuaded reluctant firms to undertake the production of — for example — jet aircraft, sulphur, titanium, and hydraulic presses).

The extent to which the government can and does influence the policies of particular firms or industries may be judged from some recent examples, taken at random. The "big Five" motor manufacturers have passed in the last five years from boom to recession and back to boom largely as a result of government decisions on purchase-tax and hire-purchase regulations: the two largest aircraft firms have recently had the whole basis of their profitability and production policy cut away by changes in government orders; many powerful industries are now being forced to abrogate long-standing collective price-agreements; the largest private joint-stock bank was recently refused permission by the Capital Issues Committee to make a new issue of shares: the last major investment project in the steel industry, affecting two of the largest units in the industry, was substantially decided, in respect both to its size and its location, by the government, and so on.

Some people may doubt whether the government always uses its power with perfect wisdom, and critics often accuse it either of infirm purpose or ambivalent intention. But there can be no doubt as to the power itself (though if it were thought insufficient, there would be no great difficulty about reintroducing some of the physical controls which were dismantled after the war). Broadly, any government can now impose its will (provided it has one) on the private corporation, and the actions even of a Conservative Government do in practice impinge on industry to an extent which would have been thought outrageous a generation ago. This new economic activism of governments profoundly affects the policies, and restricts the autonomy, of the large British corporation.

Nor is it nullified, as some people on the Left still fear, by the *political* power of large-scale industry. There is little evidence that such power is either decisive or dangerous. Industry was quite unable to prevent the nationalization program of 1945–1951, the postwar laws against monopoly and restrictive practices, and a level of profits taxation which continues to be described as "penal." The Aims of Industry, a body set up by private business to conduct free-enterprise propaganda, has made a negligible impact; indeed what is surprising about the postwar era of government intervention is how ineffective most such propaganda has been. A few publicity campaigns against nationalization, such as those of Tate and Lyle in 1950 and I. C. I. in 1955, have met with success; but this was to be explained mainly by the total failure of the Labour Party to make clear to the electorate why it wished to nationalize those particular firms at those particular times. Generally there is no evidence that the British corporation wields a dangerous degree of political power.

III

The private corporation, then, is subject to considerable restraints on its behavior. Within the limits set by these restraints, what does its top management consider to be the aim of business policy, and to whom does it feel itself to be responsible?

First, does it seek to maximize profits, and if so, why? Evidently it does not now do so because its own remuneration derives primarily from profit. The divorce between ownership and control is a sufficiently familiar and well-documented fact; with a few notable exceptions, the top management of large British firms today is in the hands of salaried executives who have no substantial shareholding interest in their firms, and who owe their power to, and derive their income from, their position in the managerial structure.

Nor is there much sign that the management maximizes profits from an altruistic desire to maximize the income of shareholders. Many British managements are at the least indifferent, and occasionally even actively hostile, to the claims of shareholders for larger distributions; they prefer to give the first priority to ploughing-back for further expansion. Indeed, large firms are constantly being rebuked in the financial press for their failure to regard high dividends as the primary aim of business activity.

Yet the salaried manager is clearly still interested in high, even if not theoretically "maximum," profits. Partly, of course, this is because the level of profit still affects, even though it does not mainly determine, his own remuneration — in the long run because his promotion and salary prospects will be influenced by the rate of growth and the profitability of the firm, in the short run either because his salary contains a bonus element or because he has some shareholding in the firm.

But he is also interested in high profits because of a mixture of psychological and social motives. He tends to identify himself closely with his firm, which comes to have for him a genuine personality of its own, with interests quite separate from those of its shareholders. And not only his corporate loyalty to the firm, but all his personal motives — professional pride, ambition, self-realization, desire for power and prestige — find their fulfillment in high output and rapid growth, and hence high profits.[8] These are both the conventional test of business performance and the ultimate source of business power. They determine both the strength and prestige of the firm, and the power and social status of its executives.

High profits and rapid growth are therefore still the dominant business incentive in Britain. They are, it is true, less ruthlessly pursued, for a variety of reasons, than in the days of entrepreneurial capitalism. First, if profits are seen partly as a source of prestige, they are, in the climate of the welfare state, far from being the only such source. As I have written elsewhere,

> The business leader can also acquire prestige by winning a reputation as a progressive employer, who introduces co-partnership or profit-sharing schemes: or by being known to possess a high standing in Whitehall, and to have the ear of Ministers, an obvious candidate, perhaps, for Royal Commissions and National Advisory Councils; or by enjoying an outstanding local and civic reputation, as a benefactor, a helpful friend to the City Council, a member of the Court of a civic University: or by displaying obvious patriotism, and devoting a lot of time to the British Productivity Council. . . Such activities are increasingly common and well-regarded.[9]

They are, moreover, encouraged by the rise in the educational attainments of British top management. Today, fewer opportunities exist for rising from the bottom; and a higher proportion of executives, in the large corporation especially, have a public-school or university background. This change has bred a more suave and sophisticated attitude to business, strikingly different from the ruthless, obsessive single-mindedness of the older business leader. A further influence is the altered climate of public opinion, already referred to, which considerably restricts the bounds of what is socially permissible in business activity. It is for all these reasons that British businessmen now like to talk, not of their duty to maximize profits, but of the social responsibilities of the corporation, and of how it exists to serve not the shareholder alone, but also the consumer, the worker, and the public at large.

But at this point we must beware. Such talk may be treated as genuine if it is taken to reflect a mood, but not if it is taken to define a new objective. The objective remains high profits and rapid growth. It is pursued, it is true, in a more civilized and less aggressive manner; perhaps, in consequence, profits are not fully maximized.[10] But the corporation still seeks an extremely high level of profit — high enough both to finance much or all of its current expansion plan and to cover a rate of dividend which will facilitate future new issues of shares; and with this in view it obeys the profit-motive in the majority, at any rate, of its business decisions. We certainly do not need to search for some completely new motivation, least of all one so ambivalent and potentially contradictory as the much-talked-of joint responsibility to workers, shareholders, customers, and the public. Such talk reflects a change in the rules of the game, not in the objective.

IV

The public attitude to the corporation has been influenced, not only by the changes summarized above, but also by developments in the nationalized sector of industry. The main nationalized industries, and the numbers employed in them, are transport (800,000), coal (750,000), electricity supply (180,000), and gas supply (140,000).[11] Each of these industries is managed by one or more public corporations, this form of organization having become the chosen instrument for nationalization after the rejection of management by the workers, on the one hand, and by a civil service department, on the other. The public corporation is naturally subject to many of the same influences as the private corporation. But we are here mainly concerned with the differences, and especially with its relationship to Parliament and the government.

The accepted theory was that the public corporation should

be largely independent in its day-to-day operations; untrammeled either by continuous political interference or niggling, bureaucratic control by the civil service, it was to be permitted normal commercial freedom and scope for initiative. It would, on the other hand, be ultimately accountable to a Minister, and through him to Parliament. He would appoint and dismiss the Board, issue general directions as to policy, and receive the annual report and accounts; and his actions would be debatable in Parliament. By this compromise it was hoped to combine business efficiency with public accountability.

By no means everyone is content with the way in which the theory has worked out in practice. First, many politicians are gravely dissatisfied with the extent of Parliamentary accountability. On matters of day-to-day administration, Ministers refuse to answer Parliamentary questions on the grounds that they are not responsible. Even on matters of major policy, Parliament has (until recently) been restricted to a single day's debate each year on the Annual Report of the industry, an occasional half-hour's debate "on the adjournment," and one or two other minor opportunities for discussion.

This of course is quite inadequate for any effective supervision. There has, in consequence, been a growing resentment and frustration among Members of Parliament, who feel that the corporations have become remote, irresponsible bodies, immune from public scrutiny or democratic control. This frustration grew so strong that in 1956, after much heart-searching, a permanent Select Committee on the Nationalised Industries was established. But whatever its future role, the public corporation has not up to the present been in any real sense accountable to Parliament, whose function has been limited to fitful, fragmentary, and largely ineffective ex-post-facto criticism.

Nor, on the other hand, have the corporations been permitted to act in a normal commercial manner, seeking to maximize their profits without political interference. I discuss below whether such a policy would be theoretically desirable. It has been ruled out in practice by two factors. First, the corporations cannot maximize their profits, because they are forbidden to do so by law. The Nationalisation Acts enjoin them merely to break even

— to cover their costs "taking one year with another." This injunction has several disadvantages (for example, its effect on the possibilities of self-finance). But the relevant consequence here is that the level of profit cannot reflect (though the level of losses may) either operating efficiency or consumer preferences; it reflects only the provisions of an Act of Parliament.

Secondly, Ministers intervene regularly, and indeed increasingly, in the affairs of the corporations. Under the Nationalisation Acts, the Minister has the power to give the Board "directions of a general character on matters affecting the national interest." This was intended to be a power of last resort, for use only when a major divergence of policy had arisen between the Minister and the Board; and in fact only one such direction has ever been given — in April 1952, when the Minister directed the British Transport Commission not to increase certain charges.

But a development has occurred which was not foreseen in the discussion prior to nationalization. This is the increasing propensity of Ministers to intervene, not by means of open "directions," but through informal consultation and pressure over the lunch table or at private meetings. Ministers now not only exercise a continuous general supervision over the corporations, but they also intervene to alter or influence specific decisions on major policy; and no Board today would take such a decision without first "clearing" it with the Minister.

Many observers are disturbed by this development. First, it makes it harder for the corporations to pursue a normal commercial policy, not only for the general reason that it subjects them to continuous "political" interference, but in particular because the interventions often run counter to their commercial interests. Thus, to take the best-known examples, there is an informal "gentleman's agreement" that the Coal Board will not increase prices without the consent of the Minister; of ten applications to him for a price increase, one has been refused and four approved only at a lower level of increase. Again, on two critical occasions the Minister, in order to avoid the political odium of a national railway strike, has compelled the Transport Commission to grant a larger wage increase than it proposed or wished. On other occasions Ministers have brought pressure on Boards to keep open marginal enterprises. Such actions naturally lead to lower profits or heavier losses, and also, because the Boards come under public criticism for losses or wage increases which are not in fact their fault, lower managerial morale.

We are discussing here interventions which have a "political" motive, such as the desire to avoid an unpopular strike or price increase, not those which have an "economic" or planning motive. The latter are of course inevitable with such basic, public-utility industries. Indeed, the criticism is that in this field successive Governments have been, not too active, but too supine. There has been, for example, little real attempt to plan, whether through prices or physical controls, the coordination either of road and rail transport or of the three fuel and power industries. Again, all the nationalized industries were committed to huge investment programs, but these were never satisfactorily coordinated either with each other or with the level of investment activity in the private sector. The result has been an unfortunate combination of too much political interference and too little planning control.

The second objection to this pervasive behind-the-scenes influence of Ministers is that it appears to run counter to any doctrine of public accountability. Being exercised in secret, it cannot be debated in Parliament and the press; it is the Board which nominally takes the decision, and there is no overt act for which the Minister can be held responsible. We are thus in danger of reaching a situation where the Boards are neither publicly accountable nor free commercial agents, but semicommercial bodies privately accountable to an individual Minister.

v

Many proposals are made for altering this state of affairs. The first is to increase the degree of Parliamentary control and accountability. But Parliament can never effectively control the nationalized industries. It lacks the time — it is doubtful if it could find even three whole days per year for discussing each industry. It lacks the objectivity — any discussion on these industries is inevitably colored by political loyalties. It lacks the requisite caliber of M. P. — the man who, well-versed in the problems of large-scale industry, can discuss major policy in an informed manner instead of merely voicing trivial constituency complaints. Lastly, Parliamentary control would force the Minister, who alone is answerable to Parliament, to become directly responsible for almost every action of the Board; the consequence would be a degree of Ministerial supervision which, besides its other obvious drawbacks, would certainly repel able potential recruits to the Boards. No doubt some minor improvements can be made in the present arrangements; but effective Parliamentary control is a myth.[12]

A second school of critics, going to the opposite extreme, would have both Parliament and the Minister take *less* active interest in the corporations than they do today. On this view, the political authority should behave like the typical private shareholder, content to remain passive so long as the results are satisfactory. The Boards, for their part, should be allowed a free hand to operate commercially. They should attend rigidly to marginal cost and the rate of return on capital; and their price and output policies should follow normal profit-maximizing lines. They would then be, at least in a crude sense, accountable to the consumer, while their efficiency could be assessed by the traditional criterion of profit.

As a complete solution, this is not feasible. First, it is not theoretically desirable. The public corporations are statutory monopolies, wholly protected from direct competition or new entry into their industries. They are, it is true, often subject to severe competition from close substitutes (coal from oil, the railways from road transport, gas from electricity); and coal and the railways in particular have now been made painfully aware of the consequences of free consumers' choice. Nevertheless, the corporations do hold a monopoly position within their own industries; and it follows that a high level of profit might reflect, not business efficiency or the strength of consumer demand, but merely monopoly pricing.

Second, the government has a more active responsibility than the private shareholder in respect of new finance. The public corporations are self-financing to a much smaller degree than most private firms, and they borrow, not directly from the capital market, but either from the Treasury or under Treasury guarantee. It is now widely agreed that they should, by a more realistic and commercial pricing policy, finance a higher proportion of their capital expenditure out of ploughed-back profits. But in view of the size of their investment program, complete self-finance is hardly possible; and if they must borrow, they should borrow on government credit if only because ultimately the government has either to authorize an increase in charges or meet the deficit. They must therefore remain financially dependent on the government, which in consequence should exercise some supervision over their capital programs.

Third, it is sometimes argued that the Boards cannot simply be left to get on with their jobs, since they have no financial inducement to do these jobs efficiently; that is, their incomes are not affected by the financial results of the enterprise. But of course this is also true of some proportion of private managers; and moreover the factor of prestige operates powerfully in the nationalized sector. If a public corporation makes a loss, its top management is subjected not only to severe and unsympathetic criticism in Parliament and the press, but also to a certain contempt and derision on the part of the business fraternity generally; and this provides a distinctly strong inducement to produce creditable financial results. The contrast, for example, between the prestige of the electricity industry (which has consistently made good profits) and that of the Transport Commission (which has incurred continuous deficits) is most noticeable. The difference in incentives between the public and private sector may therefore not be very great. However, to the extent that it exists, it justifies the political authority in taking a more active interest than the normal private shareholder.

Fourth, a considerable measure of planning control is necessary over industries of such basic importance to the whole economy. And, last, it is not realistic to suppose that these industries can ever be wholly free of "political" interference. Unlike private shareholders, Parliament and the Minister are in almost continuous session; they are subject to strong pressures from both workers and consumers; their constituents are closely affected by the operations of the industries; and moreover many Labour M. P.'s still think of "public accountability" as the prime object of nationalization.

It is therefore neither practicable nor desirable that the corporations should pursue a completely independent, profit-maximizing, commercial policy. Nevertheless, most observers would like to see a major move in this direction. The first essential would be a much clearer division of function between the Minister and the Board. It should not be primarily the function of the Minister, driving from the back seat, to guide or supervise normal operating policy. For the reasons given above, he must no doubt supervise rather more closely than the shareholders in a private firm; and for this purpose he will call to his aid techniques such as the periodic outside committee of investigation. But he should rely mainly on choosing the right people for the Board and then allowing them to operate on normal business principles; especially, they should be given more freedom than they now have in respect to price determination, wage policy, and the closure of marginal enterprises. The Minister should then intervene only when considerations either of economic planning or consumer protection or social cost are thought to require a clearly noncommercial policy on the part of the industry.

Many critics, moreover, would prefer these interventions to be made openly, in the form of "directions" under the Act, rather than in private as they are today. This would have two advantages. First, it would improve the morale of the Boards, which would not then be exposed to public obloquy for poor results or noncommercial actions which in fact were foisted on them by the Minister. Second, the directions would be debatable in Parliament, so that at least someone would be publicly accountable whenever the Boards were forced to act against their commercial interests. Such a policy would not be without its practical difficulties — for example, it might bring Ministers into open conflict with the trade unions over wage claims. But the combination of normal commercial freedom with public accountability for noncommercial directives is increasingly thought to be sound in principle.

VI

The Labour Party's attitude toward nationalization has been profoundly affected by these various developments in the private and public sectors. It has of course also been affected by other considerations, not discussed in this essay. First, many traditional Labour objectives, to the fulfillment of which nationalization was at one time thought to be essential, have either been achieved, or manifestly could be achieved, by other methods — for example, the objectives of full employment, economic planning, a transfer of power to labor, redistribution of incomes, and so on. Second, if the Party were to proceed with nationalization, using the obvious criterion of size, the next industries on the list (automobiles, aircraft, chemicals, shipbuilding, radio, electrical equipment) are not "natural" candidates in the sense that the 1945–50 list of industries could reasonably be held to be. They are neither public utilities, nor basic industries (in the sense that coal and railways are basic), nor natural monopolies, nor in need of central coordination; moreover, they have indistinct boundaries, and they are heavily involved in export markets. Third, the efficiency criterion, which assumes a greater importance in the light of the British postwar balance-of-payments problem, does not point clearly to further large-scale nationalization. On the one hand, the obvious next candidates (those mentioned above) are performing in a tolerably efficient and expansive manner; on the other hand, the record of the nationalized industries, while certainly better than many critics allow, is at least not beyond reproach. Last, the Labour Party, being human, is not uninfluenced by the clear evidence that large-scale further nationalization would not be electorally popular.

But the Party has also been strongly influenced by the developments discussed in this essay. On the one hand, the public corporation does not at present appear to be satisfactorily accountable to anyone. Parliament exercises only a fitful power of debate (usually long after the event); the Minister exerts some unknown degree of control behind the scenes; while the corporations are less sensitive than their private counterparts to the normal pressures of the profit motive and the price mechanism. It may well be, of course, that too much importance has been attached to "public accountability," and that the sensible attitude would be to insure simply that the corporations should get on with their jobs in a businesslike manner. But to the extent that accountability is judged important, it has evidently not been satisfactorily achieved in the nationalized sector.

The private corporation, on the other hand, gives less offense to the Left from this viewpoint than it did before the war. It appears more sensitive to public opinion and social considerations. Its actions are more circumscribed by the counter-power of labor. It responds in a broad way to individual consumer preferences. And, above all, it has proved itself easily amenable to government control. Whereas before the war it was assumed (surprisingly, in the light of the total control of the Nazi Government over a privately-owned economy) that a change in ownership was an essential condition of government control, today it is realized that control can be made effective without nationalization. Operating by legislative, fiscal, physical, or monetary methods, the government can, broadly speaking, make private industry dance to any tune it wants. Frequently it has no tune, or only a discordant one. But whenever it believes that the policy of the private corporation runs counter to the public interest, it has plenty of ways in which it can impose its will. This is of course only a reflection of the broader truth that in Britain today industrial ownership is not the main determinant of political or economic power.

For these various reasons, the Labour Party's program of future nationalization is a distinctly modest one. It embraces the renationalization of steel and long-distance road-haulage, and a major nonindustrial project in the shape of the "municipalization" of much rented property. For the rest, the Party merely "reserves the right to extend public ownership in any industry or part of industry which, after thorough inquiry, is found to be seriously failing the nation." [13] In the present climate of opinion, this right is not likely to be exercised in respect of any large number of corporations.

It does not of course follow that all socialists are wholly content with the private corporation, and wish to make no further changes. It is only that these further changes, which in any event (with the one exception mentioned below) are not very far-reaching, are now seen to be realizable by methods other than traditional nationalization. For example, some socialists would like the government to exercise a firmer planning control over the investment decisions of private industry; others propose that it should take steps to reduce the amounts spent on advertising; others, again, wish to restrict the extent to which corporate funds are used to provide tax-free privileges for top management. But all such matters could be attended to without a change in ownership.

There is, it is true, one respect in which industrial ownership is still important. Private property in Britain is most unequally distributed; and industrial shares are more unequally distributed than other private property. The Labour Party wishes to achieve a more equal distribution both of existing property and future capital gains. There are a number of ways in which it could do this. But one method which is now attracting support on the Left is the direct acquisition of industrial shares either by the state (through the acceptance of death-duties in kind) or by a state-owned body such as a government investment trust or a national superannuation fund.

This would not, however, involve, nor is it intended to involve, nationalization in the traditional sense. Nationalization implies the compulsory purchase, under an Act of Parliament, of the entire capital of a firm or industry, the object being to acquire control. Share-buying is directed solely toward obtaining income and capital gains. For this there is no need to assume compulsory powers, or to buy out whole firms, or to interfere with the existing management, or to seek in any way to exercise control. The role of the state would be that of the normal pension fund or investment trust, buying and selling stock in the open market, and acting generally as a purely passive shareholder.

To sum up, there is now no strong desire in the Labour Party to nationalize a further large sector in industry. In the words of a recent policy statement — words which would have been unthinkable twenty years ago — "The Labor Party recognizes that, under increasingly professional managements, large firms are as a whole serving the nation well." [14] Let them be subject to essential social and governmental controls — more, if necessary, than exist today; but nationalization itself will be kept as a reserve power of last resort, to be used, in practice, most sparingly.

14

INDUSTRIAL ENTERPRISE IN SOVIET RUSSIA

ALEXANDER GERSCHENKRON

Soviet Russia describes itself as a socialist country and its economy as a socialist economy. Those claims are seldom disputed. And yet, on reflection, they may well appear less valid than is generally assumed. In casting doubt upon them, our purpose is not merely to accuse the Russians of conceptual perversion and to defend some "correct" concept of socialism against Soviet encroachments. There may be indeed much need for, and justification of, tidier semantics; but what primarily matters within the present context is to elucidate some aspects of industrial enterprise and industrial management in Soviet Russia, and one way to approach the problems involved is to look briefly for the ideological antecedents of policies in the course of which the industrial organization in Soviet Russia has been shaped and reshaped.

To do this, let us have recourse to an expository device the attractiveness of which is attested by long centuries of use and abuse. Imagine an average Russian intellectual in the very early years of this century, preferably a university student, who, like a famous fictional figure of another age and continent, most likely would have "an insuperable aversion to all kinds of profitable labor." On the other hand, he would be passionately interested in politics and political debates and speculations and would consider himself an implacable enemy of the Russian autocracy. Imagine further that like the princess in the Grimms' fairy tale, or like St. Vladimir's knight in the Russian ballad, or like the hero in Edward Bellamy's novel, he was put to sleep, say in 1902, and slept several decades in pleasant isolation from highly unpleasant world history, dreaming happily the dream of a future Russia, free from the stupors of starvation, drunkenness, and illiteracy. True to our patterns, let him awaken as the Kremlin chimes strike the first hours of the century's second half. Let us agree that time had stood still with him and that, unlike the Catskill villager who had taken such a deep draught out of the mysterious flagon, he found his youthful vigor undiminished. We can therefore at once dispatch him upon an extensive journey through the highways and byways of Soviet industrial landscape. Finally, let us posit — making the most fantastic assumption of them all — that he is allowed to give free vent to his observations, comparisons, and reactions.

Our traveler's first impressions are general but very exciting. He quickly discovers that private property in capital goods has been abolished. He feels that this is indeed a negative but very convincing proof that the previous "system of capitalism" has been replaced by the "system of socialism." In forming this view he feels corroborated by what he remembers from his perusal not only of socialist books and pamphlets but also from very scholarly and quite nonsocialistic treatises of the subject.[1] They all regarded the question of ownership over the means of production as the separating line between the two economic systems, the great watershed clearly and firmly drawn on the maps of social geology. Our explorer not only fails to be shocked by the change but tends to welcome it. His previous political views are not ascertainable in great detail. It is clear, however, that despite his dreams he was not connected with any of the then existing socialist groups; a fact which tends to set him somewhat apart, since in those days the average Russian intellectual liked to view the world through socialist spectacles with a better than fifty-fifty chance that the precise hue of his glasses had a Marxian rather than an agrarian or populist tinge. Yet, although not a socialist, he tended to contemplate socialism in its different connotations with a good deal of sympathy. In this, no doubt, he was very Russian and very un-American. He never felt the average American's aversion to the term which Bellamy once expressed so well and so forcefully, inviting the inevitable *a minori ad maius* inference.[2]

Per contra, for our man socialism always has been an "okay word." He never doubted that socialist ideas contained considerable ethical values. He felt that the socialist movement tried to satisfy age-old yearnings for justice and goodness. He had heard others use and was himself not past using the sacral phrase: "In a sense, of course, we are all socialists." At the same time, perhaps paradoxically and inconsistently, he was also attracted by the anethical tenets of Marxism which stressed the inevitable rise of Russian society from the barbarous depth of a primitive agrarian economy to the heights of a civilized industrial community. It was pleasant to have the certainty of economic progress assured by what he, along with many members of the intelligensia, was glad to regard as the "last word of modern science." [3] But neither respect for socialist values nor the thesis that Russia "was bound to pass through the stage of capitalism," to use the parlance of the time, had led him to a complete espousal of the socialist cause. What kept him from joining one of the many clandestine socialist groups, his strong individualism aside, were grave doubts as to the practicability and feasibility of the socialist system, particularly with regard to its ability to discipline and to organize.

Let us inject here that our man's surprise in seeing a socialist system established and working in his country is not paralleled by similar astonishment at the extent of industrialization which had taken place in the interval. He remembers well Count Witte's policy of rapid industrialization in the 1890's and his own conviction derived both from Witte's exploits and Marxian expositions that by mid-century Russia would become an industrialized country. When it is explained to him that the process of industrial growth had been interrupted by great wars, both foreign and civil, which left great destruction in their wake and presented vast and difficult problems for reconstruction, our traveler manages to requite this intelligence with a critique of a Russian statesmanship that did not know how to stay out of two world wars. Faithful to traditions of his youth, he is always willing to criticize the government. Yet his interests lie in a different direction. It is not the magnitude of the industrialization effort, which he persists in taking for granted, but the specific organization of Soviet industry that arouses his curiosity. Here he quickly discovers much reason for surprise.

As a young man, he used to read in many a treatise on political economy an expression of doubt that a socialist society would be able to increase or even to maintain its capital stock. Such a society, it was argued persuasively, would not be able to control its desires and would tend to squander its resources in excesses of consumption: "Men first feel necessity, then look for utility, next attend to comfort, still later amuse themselves with pleasure, thence grow dissolute in luxury, and, finally, go mad and waste their substance." [4] This side-circuit of Vico's *corsi e ricorsi* was felt to foretell the nature, and to spell the doom, of a socialist society. Indeed, the socialist literature had seemed to place all weight of emphasis on redistribution of wealth and greater equality of income. Its interest in growth of production seemed quite overshadowed by its interest in distribution. But the Soviet society seems never to have been in danger of overconsumption. The traveler learns with amazement that, over the period of almost a quarter of a century, industrial output increased about six times, whereas the real wages of industrial workers actually declined absolutely, even though statistics for the magnitude of the decline would vary depending on the system of valuations used in making the comparison. Some preliminary conclusions begin to form themselves, though vaguely, in the traveler's mind. He begins to think that possibly his concept of socialism requires some readjustment if it is to be made to fit Soviet reality.

As he wanders from factory to factory and gathers his impressions of the way in which the Soviet industrial enterprises are organized and managed, this need for conceptual reassessment becomes stronger and stronger. He finds out that the enterprises are managed by individuals called "directors" as they had been in presocialist times. He sees those directors arrive at the factories in large chauffeured automobiles. He hears them in their conversations with their subordinates employ the old feudal *ty* (thou) while they are being addressed with the respectful *vy* (you). His confusion grows as he hears them speak of "profits," a category he had thought quite alien to socialist economy and for a long time a central target for socialist attacks upon capitalism. He is astonished to hear occasional references to "trusts," an organizational form which he was wont to associate with monopolistic exploitation of both workers and consumers by an aggressive capitalist enterprise.

He discovers that the director wields what in theory at least

appears an undivided power within the plant. In explaining the
director's position to him they use the term *yedinonachaliye*, and
our explorer cannot help reflecting that while the Russian language has a different word reserved for a rendition of the Greek
word "autocracy" (that is, *samoderzhaviye*), the Greek version
of the term actually employed to characterize the director's status
would be *monocracy*, and whatever the difference between *auto*-
cracy and *mono*cracy, either seems sufficiently removed from
*demo*cracy. Yet before he has absorbed the idea of a director of a
socialist enterprise who acts so fully the part of being the master
in his own house, our traveler is again jolted by hearing that the
power of the director essentially consists in acting under orders and
his main function lies in being responsible for the exact execution
of those orders. That, he is told, is the essence of socialist planning
and the natural opposite of capitalist chaos. After having watched
directors of huge enterprises upbraid their subordinates in a
thunderous bass and immediately thereafter conduct a telephone
conversation with their superiors in a softly ingratiating tenor, the
tourist is ready to accept the fact of a duality in the director's social
role. But while he marvels at the flexibility of human nature and
the range potentiality of a man's voice, he finds it more and more
difficult to bring his impressions into harmony with his admittedly
preconceived ideas about the nature of the socialist system. In
fact, he finds he has reached a point at which he must try to re-
read what the socialist literature had to say on the problems of
management and entrepreneurship and to see how it may have influenced the creation of the enterprise system in Soviet Russia.
Accordingly, he interrupts his industrial tour and betakes himself to a library, anxious to spend some time buried in volumes of
ancient and not-so-ancient lore.

Unfortunately, the very next day as he tries to order Oskar
Lange's brilliant pamphlet *On the Economic Theory of Socialism*
he finds himself questioned about his interest in counterrevolu-
tionary literature in general and bourgeois theories of socialism
in particular. The interrogation is stern and menacing, and at its
close the disenchanted explorer quickly resumes his enchanted
sleep, expecting to reawaken in more civil and less bewildering
times.

Even so, he has been able to arrive at some helpful though negative conclusions. It appears that the great figures of socialist literature had paid very little attention to the problems of enterprise and its management. To the extent that they did, the chief purpose was to separate "administrative wages" from "entrepreneurial profit" (that is, *Verwaltungslohn* from *Unternehmergewinn*).[5] The latter was seen as flowing from ownership over capital; the former included both managerial and entrepreneurial rewards and did not seem to constitute much of a problem. Marx may have praised in passing the "shrewd expert eye" of the capitalist selecting and combining the factors of production.[6] But the emergence of both the workers' producer cooperative and the joint-stock company made it perfectly clear to him that the exercise of the managerial guidance *(Oberleitung)* by the capitalist had become superfluous.[7]

Karl Hilferding, writing a generation after Marx's death, naturally had a great deal more to say on the joint-stock companies. He stressed their powerful role in the process of concentration of capital. They created, he said, a financial basis which was much broader than that usually available to an unincorporated enterprise. He did not confine himself to stressing the "superfluity" of the capitalist within the joint-stock company, but went on to suggest that the corporate form offered much more fertile fields to entrepreneurial and managerial activity, permitting greater degree of rationality, faster discarding of obsolescent equipment, and a much more aggressive policy in widening the firm's market areas. According to Hilferding, a man who administered an enterprise that was not his could be presumed to act more vigorously, more boldly, and more rationally than an individual owner-entrepreneur, whom Hilferding believed to be restrained by anxieties and personal considerations of all kinds.[8]

The political implication of this appraisal for the future socialist economy was fairly clear. If the joint-stock enterprise had facilitated so much of the task of entrepreneurship and management, the socialist economy could have been expected to simplify it further. Despite all the differences in fundamentals and approach, Hilferding's conclusion came close to Schumpeter's view of the process. Schumpeter believed that the entrepreneurial function was losing its importance because generations of innovating entrepreneurs had firmly embedded the desirability of innovations within the social value system. As innovations became routine, special personal qualities and a special effort were no longer needed to overcome the resistances to change.[9] Unlike Schumpeter, the socialist writers did not treat entrepreneurs and innovations as independent variables in the process of economic growth. For them the process did not have to "become depersonalized and automatized";[10] it always had been viewed in those terms. But the final conclusion was the same: entrepreneurship and management could be taken for granted. As in so many other areas the problems of socialist management were assumed to be presolved in the course of the capitalist development. The Marxian literature was reluctant to indulge in detailed descriptions of the socialist system, but the general contours of the picture emerged with sufficient clarity: socialism meant organization of production not indeed by the state, which was to "wither away," but by the free collectives of "associated producers," the tasks of management being discharged by salaried specialists. It was this image of the economy which inspired Lenin in 1917 as he stood at the threshold of power.[11]

These basic attitudes would well serve as an ideological introduction to the views expressed by Oskar Lange in his celebrated piece.[12] The tenor of the former is in perfect harmony with the spirit of the latter. Also for Lange the managerial problem was simple indeed. The Central Planning Board is to tell the managers to minimize average cost and to produce as much of each commodity as will equalize the price of product and its marginal cost. The managers are to bid for labor in the market; similarly, consumers' preferences are to determine prices of consumers' goods, while all other prices and the rate of interest is set by the Planning Board, as far as possible so as to equalize demand and supply of producers goods and of loanable funds. Finally, the Planning Board determines arbitrarily the rate of net investment from planning period to planning period.[13]

This scheme for the organization of the socialist economy has one guiding principle and one basic aim: "to satisfy consumers' preferences in the best way possible." [14] There is every implication that in determining "arbitrarily" the rate of net investment, the Planning Board is expected to be guided primarily by the welfare of the consumers and to operate with reasonable time-horizons.

It is, of course, not clear at all in the Lange scheme how it is assured that the manager will in fact observe the two fundamental rules with regard to methods of production and the composition of output. Neither a system of supervision of managerial activity nor a system of possible incentives to induce the managers to comply with the rules is included in the scheme. This omission, however regrettable, is perhaps not altogether incomprehensible. The point is not only that the market in consumers' goods, together with the emergence of surpluses and deficits in producers' goods and loanable funds, is thought to provide objective checks for the correct functioning of the system; no less important is the implied supposition that in a system based on consumers' preferences the consumers should find ways and means to control the activities of the managers and to enforce compliance with the rules; similarly, there is the further supposition that consumers will know how to force the Planning Board not to substitute its own preferences for those of the consumers. And above it all hovers the feeling that an economy of this type would generate a social environment within which compliance with rules that are socially so desirable will be forthcoming readily and spontaneously. *Le socialisme c'est la justice et la bonté*, says one of Anatole France's heroes. It should not be difficult for such a society to find "just" and "good" managers to administer its economic enterprises. This has been the traditional view of socialism by socialists. And even Lenin, who envisaged the managers as standing under "control of the armed proletariat," considered such control quite a transitory measure. Lange's system *is* a socialist system in terms of the ideological history of the socialist movement and must be read and appraised in the context of that history. Compared with the basic stress on popular welfare, the question of collective versus individual ownership of means of production would seem altogether ancillary.

But if the Lange system of socialist economy can claim to be considered the consummate model of socialism, by the same token it impedes rather than furthers our comprehension of the Soviet system to view it as a socialist system. It is a general hazard of social science that the objects of our study time and again tend to confuse the scholarly observer by making statements about themselves. When those statements are supported by monopolistic dominance over communication media on the part of a powerful dictatorial government, their persuasive power is further enhanced. Nevertheless, however often Soviet Russia may introduce itself to the world as a socialist country, the fact remains that the social scientist may find it much more illuminating to consider Soviet Russia not as a socialist economy, but as an economy which by the will of a ruthless totalitarian government has been kept in the process of a very rapid industrialization. "Accumulate, accumulate! This is Moses and the Prophets!" [15] Those are the words in which Karl Marx tried to describe the "fifth essence" of capitalism. There is every reason to doubt that there has been any economy on modern historical record to which these words would apply with greater justification than the economy of the Union of the so-called *Socialist* Soviet Republics.

Predictions are precarious. Still so firmly has the Soviet political system been wedded to the policy of a high *and growing* rate of investment that at least this observer of its evolution has felt tempted to conclude that no other economic policy would be easily compatible with the maintenance of the Soviet dictatorship; in other words, that a policy of rapid increases of consumers' welfare either would remain unacceptable to the dictators, or, if accepted, would in all likelihood lead to the disintegration of dictatorship. It matters little in this connection whether future history will verify or falsify this hypothesis. It is referred to here in order to throw into relief the antagonistic nature of an allegedly classless economy in which the investment interest of the government has been continually opposed by the consumption interest of the population.

To return to the problem of management and enterprise: the socialist literature could afford to pay scant attention to the problem of management because it operated with the vision — or illusion — of a harmonious society unrent by any serious cleavage of interest. The antagonistic Soviet society was forced to pursue a different policy. Far from being able to ignore or to take lightly the problem of management, the leaders of the Soviet government came to regard the search for the appropriate degree of managerial dependence as focal to their economic policy. The position of the manager proved the all-important nucleus of the broader problem of the appropriate degree of centralization within the Soviet economy. So far, the very nature of that economy has precluded a clear and lasting solution to either problem. Thence came the uneasy compromise between the preached principle and the tolerated practice; thence came also the continual wavering to and fro in organizational structure, in the course of which the lines of command were alternatively lengthened and shortened, loosened and tightened. Quite recently, the Soviet government has embarked upon a far-reaching scheme of organizational reform, thus making dramatically apparent the inherent instability of the previously existing arrangements. The remainder of this paper will be devoted to a sketch of those arrangements and an apraisal of the probable motivations and effects of the present reforms.

The attempt is constantly made in Soviet writings to view the evolution of management and enterprise *over the whole Soviet period* as determined by one unvarying and unerring purpose. Such claims do not stand up under investigation. After the October Revolution, the institution of Workers' Control over economic enterprises was established by a rather perplexed and bewildered government. Even today the Workers' Control of those days (1918–1919) is still praised in Soviet literature as an important step on the road of Soviet managerial progress.[16] In reality Workers' Control very quickly led to the diffusion of syndicalist tendencies; it served to hasten the disintegration of the country's economy, and, probably even more than the simultaneous resistance of factory owners, forced the government, then in the throes of the civil war, to proceed with an otherwise unintended nationalization of industrial enterprises.

On the other hand, during the N. E. P. period of the twenties, the centralized grip on industry was considerably relaxed, even though large-scale industry remained in the hands of the state. "Trusts" which combined a number of connected industrial enterprises assumed some managerial decisions, while at the level of individual enterprises managerial activity was largely exercized by the so-called "triangle" or "trio" (troyka), consisting of the director of the enterprise, the local party cell, and the local trade-union group. This tripartite organization of factory management no doubt reflected some general socialist ideas concerning democratization of management. In the West, such ideas became mildly articulate in the socialization debates after World War I and affected various legislative acts.[17] They continued to play a considerable part in the literature of the interwar period, in which "extension of democracy into the economic sphere" was advocated.[18] After the last war those modest beginnings were further amplified in the various codetermination or cooperation schemes which were designed to give the workers of the enterprise some sense of participation in the conduct of the enterprise.[19]

In Soviet Russia, this legacy of socialist ideas did not survive the end of the New Economic Policy. It was clearly at variance with the policy of superindustrialization. "The year of the great change" was Stalin's apt description of the year 1929. It was in 1929 that the thorough purge of the Central Trade Union Council took place. The emasculation of the unions as a representation of labor's interests was the result. Thereafter, Soviet industrial labor appeared reduced to the passive role of a "factor of production" and the unions were transformed into an arm of the management, designed — to use Marxian terms — to extract out of labor the greatest possible amount of surplus value. The readjustment of the unions was swift and far-reaching, and neglect of the interests of labor quite unhesitating. It was left to Stalin a few years later to follow his usual practice and to shift the blame onto subordinate shoulders by stressing the forgotten connection between incentives and output. It was only then that the unions began to proclaim some concern for the workers' living needs, although dealing with those needs "chiefly if not exclusively in terms of production needs." [20]

It was the same year, 1929, in which the "triangle" was loudly denounced and the aforementioned principle of director's monocracy proclaimed. Henceforth neither the trade union nor the party cell was to interfere with the decisions of the manager.

This "strengthening" of *local* authority naturally was not an act of decentralization but, on the contrary, an important precondition for a greatly enhanced centralization in the management of Soviet industry. Within the "triangle" the responsibility had been divided and hence diffuse and elusive. The management was to become a stable, more easily supervised and more readily apprehended recipient and executor of the orders that came from the center. The intention no doubt was a fully centralized organization in which the factory manager was no more than a transmission belt in the formidable industrialization machine whose prime movers and control levers were concentrated in Moscow. It was in this spirit therefore that, in 1929, the individual enterprise was solemnly pronounced an "independent productive and commercial unit," which became fully dependent upon the decisions in the administrative center. At the same time, the "center" was appropriately reorganized so as to establish the closest possible connection with the individual enterprises. As a part of this process, the Supreme Economic Council was split into three People's Commissariats (much later, in 1946, renamed Ministries) with a rapid proliferation in the following years of special People's Commissariats for every important branch of Soviet industry. In 1934, the previously existing intervening links were abolished and, at least in the rapidly growing heavy industry, the enterprise became directly subordinate to the respective People's Commissariats in Moscow, thus consummating the centralization of the industrial structure.[21]

The formidable effort at centralization is a historical fact. Nor is there any doubt that a complete subjugation of the manager of the individual enterprise was the aim. And yet, even for an omnipotent and ruthless dictatorship the coefficient of "will enforcement" rarely equals unity. What is so striking about the outcome of this process is that dictatorial order and resistance inherent in men and things combined to produce an organizational structure whose lines possessed neither the charming simplicity of Oskar Lange's pair of rules nor the uncharming straightforwardness of an absolute "I order, you obey" economy. To understand the position of the manager as it was pressed into shape in Stalin's organizational rolling mill, it is advisable to present first an image of Soviet industrial management as seen through the wishful spectacles of the official theory of that period. One may proceed then to compare the image with a more concrete presentation of Soviet reality.

In the official view, the manager's activity in his enterprise was regulated by a linguistic monstrosity known as the annual *Tekhpromfinplan*, which was a complex of targets for the prospective plan period, comprising quantities and values of output, utilization of workers of different categories, use of different types of raw materials and fuels, magnitudes of gross and net investment, data on cost, prices and profits, and finally a description of technological and organizational innovations. That plan, prepared within the enterprise, upon central directives, and then approved by central authority, was regarded as an integral part of the annual over-all plan for the development of the Soviet economy. For the manager it possessed the force of law.

An appropriate avenue leading to an understanding of that plan and the manager's official position within its framework may be found in the concept of profits, an obvious curiosity within an allegedly socialist system, which caused so much surprise to the errant intellectual who haunted the introductory pages of this essay. Originally introduced for ambitions of imitative respectability as a symbol of American business-like matter-of-factness (*delovitost'*), the category of profits has become a carrying pillar of the system of economic accounting (*khozraschet*), which in turn is identified with the aforementioned "independence" of the enterprise. Having been supplied from the state budget with fixed capital, receiving a modicum of working capital from the state budget, and covering the balance of its needs in working capital through credits from the State Bank, the manager of the Soviet enterprise as a rule is expected to husband his resources in such a way as to produce the planned quantity of output without exceeding the prescribed planned cost of that output; since, again as a rule, unit prices exceed unit cost and sales are assured, the enterprise is expected to achieve a certain planned profit. If, in addition to achieving the planned profit, the enterprise should succeed in achieving some "unplanned" profit, so much the better and this achievement is appropriately rewarded.

In this way, even though every industrial enterprise in Soviet Russia is owned by the state, its budget is kept discrete from the state budget; the revenues and the expenditures of the firm do not enter the state budget, except for the investment funds (and subsidies) received from, and for taxes (on turnover and profits) paid into, the state budget.

What then is the function of profits within this system? A simple answer distilled from the official writings may be formulated as follows. Just as the main function of prices for producers' goods in the Soviet economy — consumers' good prices are a different matter — is said to lie in their role in planning output and in supervising the degree to which plans have been fulfilled, also the role of profits — as distinguished from taxes on turnover — lies in their serving as an index of the degree to which resources have been used in accordance with the plan. Needless to add, the indicator is a very crude one. Very different combinations of the individual cost factors are, of course, compatible with a given level of profits and the planners' point of view of the desirability of the individual combination might differ very widely. Yet, such as it is, the category of planned profits has provided the central authorities with a simple global check on the use of resources by the individual enterprises.

To gauge an industrial manager's freedom of decision, it is useful to turn for a moment from planned profits to unplanned profits. Obviously in order to overfulfill the plan — be it in the quantity of output or in the sum of profits — the manager must be able to display freedom of initiative outside the area circumscribed by the prescriptions of the plan. But how can the manager increase profits beyond the level provided for in the plan? Theoretically, numbers of workers, wage rates, cost of available raw materials, selling prices, funds available for technological improvement — all those are circumscribed by the plan and must be regarded as "givens." The manager cannot vary any of those magnitudes as might his counterpart — the Western manager operating within a more free competitive structure. As long as total output is held constant, the only way open to a Soviet manager who wishes to achieve unplanned profits is through introduction of innovations which reduce cost while costing nothing. More rational arrangement of men and machinery within a plant, less wasteful handling of materials and machines, insistence on greater diligence on the part of the workers — those are the primary methods of increasing unplanned profits which are at the disposal of a Soviet industrial manager, as pictured by official writings. It is difficult to avoid the conclusion that his range of freedom is severely limited.

It is true, of course, that output need not be considered constant. No Soviet manager in his right senses will contemplate an increase of profits by reduction of output below the planned level. On the other hand, overfulfillment of the plan is not only permissible; it is enthusiastically encouraged by multifarious rewards. An increase in output may increase or decrease profits, but it is fair to say that in all probability a Soviet manager will be willing to swap some decrease in profits for some increase in output; if an increase in output would bring the enterprise across the magic line that separates underfulfillment from overfulfillment of output, the probability becomes a certainty. Yet what has been said of higher than planned profits largely holds also of higher than planned output. How can a Soviet manager, officially described as narrowly circumvallated by the plan, find labor, and raw materials, and semifabricates, and possibly also some investment goods that are needed in order to increase output? Would not overfulfillment of the output plan in one area of necessity lead in this fully employed system to underfulfillment of the plan in other areas? And if the plan provides, as is claimed, for balanced growth of the economy as a whole, would not such lopsided sallies beyond the plan targets disrupt the functioning of the economic system, leading to useless surpluses in some spots and badly missed deficits in others? And is it not correct to infer that in an economy in which individual enterprises are allowed to indulge in such disruptive activities, the position of those enterprises and particularly that of the leaders of those enterprises must be a good deal less restricted than might appear from our official image of the Soviet economy?

It is half a century since a brilliant German sociologist put on paper what certainly has proved to be a profound insight: "The elimination of any spontaneity in a subordinate position is in reality much rarer than one might assume from popular speech which uses very freely such terms and phrases as 'compulsion,' 'no other choice,' 'absolute necessity,' and so on. Even in the most cruel and oppressive states of subordination, there usually exists a considerable measure of personal freedom." [22] Recent studies on Soviet industrial management by Western economists have well borne out the truth of Simmel's generalization.[23]

The conclusion is inescapable that the official theory is a poor guide in assessing the true role of Soviet industrial managers. Far from being bound, rump and limbs, by the plan, the manager enjoys a large sphere of independent activity. On the one hand, he is able to influence the targets of the plan. In so doing he tries to maneuver in such a way as to achieve two disparate ends: to establish for himself a reputation of a bold administrator insisting on high rates of growth and at the same time to keep the planned rates of growth well within the capabilities of the enterprise so that they can be attained with a good deal of certainty and without undue stress and strain. In Soviet conditions where inter-industry supplies have remained the weakest point of the whole economic system,[24] and where on the other hand, the policy of high rates of growth keeps the enterprises at a very low level of inventories, the managers are almost forced to hold hidden reserves. To carry on such a policy it is necessary first to convince the central authorities that the input-output coefficients are higher than they actually are; it is necessary, second, to engage in various strictly illegal dealings, in the course of which materials and goods produced are bartered away to neighboring factories in an attempt to provide substitutes for the shortcomings of the central system of allocations. To be able to do this effectively, the manager must also deceive the central authorities as to the actual level of his plant's output. Only in this way can he accumulate a stock of finished goods of which he can dispose through other than the planned channels.

Those who are interested in the details of these evasive arrangements may refer to the two excellent works mentioned in Note 23. What matters here is only to throw light on a fundamental peculiarity of the Soviet industrial system — that is, the well-built-in discrepancy between plan and reality. In the light of this discrepancy it is easy to see that the manager as a rule has many ways of achieving unplanned profits or of increasing output above the plan figures or of deciding between the one and the other course of action. Thus the actual situation no doubt is a great deal more complex than it appeared to be on the basis of the official descriptions of Soviet planned economy. It is safe to conclude that the Soviet government's power over the economy is somewhat less complete than Soviet literature would make us believe.

The reason for this bashfully concealed but nonetheless very real limitation on the power of a ruthless dictatorial government is not far to seek. The official view of the Soviet economy is premised upon the assumption of unrestricted knowledge and foreknowledge on the part of the central planners. Needless to say, this assumption is far from realistic. The stream of paper reports that flows from the plants to the central authorities may belittle the majesty of the Volga River, but it provides no assurance of real insight into the conditions within the individual plant. The fundamental ignorance of the central authorities restricts their ability to enforce their will. Obversely, it is the knowledge of the manager that assures for him his area of freedom. Once the assumption of complete knowledge is dropped it becomes immediately clear why the Soviet system in the past had frequent recourse to the price system of producers' goods, not just in order to check and supervise, but in order to change the allocation of scarce resources. Increases in prices of commodities such as oil or copper were cases in point. The purpose was to induce the managers of industrial enterprises to economize on those commodities in favor of the more plentiful substitutes. And the reason why the device of a price increase, so much less direct and so much less transparent in its effects than that of a change in quantitative allocations as among firms, was chosen must be sought precisely in the ignorance of the authorities, who were in the dark as to what allocation claims of what plants to accept or reject. Presumably, once the prices have been changed and the managers have adjusted their decisions accordingly, the plan targets for the utilization of the relevant materials were also appropriately adjusted. But the process reveals both the importance of the area of free managerial decision and the *mirabilia* of such decision determining the plan, rather than vice versa — surely a rather perverse sequence from the point of view of the official theory.

The Soviet government is not known for its tolerance. Nor does it readily brook disobedience to its orders. If it has been acquiescing in a widely diffused system of plan evasion, the reason is that — aware of the extent of its ignorance — it has recognized that a measure of managerial freedom from the plan was a prerequisite to the fulfillment of the plan. The price it pays is not simply in terms of abdication in favor of abstract managerial independence. Up to a point, evasions of the plan are indeed designed to fulfill the plan. But some of the evasions are dictated by very different motives, including the managers' personal enrichment, something that is not easily compatible with the Soviet ethos of absolute devotion to the state.

Thus the Soviet system of industrial management defies an easy circumscription of its contours. For it has no fixed contours at all. The zone of managerial freedom is largely *extra legem.* Hence its boundary is in perpetual motion, being continually adjusted and readjusted. At the level of each individual enterprise, a managerial sally into greater independence is followed by retreat toward greater obedience. Shifting the managers from factory to factory, maintaining a well-developed system of informers, increasing control over the "monocrat" by the local party organs — those are some of the devices by which the central authorities have often attempted to shorten a manager's tether, or at least to control its length. Yet as managerial disobedience is eliminated, so is his free initiative. And since the latter soon proves indispensable for the successful operation of the enterprise, the rope must be played out again, starting a new cycle, the regularity of which would have surprised and delighted Polybius or Vico.

But is the Soviet government really doomed to keep this zigzag course, which no doubt is wasteful of time and effort? Must it continue living in fear of managerial autonomy? Cannot it rather face up to its necessity and mete out to managers an openly recognized generous measure of freedom? There is little doubt that tendencies in this direction have been present within the Russian economy long before Stalin quit the stage. This should not be surprising. Apart from the reasons just mentioned, existence of a twilight zone of tolerated illegality agrees ill with the nature of Soviet dictatorship. And yet it is the mechanics of power exercise by the self-same dictatorship that make it so difficult to take the step from grudging acquiescence to open recognition.

It is very often not recognized that dictatorial power requires incessant exercise. It is maintained and asserted by ruling and regulating. A decrease in regimentation therefore tends to be tantamount to a decline in power. Even more important, however, is the previously mentioned connection between the dictatorship and the high rate of growth. If it is true that the Soviet dictatorship not only makes rapid industrialization possible but continually derives from rapid industrialization new strength and new vindication, then it is also true that the high rate of investment and, obversely, the low rate of consumption must remain characteristic of the Soviet economy. Yet, because of the relative neglect of consumption, the path of an industrial manager is strewn with manifold temptations. Wherever technically possible, there is a strong urge to deflect resources into consumption and away from investment. A recognized and firmly established sphere of managerial autonomy is therefore very likely to produce results that would be most undesirable from the point of view of the basic interests of Soviet dictatorship. To give an example: in 1934, the Soviets decided to grant increased freedom of action to the so-called "local industry," producing for the local market with the help of local fuels and local raw materials. Stalin spoke of the need to "liberate its initiative." Appropriate resolutions were adopted.[25] And yet, after a short period the policy was abandoned, because even in the limited sphere of "local industry" freedom from regulation soon clashed with the basic principles of Soviet policy.

There were other similar oscillations. But what has been taking place in the Soviet Union during the past few years is an effort at organizational reform without precedent and parallel in the history of the country since the inception of central planning. It seems to introduce far-reaching changes in the distribution of economic authority and, possibly, to affect the position of industrial managers as it developed under Stalin and has been described in the preceding pages. The reform originated as an attack upon the central organs of economic administration which began within less than a year after Stalin's death and proceeded to gather momentum at great speed.[26]

About a year later (August 9, 1955) the scope of managerial rights was expressly expanded through a resolution of the Council of Ministers.[27] In this way, some of the activities previously proscribed, though tacitly tolerated, were solemnly legalized. Among these activities were unplanned purchases and sales of materials, equipment, and finished goods to other enterprises, even though in moderate amounts. Furthermore, the managers became entitled to more flexibility in adjusting wage rates and wage payments and they also received the right to shift outlays from one category to another, and from one period to another. All this is to be done within certain narrow limits. It is quite doubtful, therefore, that the resolution brought any substantive change into the management of the Soviet enterprise, even though it may have had the effect of providing to managerial consciences some relief from the burdens of evasions and collusions.

Finally, in May 1957, the Supreme Soviet of the U.S.S.R. passed an Act dealing with "Further Perfecting the Organization of Administration in the Sphere of Industry and Construction." [28] Under the terms of the act most of the central economic ministries of either description (see above) were abolished. The area of the U.S.S.R. has been divided into more than one hundred administrative regions, and in every region a National Economy Council (*Sovnarkhoz*) has been entrusted with the local administration of industrial enterprise. The *Sovnarkhoz* reports to the Council of Ministers of the individual republic, which in turn is subordinated to the Council of Ministers of the U.S.S.R.[29]

The sphere of competence of the *Sovnarkhozy* as defined in a special charter is vast indeed.[30] Particularly striking is the right bestowed upon them to change both output and investment targets, apparently not merely by shifts as among enterprises of the same industrial branch but also by shifts as among industrial branches. At the same time a considerable increase in "local industry" is envisaged, which is to be supervised by the local rather than regional organs.

The central guidance of Soviet industry henceforth is to reside in the Council of Ministers and to proceed on the basis of a unified plan prepared by the State Planning Commission (*Gosplan*). The latter institution is called upon to watch over the "rational location of industry," to assure a unified policy in developing the leading branches of Soviet industry, to supervise the rate of economic progress, and so forth.[31] It is intended that the most crucial economic decisions for the Soviet economy as a whole should continue to be taken in Moscow. In particular, the basic determination of the rate of investment and the rate of consumption will remain reserved to the central organs. Similarly, the central quantitative allocation of scarce materials (which used to be called "funded commodities") is to continue, possibly even on a somewhat expanded scale. Khrushchev solemnly announced that the organizational reform would not weaken the central guidance of the Soviet economy.[32]

It cannot be the purpose of this essay to go into details in describing the organizational transformation that is being carried out. It is more important at this point to form some idea with regard to the possible motivations of the reform. In this connection it might be possible to appraise both the correctness of Khrushchev's prediction and the probable durability of the change.

In reviewing the possible aims of the reform, what comes to mind first is its potential military aspect: to split the Soviet economy into a large number of more or less watertight compartments may enhance its power of resistance in case of war. If this be true, the reform may be somewhat comparable in character, though not in dimension, to the change in attitude adumbrated in the Third Five-Year Plan with regard to scale of enterprise and location of industries. This explanation, however, is at variance with the reasonable hypothesis that the Russians indeed desire a continuation of the "cold war," with its periodic recrudescence of tensions which are so congenial to dictatorial rule; but that at the same time they both do not want "hot war" and feel safe in the knowledge that an attack upon them by the West is very improbable. This does not mean that the mechanics of exercise of dictatorial power might not at some juncture lead Russia into the impasse of an open military conflict, but it is unlikely that the

Soviets should be willing to pay a heavy price in terms of economic cost for what must seem to them a remote contingency.

It is therefore more plausible to assume that the reform is a recurrence of the cyclical swing away from central control, except that the previous rate of Soviet economic growth as well as the great disturbances of the succession crisis served to magnify the cyclical swing out of all historical proportions. On the one hand there was the feeling that the growing size of the Soviet industrial establishment rendered continuation of its direction from one single center more and more difficult. On the other hand, Khrushchev may have had very excellent reasons to get rid of the ministerial bureaucracy, whose bulk had been bred in loyalty to Khrushchev's competitors in the struggle for personal power. Nevertheless, if the aggregate weight of these considerations was sufficient to cause the change, it may not suffice to perpetuate it. For the centripetal forces, which for the moment appear subdued, almost inevitably will reappear and are likely to reassert themselves.

At the time of this writing, the reform still receives high praise in Russia; it is even said to have accelerated the rate of industrial growth.[33] The satisfaction of having eliminated ministerial inefficiency still dominates the picture. However, the new brooms of the *Sovnarkhozy* will also very soon be covered with bureaucratic cobwebs. Then the risks of decentralization, including the great difficulty of reconciling the vast decision power of the *Sovnarkhozy* with *consistency* in central planning, will become increasingly conspicuous. Even now, the Soviet press and literature are full of warnings against the dangers of "localism" *(mestnichestvo)*. The intensified intraregional division of labor is likely to proceed at the expense of specialization on a national scale and to lead to a malallocation of resources. It was a peculiarity of the industrial managers' illicit activities that they were displayed within a narrow area bounded by personal connections and acquaintances. One consequence of the reform is to enhance further this quaint element of medieval narrowness within an economy whose "modernity" is so incessantly glorified.

And what about the position of the manager within the new organizational framework? Obviously, the *Sovnarkhozy* will be closer to the individual enterprise than were the abolished ministries in Moscow. But it is not obvious at all that they will be close enough to give the regional authorities a real insight into the inner workings of the enterprise. Some of the regions represent formidable industrial complexes.

Moreover, the reform began in an atmosphere in which increase rather than decrease in managerial freedom seemed to be the aim.[34] There is, for instance, no question that the managers were accorded more flexibility in their relations with the labor force. This is bound to intensify the inflationary pressures within the economy. It will be recalled that the wartime legislation which had tied the worker to the factory for long years after the war finally melted away in the years of the Soviet thaw. As a result, the managers are able to bid for labor, with the inevitable effect upon wage rates. It would seem that the greater flexibility inherent in decentralization will make it more difficult for the authorities to resist the enterprises' demands for additional funds.

Even during its periods of strictly centralized administration, the Soviet authorities found the inflationary cost and price changes of the thirties a very real obstacle to their attempts to check on whether or not resources had been used in accordance with the plan. In conditions of decentralization, the inflationary change in yardsticks by which performances are measured must reduce the central authorities to the state of groping helplessness.

More fundamental, however, than the problem of inflation is that of a high rate of investment. In the past, it was the iron grip of central authorities that forced upon the economy the low rate of output of consumer goods. It would seem that any step along the road of decentralization is likely to relax the grip and to jeopardize adherence to the traditional policy. The managers of industrial enterprises in all likelihood will be strongly tempted by the pent-up demands for consumer goods, and it is not clear at all that the *Sovnarkhozy* will know how to resist that demand and will not become a sheltering wall between the central authority and the individual enterprise. If that should happen, however, central direction of the economy by means of the plan will become quite problematic and the urge to relieve the situation by an organizational reversal irresistible. Mergers of two or more *Sovnar-*

khozy would appear as the most natural first steps toward such a *restitutio in integrum.*

To be sure, it is at least imaginable that the Soviet government might decide upon a radical revision of its economic policy. A drastic increase in the rate of consumption would reduce the inflationary pressures *and* provide the preconditions for the successful perpetuation of a decentralized economy, subject to a limited but effective degree of planned control. A Soviet economy, so transformed, would be much more readily understood and appreciated by Western observers. It would prove much less confusing to our prerevolutionary intellectual, should he wish to return for a renewed inspection tour.

Yet the chances for such an evolution are slim indeed. In the west the transition from an industrialization economy to a consumption economy has been gradually achieved. *Sine littera* and with varying ingredients, the western economies have come to combine liberal (in the original sense) and socialist elements — that is to say, the elements of the two humanitarian movements that dominated the nineteenth century. It is doubtful that a consumption economy can be established in Soviet Russia. A decentralized economic system geared to a steady rise in the levels of consumption would leave the Soviet dictatorship without a social function, without a justification for its existence. It is much more likely that the dictatorship will continue the policy of wilfully provoking one international crisis after the other and of maintaining a high rate of investment as the economic *pendant* to such a policy. Then a renewed curtailment of such managerial freedoms as have been granted since Stalin's death,[35] followed by a general reversal of the decentralization policy, should be only a matter of time, and enterprise and management in Russia should once more return to the normalcy of Soviet mercantilism, concealed beneath a generous veneer of socialist phraseology.

NOTES

Chapter 1. Introduction

1. A. A. Berle, Jr., *Economic Power and the Free Society* (New York, 1957), p. 15.

2. Clark Kerr, *Unions and Union Leaders of Their Own Choosing* (New York, 1957).

3. Cf. Robert Brady, *Business as a System of Power* (New York, 1943).

4. Editors of *Fortune*, with the collaboration of Russell W. Davenport, *U. S. A.: The Permanent Revolution* (New York, 1954).

5. C. Wright Mills, *The Power Elite* (New York, 1956), p. 133. Cited by Earl Latham, below, p. 229.

6. Chester I. Barnard, *The Functions of the Executive* (Cambridge, Mass., 1938), p. 224. Cited by Earl Latham, below, p. 230.

7. Cf. Kingman Brewster, Jr., "The Corporation and Economic Federalism," below.

8. Berle, *Economic Power and the Free Society*, p. 3.

9. J. M. Keynes, "The End of Laissez-Faire" (1926), republished in *Essays in Persuasion* (London, 1931), pp. 314–315.

10. C. A. R. Crosland, *The Future of Socialism* (London, 1957), p. 480.

11. Don K. Price, "Creativity in the Public Service," to be published in the yearbook of the Harvard Graduate School of Public Administration, *Public Policy*, Vol. IX.

Chapter 2. The Modern Corporation and the Rule of Law

1. Peter Drucker, *Concept of the Corporation* (New York, 1946), p. 11.

2. William T. Gossett, *Corporate Citizenship* (Washington & Lee University, 1957), p. 157.

3. Drucker, *Concept of the Corporation*, n. 1, pp. 6–7.

4. A. A. Berle, Jr., *Economic Power and the Free Society* (New York, 1957), p. 15.

5. Letter from Engels to Conrad Schmidt dated October 27, 1890, printed in *The Correspondence of Marx and Engels* (New York, 1937), pp. 477, 481.

6. Bertrand de Jouvenel, *Power, The Natural History of its Growth* (London, 1952), p. 88.

7. The classic works on the early history of the business corporation remain William R. Scott, *The Constitution and Finance of English, Scottish and Irish Joint Stock Companies to 1720*, 3 vols. (Cambridge, 1912), and DuBois, *The English Business Company after the Bubble Act, 1720–1800* (New York, 1938). A compact summary including American developments will be found in E. Merrick Dodd, Jr., and Baker, *Cases and Materials on Corporations*, 2d ed. (Brooklyn, 1951), pp. 1–33.

8. Oscar Handlin and Mary Handlin, *Commonwealth, A Study of the Role of Government in the American Economy: Massachusetts, 1774–1861* (New York, 1947), p. 194.

9. A classic statement of the hypothesis is Justice Brandeis' in Liggett Co. v. Lee, 288 U. S. 517, 548 (1933) (dissent). A more recent one is in Berle, *Economic Power and the Free Society,* n. 4, pp. 5–6.

10. Berle, *Economic Power and the Free Society,* n. 4, p. 9.

11. For a similar reaction, more elaborately stated, see Bayless Manning, Review of Livingston, *The American Stockholder, Yale Law Journal,* 67: 1477 (1958).

12. With perhaps an execption for those corporate actions which alter the security holder's position as such.

13. *E.g.,* Mass. Gen. Laws, c. 156, § 23 (1932).

14. A rather full recent statement may be found in Archibald Cox, "The Legal Nature of Collective Bargaining Agreements," *Michigan Law Review,* 57: 22–25 (1958).

15. Lon Fuller, "Human Purpose and Natural Law," *Natural Law Forum,* 3: 68, 74 (1958).

16. *E.g.,* J. K. Galbraith, *American Capitalism: The Concept of Countervailing Power* (Boston, 1952), pp. 196–200.

17. For some current discussion see Archibald Cox, "The Role of Law in Preserving Union Democracy," *Harvard Law Review,* 72: 609 (1959); Harry H. Wellington, "Union Democracy and Fair Representation: Federal Responsibility in a Federal System," *Yale Law Journal,* 67: 1327 (1958); Clark Kerr, *Unions and Union Leaders of Their Own Choosing* (Fund for the Republic, 1957).

18. Dealer grievances were aired in *Hearings* before the Antitrust Subcommittee No. 5 of the House Committee on the Judiciary, 84 Cong., 2 Sess., ser. 26 (1956) and *Hearings* before the Subcommittee on Automobile Marketing Practices of the Senate Committee on Interstate and Foreign Commerce, 84 Cong., 2 Sess. (1956). The federal law is 70 Stat. 1125, 15 U.S.C.A. § 1222 (Supp. 1956). This legislation as well as state legislation and the common law background is discussed in note, "Statutory Regulation of Manufacturer-Dealer Relations in the Automobile Industry," *Harvard Law Review,* 70: 1239 (1957).

19. These very tentative observations are based on unsystematic interviews with a few dealers in the Boston area. I am indebted to Mr. Bernat Rosner for assistance in opening up this line of inquiry.

20. See below, p. 79.

21. See below, p. 72.

Chapter 3. To Whom and for What Ends is Corporate Management Responsible?

1. The word "purchase" is never used in this context.

I enjoyed the benefit of talking about this paper with my colleagues Joseph W. Bishop, Jr., Francis W. Coker, Jr., and Bayless Manning, who are in no way accountable for its heresies. Neale M. Albert, a student at the Law

School, helped prepare the notes. My ingenious friend, Herman W. Liebert, suggested the use of the words "endocratic" and "exocratic," explained in Note 2.

2. Our language contains no word to identify the large, publicly-held corporation, whose stock is scattered in small fractions among thousands of stockholders. I shall refer to such corporations here as "endocratic" corporations or enterprises, to distinguish them from small or large corporations controlled by substantial stock ownership — "exocratic" corporations. The problems presented by these aggregates are the same, of course, when the enterprise is carried on in noncorporate forms: for example, some real-estate syndicates which mobilize the funds of the investing public.

3. Northern Securities Co. v. United States, 193 U.S. 197 (1904); Hamilton Watch Co. v. Benrus Watch Co., 114 F. Supp. 307 (D. Conn., 1953), aff'd 206 F.2d 738 (2nd Cir., 1953); American Crystal Sugar Co. v. Cuban American Sugar Co., 152 F. Supp. 387 (S.D.N.Y., 1957); Affirmed 259F 2nd 524 (2nd Circ., 1958). For a vivid account of the background of the Northern Securities case, see A. R. Burr, *The Portrait of a Banker: James Stillman* (1927), pp. 163–179.

4. See, *e.g.*, N.Y. Gen. Corp. Law sect. 61; Calif. sect. 834 (1); Del. sect. 327; Federal Rules of Civil Procedure, Rule 23(b). See Duncan v. National Tea Co., 14 Ill. App. 2nd 280, 144 N.E. 2d 771 (1957).

5. Review of Joseph Livingston, *The American Stockholder* (1958), *Yale Law Journal*, 67: 1477 (1958).

6. If Professor Manning means that the purely buccaneering raid can be, and often is, an unsavory affair, involving no more than a contest over which band is to milk the corporation, I quite agree. Similarly, if his comment is meant to reinforce the conclusion that proxy battles "cannot be relied upon as an effective device for regularized supervision of management's stewardship." *Ibid.*, p. 1489. Aliter, however, if his sentence means what it seems to say, in one inflection — that is, that shares acquired for the purpose of gaining or seeking corporate control are improperly acquired.

7. *Ibid.*, p. 1494, n. 32.

8. Joseph Livingston, *The American Stockholder* (1958); A. A. Berle, Jr., *The Twentieth Century Capitalist Revolution* (1954).

9. Rosenfeld v. Fairchild Engine & Airplane Corp., 284 App. Div. 201, 132 N.Y. Supp. 2d 273 (1954), aff'd, 309 N. Y. 168, 128 N. E. 2d 291 (1955). See also Steinberg v. Adams, 90 F. Supp. 604 (S.D.N.Y., 1950); F. D. Emerson and F. C. Latcham, "Proxy Contest Expenses and Corporate Democracy," *Western Reserve Law Review*, 4: 5 (1952); Aranow and Einhorn, *Proxy Contests for Corporate Control* (1956).

10. See Note 4, above, and George D. Hornstein, "The Death Knell of Stockholders' Derivative Suits in New York," *California Law Review*, 32: 123 (1944); "The Future of Corporate Control," *Harvard Law Review*, 63: 476 (1950); "New Aspects of Stockholders' Derivative Suits," *Colorado Law Review*, 47: 1 (1947). S. Solomont & Sons Trust, Inc. v. New England Theatres Operating Corp., 326 Mass. 99, 93 N.E. 2d 241 (1950); Pomerantz v. Clark, 101 F. Supp. 341 (D. Mass., 1951); Note, *Boston University Law Review*, 36: 78 (1956).

11. See, for example, E. Merrick Dodd, Jr., *American Business Corpora-*

tions Until 1860 (1954); Brandeis, J., in Liggett v. Lee, 288 U.S. 517, 548ff. (1933) (dissent); Joseph S. Davis, *Essays in the Earlier History of American Corporations* (1917). See also B. C. Hunt, *The Development of the Business Corporation in England 1800–1867* (1936).

12. F. D. Emerson and F. C. Latcham, *Shareholder Democracy* (1954); Wilber G. Katz, "The Philosophy of Midcentury Corporation Statutes," *Law and Contemporary Problems*, 23: 177, 188–192 (1958); F. D. Emerson, "The Roles of Management and Shareholders in Corporate Government," *ibid.*, 231; Sheldon E. Bernstein and Henry G. Fischer, "The Regulation of the Solicitation of Proxies: Some Reflections on Corporate Democracy," *University of Chicago Law Review*, 7: 226 (1940); Mortimer M. Caplin, "Proxies, Annual Meetings and Corporate Democracy," *Virginia Law Review*, 37: 653 (1951); Lewis D. Gilbert, "Wanted: A Program for Fair Corporate Suffrage," *Investor* (June 1953), p. 28; "Stockholder Participation in Corporate Affairs," *Virginia Law Review*, 37: 595 (1951).

13. The proxy provisions of the Securities Exchange Act, and the rules of the Securities and Exchange Commission adopted under them, impose a far more severe standard of propriety in the corporate electoral process than prevails in political elections. Correspondingly, these regulations raise delicate problems under the First Amendment.

14. Most recently reported in Livingston, *The American Stockholder*, chap. iv, p. 12.

15. W. O. Douglas, *Democracy and Finance* (1940), p. 53.

16. Lewis D. Gilbert, *Dividends and Democracy* (1956).

17. A. A. Berle, Jr., *Economic Power and the Free Society* (1958), pp. 12–13.

18. Scott Buchanan, *The Corporation and the Republic* (1958).

19. Berle, *The Twentieth Century Capitalist Revolution;* D. E. Lilienthal, *Big Business, A New Era* (1953); P. F. Drucker, *Concept of the Corporation* (1946); H. R. Bowen, *Social Responsibility of the Businessman* (1953).

20. See, however, Theodore Levitt, "The Dangers of Social Responsibility," *Harvard Business Review*, 36: 41 (1958). Edward S. Mason, "The Apologetics of Managerialism," *Journal of Business, University of Chicago*, 31: 1 (1958).

21. *Economic Power and the Free Society* (1958), p. 16.

22. See note 18.

23. Manning, Review, *Yale Law Journal*, 67: 1478 (1958).

24. *Ibid.*, p. 1494.

25. *Ibid.*

26. See Wilbur T. Blair, "Appraising the Board of Directors," *Harvard Business Review*, 28: 101, 150 (1950) ("the principle is unworkable").

27. Carl Kaysen, "The Social Significance of the Modern Corporation," *American Economic Review*, 47: 311, 313 (1957), "No longer the agent of proprietorship seeking to maximize return on investment, management sees itself as responsible to stockholders, employees, customers, the general public, and, perhaps most important, the firm itself as an institution . . . Its responsibilities to the general public are widespread: leadership in local charitable enterprises, concern with factory architecture and landscaping,

provision of support for higher education, and even research in pure science, to name a few."

28. Quoted by Mason, "The Apologetics of Managerialism," p. 3.

29. Douglas, *Democracy and Finance*, p. 53.

30. Richard Eells, *Corporate Giving in a Free Society* (1956), reviewed by Manne, *University of Chicago Law Review*, 24: 194 (1956); "Corporate Giving: Theory and Policy," *California Management Review*, 1: 37 (1958).

31. "Mouse with a Leer," *The Economist* (July 20, 1957), p. 191.

32. A. A. Berle, Jr., "Corporate Powers as Powers in Trust," *Harvard Law Review*, 44: 1049 (1931); E. Merrick Dodd, Jr., "For Whom are Corporate Managers Trustees?" *Harvard Law Review*, 45: 1145 (1932); Berle, "For Whom Corporate Managers are Trustees," *Harvard Law Review*, 45: 1365 (1932); E. Merrick Dodd, Jr., "Is Effective Enforcement of the Fiduciary Duties of Corporate Managers Practicable?" *University of Chicago Law Review*, 2: 194 (1935); Berle, *The Twentieth Century Capitalist Revolution*.

33. Berle, "Corporate Powers as Powers in Trust," p. 1049.

34. Dodd, "For Whom are Corporate Managers Trustees?" pp. 1145, 1161.

35. Berle, "For Whom Corporate Managers are Trustees," pp. 1365, 1367.

36. Dodd, "Is Effective Enforcement . . . Practicable?" pp. 194, 206–207.

37. Berle, *The Twentieth Century Capitalist Revolution*, p. 169.

38. J. K. Galbraith, "Market Structure and Stabilization Policy," *Review of Economics and Statistics*, 39: 127 (1957); Eugene V. Rostow, "Market Organization and Stabilization Policy," in Max F. Millikan, ed., *Income Stabilization for a Developing Democracy* (1953), pp. 439, 460–469.

39. Economic Report of the President, January 1959, p. v.

40. "Economics by Admonition," *American Economic Review*, Supplement, 49: 384, 395 (1959).

41. I have attempted to develop this thesis in a book of lectures, "Planning for Freedom," to be published this year by the Yale University Press. This paper develops a theme which appears on several pages of that manuscript.

Chapter 4. The Corporation and Economic Federalism

1. The literature is legion. One of the earliest and most prophetic is one of the most unsung, perhaps because it appeared in 1942 when the operational jurisprudes were busy with other things: Peter F. Drucker's *The Future of Industrial Man* (New York, 1942).

2. For the flavor of this antipathy and its widespread hold on all walks of American life in an earlier day see *Proceedings of the National Conference on Trusts and Combinations* (New York, 1908).

3. See Joseph A. Livingston, *The American Stockholder* (Philadelphia, 1958); Bayless Manning, book review of Livingston in *Yale Law Journal*,

67:1477 (1958); Victor Perlo, " 'People's Capitalism' and Stock Owner-ship," *American Economic Review*, 333 (June 1958).

4. See Edward S. Mason, "The Apologetics of Managerialism," *Journal of Business, University of Chicago*, 31: 1 (1958).

5. See A. A. Berle, Jr., *The Twentieth Century Capitalist Revolution* (New York, 1954), chap. iii.

6. Carl Kaysen, "The Social Significance of the Modern Corporation," *Proceedings of the American Economic Association* (May 1957).

7. J. K. Galbraith, *American Capitalism, the Concept of Countervailing Power* (Boston, 1952).

8. *E.g.*, U. S. v. E. I. Dupont de Nemours, 351 U. S. 377 (1956).

9. See Edward S. Mason, "The Current Status of the Monopoly Problem," *Harvard Law Review*, 62: 1265 (1949); Clare E. Griffin, *An Economic Approach to Antitrust Problems* (New York, 1951).

10. See Carl Kaysen and D. F. Turner, "Antitrust Policy: An Economic and Legal Analysis" (to be published by Harvard University Press, Cam-bridge, Mass.).

11. See David E. Lilienthal, *Big Business, a New Era* (New York, 1952), pp. 181–189.

12. D. F. Turner, "Antitrust Policy and the Cellophane Case," *Harvard Law Review*, 70: 281 (1956).

13. W. Adams, "Competition, Monopoly, and Countervailing Power," *Quarterly Journal of Economics*, 67: 469 (1953).

14. See Kaysen and Turner, "Antitrust Policy: an Economic and Legal Analysis."

15. See K. Brewster, "Enforceable Competition, Unruly Reason or Reasonable Rules?" *American Economic Review* (May 1956), p. 482.

16. Berle, *The Twentieth Century Capitalist Revolution*, chap. iii.

17. A. A. Berle, Jr., "The Developing Law of Corporate Concentra-tion," *University of Chicago Law Review*, 19: 639, 656–660 (1952).

18. The "social laboratory" virtues of federalism echo throughout the literature of the subject. More subtle but perhaps more important is Henry Hart's observation that "Official law must do more than 'eliminate the nega-tive' of undue disparity between the criteria of official and of private action. It must 'accentuate the positive' of so guiding and channeling the processes of private autonomy and adjustment as to release to the utmost the enor-mous potential of the human abilities in the society — its ultimate and most significant resource." "The Relations Between State and Federal Law," *Columbia Law Review*, 54: 489–490 (1954).

19. Berle, "The Developing Law of Corporate Concentration," pp. 639, 657.

20. 49 Stat. 1526 (1936), 15 U.S.C. #13 (a)–(f), 13a, 13b, 21a (1952). Perhaps its most virulent economic critic is Morris Adelman; see, e.g., Adelman, "Consistency of the Robinson-Patman Act," *Stanford Law Review*, 6: 3 (1953).

21. 70 Stat. 1125, 15 U.S.C. #1222 (Supp. 1956).

22. It was on this ground that the Antitrust Division of the United States Department of Justice opposed the legislation; see *Hearings* before the Antitrust Subcommittee (Subcommittee Number 5) of the House Committee on the Judiciary, 84 Cong. 2 Sess., ser. 26, p. 243 (1956).

23. U.S. v. Great A & P Tea Co., 173 F.2d 79 (1949).

24. Eastman Kodak Co. v. Southern Photo Material Co., 273 U.S. 359 (1927).

25. A. M. Ross, "A New Industrial Feudalism," *American Economic Review*, 48: 903 (December 1958).

26. C. A. Hall, *Effects of Taxation on Executive Compensation and Retirement Plans* (Cambridge, Mass., 1951).

27. *Ibid.*

28. *Ibid.*

29. See Adelman, "Integration and Antitrust Policy," p. 27.

30. W. Lloyd Warner and James C. Abegglen, *Big Business Leaders in America* (New York, 1955) is one of the more recent studies of this problem.

31. See Mabel Newcomer, "Professionalization of Leadership in the Big Business Corporation," *Business History Review*, 29: 54 (1955).

32. See James C. Abegglen, "Big Business Leaders, Comment on the Newcomer and Rae Papers," *Business History Review*, 29: 75 (1955).

33. See "Financing the Expansion of Business," *Survey of Current Business* (September 1957), p. 6.

34. These issues are discussed below by John Lintner, p. 166.

35. The notion of penalizing the retention of earnings as a check on business power was in political vogue twenty years ago. See Message to Congress, April 29, 1938, quoted in *T.N.E.C. Final Report and Recommendations*, Senate Doc. 35, 77 Cong. 1 Sess. (1941), pp. 18–19.

36. *Congressional Record*, 51 Cong. 1 Sess. (1890), p. 2457.

Chapter 5. The Corporation: How Much Power? What Scope?

1. The sources for the figures quoted are listed in order below.

Total business population: 1956, 4.3 million; 1954, 4.2 million, whence my current estimate. See U. S. Department of Commerce, Bureau of the Census, *Statistical Abstract of the United States 1957* (Washington, D. C., 1957), p. 482.

Corporate share and size distribution: U. S. Department of Commerce, Office of Business Economics, *Survey of Current Business* (April 1955); figures refer to January 1, 1952, for share, and January 1, 1947, for size distribution. If anything, the figures understate the numerical preponderance of small unincorporated enterprises today.

The census figures refer to 1954. See U. S. Department of Commerce, Bureau of the Census, *Company Statistics 1954*, Bulletin CS–1 (Washington, D. C., 1958).

Asset holding of large corporations: U. S. Treasury, Internal Revenue Service, *Statistics of Income, Part 2 1955* (Washington, D. C., 1958), Table 5, pp. 41ff.

Research and Development Expenditures: U. S. National Science Foundation, *Science and Engineering in American Industry* (Washington, D. C., 1956).

Defense Contracts: "100 Companies and Affiliates Listed According to Net Value of Military Prime Contract Awards, July 1950–June 1956." Department of Defense, Office of Assistant Secretary of Defense (Supply and Logistics), mimeo release dated 10 April 1957.

For a fuller but slightly dated discussion, see M. A. Adelman, "The Measurement of Industrial Concentration," *The Review of Economics and Statistics*, 23: 269–296 (1951), reprinted in *Readings in Industrial Organization and Public Policy*, ed. R. B. Heflebower and G. W. Stocking (Homewood, Ill., 1958).

2. The figures on the relative importance of corporations come from R. A. Gordon, *Business Leadership in the Large Corporation* (Washington, D. C., 1946), p. 14, and Appendix A. These figures refer to 1939; no more recent ones are available and they almost certainly understate the relative importance of corporations. The shares of the sectors in national income are calculated from the figures for national income by industrial origin for 1956 given in *Statistical Abstract of the U. S. 1957*, p. 300. The shares of large corporations in asset holdings of all corporations are from the *Statistics of Income, Part 2, 1955*, table 5, pp. 41ff.

3. See Adelman, "The Measurement of Industrial Concentration," S. Friedland, "Turnover and Growth of the Largest Industrial Firms, 1906–1950," *Review of Economics and Statistics* (February, 1957), and J. F. Weston, *The Role of Mergers in the Growth of Large Firms* (Los Angeles, 1953).

4. These estimates are taken from Carl Kaysen and D. F. Turner, "Antitrust Policy, an Economic and Legal Analysis" (to be published by Harvard University Press, Cambridge, Mass.). See chap. ii and the appendices. The figures are based on data for 1954 for manufacturing, and on scattered years for other industries.

5. See Otto Eckstein, "Inflation, the Wage-Price Spiral, and Economic Growth," *The Relationship of Prices to Economic Stability and Growth*, papers submitted by panelists appearing before the Joint Economic Committee, 85 Cong., 2 Sess. (Washington, D. C., March 1958).

6. See R. Maclaurin, *Innovation and Invention in the Radio Industry* (New York, 1949); A. A. Bright, Jr., *The Electric Lamp Industry* (New York, 1949); C. Kaysen, *United States v. United Shoe Machinery Co.* (Cambridge, Mass., 1956); J. Jewkes *et al.*, *The Sources of Invention* (London, 1958).

7. See, on automobiles, the *Hearings* on Automobile Marketing Practices before the Interstate and Foreign Commerce Committee of the Senate, 84 Cong., 2 Sess. On aluminum, see the *Hearings* before Subcommittee No. 3 of the Select Committee on Small Business, House of Representatives, 84 Cong., 1 Sess. (1956) and the *Hearings* before the same Subcommittee, 85 Cong., 1 and 2 Sess. (1958).

8. See Kaysen and Turner, "Antitrust Policy."

9. A. A. Berle, Jr., *The Twentieth Century Capitalist Revolution* (New York, 1954); A. D. H. Kaplan, *Big Enterprise in a Competitive System* (Washington, D. C., 1954), and A. D. H. Kaplan, J. Dirlam, and R. Lanzilloti, *The Pricing Policy of Big Business* (Washington, D. C., 1958).

10. See E. S. Mason, "The Apologetics of Managerialism," *Journal of Business, University of Chicago*, 31: 1 (1958).

Chapter 6. The Corporation Man

1. By business leaders, the managers of great corporations, is meant those who occupy policy-making positions of high authority, from Chairman of the Board down to and not below Secretary and Treasurer. They are in corporations which are the largest (in terms of their share of the gross national product) within their type of enterprise (marketing, transportation, finance, for example).

2. The principal sources for the factual materials in the chapter are W. Lloyd Warner and James Abegglen, *Big Business Leaders in America* (New York, 1955), and Warner and Abegglen, *Occupational Mobility in American Business and Industry 1928–1952* (Minneapolis, 1955). Research on 8300 executives covered every type of industry and business throughout the United States. Samples of the major types of men, in both the mobile and birth elites, were systematically interviewed and each man was given personality tests.

See also Chester I. Barnard, *The Functions of the Executive* (Cambridge, Massachusetts, 1938); Reinhard Bendix and Frank W. Howton, *Social Mobility and the American Business Elite*, reprint no. 111 (Berkeley, California, 1958); Mabel Newcomer, *The Big Business Executive* (New York, 1955); Clyde White, *These Will Go To College* (Cleveland, 1952).

3. See F. W. Taussig and C. S. Joslyn, *American Business Leaders* (New York, 1932).

4. From a random sample of 505 among the men who went to these colleges.

5. See Warner and Abegglen, *Big Business Leaders in America*, pp. 196–219, and Warner and Abegglen, *Occupational Mobility in American Business and Industry*, pp. 115–158.

6. See Jean Piaget, *Language and Thought of the Child* (New York, 1926), pp. 1–49, and *The Moral Judgment of the Child* (New York, 1932), pp. 76–103.

7. See William E. Henry, "The Business Executive: Psychodynamics of a Social Role," *American Journal of Sociology*, 14: 286–291 (1949); also W. Lloyd Warner, *American Life* (Chicago, 1953), pp. 184–190; and Warner and Abegglen, *Big Business Leaders in America*, pp. 59–83.

Chapter 8. Technological Process and the Modern American Corporation

1. As this book was going to press, Barkev S. Sanders was kind enough to send me his latest findings, derived from research he is conducting for the Patent, Trade-Mark, and Copyright Foundation, which will be published in the *Patent, Trade-Mark, and Copyright Journal*, vol. 3, no. 2 (1959). His results seem strongly to reinforce the foregoing. Sanders reports that large companies, as of the time of his study, had used or were about to use 50.6 per cent of the patented inventions under their control. By contrast, smaller companies had used or were about to use 75.5 per cent. The large companies covered by his study were those with $150 mil-

lions or more of assets, all firms owning 100 or more patents, and some firms with 75 to 99 patents.

Further investigation of the significance of these findings is, of course, essential. On their face, however, they suggest that large firms may be either less successful on the average than are small firms in the research they undertake, or less enterprising than are smaller firms in putting research results into practice. Sanders' discovery is extremely suggestive in view of the fact that whereas firms with 5000 or more employees supplied two-thirds of the private funds for organized RD in 1953, they held only half the business-owned patents. This relationship also suggests, though (especially in view of what has been said about the patent system) by no means proves, that large firms are less successful than small ones in the research they undertake. Pending qualitative evaluation of the inventions involved, no firm conclusions are justified, however. On the other hand, the proponents of bigness because of its alleged superiority in innovation confront a mounting pile of adverse evidence which no amount of casual evidence or plausible a priori argument can refute.

Chapter 9. The Financing of Corporations

1. A. A. Berle, Jr., and Gardner C. Means, *The Modern Corporation and Private Property* (New York, 1932).

2. *Ibid.*, p. 43. Mergers were said to have accounted for only one third as much of the growth of the 200 largest companies in 1922–1927 as outside securities, and only two thirds as much as retained earnings.

3. A. A. Berle, Jr., *The Twentieth Century Capitalist Revolution* (New York, 1954), esp. pp. 25–40.

4. *Ibid.*, esp. pp. 35–40. As an interesting corollary, if Berle's position in 1954 is sound, the earlier power of investment bankers and "Wall Street" had waned to the vanishing point.

Incidentally, it may also be noted that concentration through mergers is not even mentioned in the recent study, perhaps because of the changed positions noted in the next two paragraphs. The available evidence, for those interested, is summarized in John Lintner, "Tax Considerations Involved in Corporate Mergers" in *Federal Tax Policy for Economic Growth and Stability*, Joint Economic Committee, U. S. Congress (November 1955), esp. p. 691, papers by John Lintner and J. Keith Butters, and Jesse W. Markham in *Business Concentration and Price Policy* (Princeton, 1955), and references there cited. In the first reference I point out that the larger number of mergers between larger companies since 1950 probably means that mergers have been increasing concentration more in recent years than during the thirties and forties.

5. Berle, *Twentieth Century Capitalist Revolution*, p. 42.

6. In *Review of Economics and Statistics* (November 1951).

7. The quotation is from page 26. Berle's enthusiasm and moral fervor seem to have run away with him, however, in a still more recent pamphlet, *Economic Power and the Free Society* (New York, 1958). Including manufacturing and other groups, he asserts, "In terms of power . . . not only

do 500 corporations control two-thirds of the nonfarm economy, but within each of that 500 a still smaller group has the ultimate decision-making power. *This is, I think, the highest concentration of economic power in recorded history.* Since the United States carries on not quite half of the manufacturing production of the entire world today, these 500 groupings — each with its own little dominating pyramid within it — represent a concentration of power over economics which makes the medieval feudal system look like a Sunday school party. In sheer economic power this has gone far beyond anything we have yet seen" (p. 14, italics added).

The evidence is clear that concentration ratios in other Western nations (let alone the areas behind the Iron Curtain) are substantially higher than those in the United States. See Gideon Rosenbluth, "Measures of Concentration," in *Business Concentration and Price Policy* (Princeton, 1955), p. 57ff. Moreover, on the measures Berle uses, the concentration in manufacturing is substantially the same in 1955 as in 1947 and 1931, and if other groups are brought into the picture it must be recognized that the over-all concentration of assets, and still more of economic power, within the entire nonfinancial corporate sector is unquestionably lower than it was thirty years ago — notably as the result of SEC action under the death-sentence clause in the Public Utility Holding Company Act and the general economic disabilities of the railroad industry.

There is, of course, no question that concentration increased tremendously during the merger movement at the turn of the century and that it increased further during the 1920's and that it remains high both within the entire nonfinancial corporate sector and within manufacturing alone. The facts of high concentration are impressive enough as they stand; they do not need to be exaggerated for effect.

8. Robert Aaron Gordon's later *Business Leadership in the Large Corporation* (Washington, D. C., 1945) should also be mentioned.

9. These studies also indicate, however, that rather substantial numbers of the largest, best-established, and "highest-quality" companies in the recent boom period were actually paying larger dividends than stockholders would have most preferred. Both these conclusions are based on the quite plausible and common assumption that the preference of stockholders with respect to dividends can be judged in terms of their willingness to pay more or less for the security in the market as dividends are increased or decreased. Our research on these questions includes an examination of the validity of this assumption.

In appraising these results it must also be recognized that the interest of stockholders is not necessarily the controlling consideration. For instance, while stockholders appear to have preferred higher dividends most of the time from large numbers of companies, the retention of these earnings and their reinvestment in plant and equipment may have increased the rate of growth of the economy — a separate consideration of considerable current concern. Whether growth is in fact increased depends among other things on the effects increased personal-income-tax receipts would have on government expenditures and the fraction of net incremental dividends reinvested by shareholders.

10. See John Lintner and J. Keith Butters, "Effects of Taxes on Con-

centration" in *Business Concentration and Price Policy* (Princeton, 1955), esp. pp. 259–261. Later *Statistics of Income* data confirm the same relationship in more recent years. More detailed studies, taking account of varying stability of income, and other relevant issues not raised by Berle and Means are now in process.

11. The data for all years except 1955 are from Raymond W. Goldsmith, *A Study of Savings in the United States* (Princeton, 1956), III, 42–57 and 81. For 1955, data still subject to some revision have been kindly supplied by Goldsmith and Morris Mendelsohn from worksheets of their later work at the National Bureau of Economic Research.

12. The tangible property owned by these corporations was about two-thirds as large as all the property directly owned by individuals both at the turn of the century and at the end of the 1920's. It held in the range of three-fifths to two-thirds through the 1930's and 1940's; but again, the ratio has increased moderately to a little under 70 per cent in the recent years before 1955.

13. This more rapid increase recently for nonfinancial corporations primarily reflects their very heavy holdings of plant and equipment — whose prices have risen far more rapidly than values in general during the postwar years.

14. The difference in the latter figures of course reflects both the fact that corporations are not relatively heavy holders of intangible assets representing claims on others, and the companion fact that, particularly in the utility, railroad, communication, and heavy manufacturing industries, non-financial corporations are relatively quite heavy debtors to others in the economy.

15. In fairness to the Berle and Means thesis, it should again be mentioned that most of these data have become available during the years since their earlier study was prepared.

16. Daniel H. Brill, "Financing of Capital Formation" in *Problems of Capital Formation*, Studies in Income and Wealth, vol. XIX (Princeton, 1957), esp. pp. 178ff. Brill's data, based on *Statistics of Income*, go through 1952, and we have extended them through 1955.

17. In the late 1920's, the ratios ran from 25 to 27 per cent; in 1948, 31 per cent; in 1955, 35 per cent.

18. Sidney S. Alexander, "Changes in the Financial Structure of American Business Enterprise" (National Bureau of Economic Research, ms. 1943), esp. III, 16–20 and 24.

19. *Ibid.*, and Daniel Creamer, Sergei Dobrovolsky, and Israel Borenstein, "Capital in Manufacturing and Mining: Its Formation and Financing" (Natural Bureau of Economic Research, 1958, ms. VII, 4 and 24). The ratio was falling in the late 1920's and early 1930's but rose in the subsequent recovery.

20. *Federal Reserve Bulletin* (July 1953, June 1956), and supporting tables. Before World War II, the ratios ran nearly 25 per cent; in the mid-fifties they were around 40 per cent.

21. Creamer, Dobrovolsky, and Borenstein, VII-8. Debt declines with increasing size in both periods among smaller firms.

22. The great speculative boom of 1929 provides the major exception to this statement.

23. The hold which the traditional view has even in the highest professional circles is exemplified by Raymond W. Goldsmith's statement in *Financial Intermediaries in the American Economy Since 1900* (Princeton, 1958), p. 302: ". . . the increase in the proportion of internal financing, gross or net in total financing . . . is a basic development in the American economy." Yet as Irwin Friend points out in his review in *American Economic Review* 48: 702–703 (September 1958), Goldsmith's own data (which we use among others below) "do not confirm these statements."

24. Goldsmith, *Financial Intermediaries* p. 222.

25. *Survey of Current Business* (September 1957). Similarly, tabulations by the Federal Reserve Board show that large nonfinancial concerns relied on inside sources for just under 60 per cent of the total internal and external funds used in 1939–1941, and relied on these sources for approximately the same fraction of funds in the period 1951–1953.

26. Although the conclusion in the text seems clear for the period through 1953 — that discussed by previous writers and the one relevant to our appraisal of the Berle and Means thesis as it has worked out over long periods — the fresh revisions ([January 1959] Economic Report of the President, p. 207) suggest a higher ratio (65 per cent) for 1955–1957. It is too early to assess the significance of the figure: the new estimates may not stand up in subsequent revisions, and these three years may have been a sport. Also the ratio may have been higher because of the reduced rate of asset growth in these years. Nevertheless the possibility is raised of a *very recent* shift toward relatively heavier reliance on internal funds. If so, the timing and other considerations suggest such a development may be closely related to more generous depreciation allowances in the 1954 Revenue Code.

27. The absolute fractions are of course larger than for all nonfinancial corporations because as previously noted manufacturing firms have always relied relatively more than nonfinancial corporations in general upon retained earnings. But our concern is with the trends — and these have, if anything, been declining. The data are given in Creamer, Dobrovolsky, and Borenstein, chap. vi, p. 51.

28. Depletion was deducted from Department of Commerce data in the January 1959 Economic Report to make them comparable with Goldsmith's data, which for this purpose properly lumped depletion with depreciation.

29. Creamer, Dobrovolsky, and Borenstein.

30. This same conclusion for the prewar period was reached by Neil H. Jacoby and Raymond J. Saulnier, *Business Finance and Banking* (Washington, D. C., 1947), esp. pp. 92–96.

31. Albert R. Koch, *Financing of Large Corporations, 1920–1939* (New York, 1943), pp. 92ff.

32. Creamer, Dobrovolsky, and Borenstein, p. 15, and Federal Reserve Board tabulations.

33. The reduced use of external funds by railroads is explained entirely by their relatively stagnant position.

34. It will now be clear why we were careful in the preceding paragraphs to say that the secular trends in reliance on internal funds for large manufacturers had either been stable or "if anything" were declining (that is, if anything, there had been increasing reliance on external funds). It is entirely possible — I would say much preferable — to explain the relatively smaller use of outside funds in the 1920's (in comparison with either the teens or the fifties) by the much lower rate of asset expansion in those years — in which case there has been a stable rather than an increasing "propensity to use outside funds." But the Berle and Means thesis can find no support in this: if high rates of asset expansion in recent years are relied upon to explain away the heavy recent dependence on outside funds, we still find no increase over four decades in the relative use of inside funds.

35. John Lintner, "Distribution of Incomes of Corporations Among Dividends, Retained Earnings, and Taxes," *American Economic Review* 46: 97–113 (May 1956).

36. The reduced use of external funds by railroads is explained entirely by their relatively stagnant position.

37. Using data for all nonfinancial corporations from Goldsmith, *Finanvial Intermediaries* p. 222, security issues and mortgages accounted for 37 per cent of total sources before 1912 and 41 per cent in the period 1923–1929; they were less than 25 per cent in 1951–1953 and 1955–1957, according to Department of Commerce data. Creamer, Dobrovolsky, and Borenstein show the decline in manufacturing and mining at p. VI-24. This relative decline in formal security issues may be the explanation of the common judgment that relative reliance on internal funds in total financing has increased, as asserted by the Berle and Means thesis; in any event, as we have seen, the assertion is confused and erroneous.

38. More detailed analysis would allow for the fact that increased tax liabilities lead to increased holdings of cash and governments, but the funding is partial at best and in itself leads at least to some increased bank borrowing and other use of private credit.

39. See Creamer, Dobrovolsky, and Borenstein, pp. 51–55.

40. See W. Braddock Hickman, *The Volume of Corporate Bond Financing Since 1900* (Princeton, 1953), esp. pp. 18–22, and 163–179, esp. 168. Further evidence of the importance of the relative costs of debt and equity financing in determining the "mix" of outside capital used by nonfinancial corporations is given in Franco Modigliani and Morton Zeman, "The Effect of the Availability of Funds, and the Terms Thereof, on Business Investment," in *Conference on Research in Business Finance* (New York, 1952), esp. pp. 280–297.

41. See G. D. Bodenhorn, "Investment and the Price System," in *The Relationship of Prices to Economic Stability and Growth*, Joint Economic Committee, 85 Cong. (March 31, 1958), pp. 335ff.

42. John R. Meyer and Edwin Kuh, *The Investment Decision* (Cambridge, Mass., 1957).

43. *Ibid.*, esp. chap. viii and pp. 176–178.

44. *Ibid.*, pp. 142ff.

45. To avoid possible misunderstanding, let it be explicit that these findings simply mean that the more sweeping and far-reaching adverse

trends in the broad patterns of financing nonfinancial corporations anticipated by Berle's and Means' basis of the separation of ownership from management of these corporations have not been borne out in more than a quarter of a century of experience; they do *not* mean that these stable patterns are ideal in any sense. This latter question is not germane to our present purpose. To illustrate the difference between the two kinds of issues, it is entirely possible, for instance, that profitability and pressure of increasing sales are more important than other things in determining what firms invest and how much they invest and still not be the sole determinants of such matters as some models of an ideal economy would require. Similarly, the profitability itself may reflect well-buttressed positions of power in product markets or the increase in sales may represent sales promotion of types that are socially undesirable on any one of various grounds. But these other matters, however important in their own right, are outside our purview in this paper.

Also, we have emphasized the broader aspects of corporate finance such as reliance on internal funds and the responsiveness of real investment to profitability and increased sales, because these were most directly involved in the financial aspects of the entire Berle and Means thesis. The reader must not be left with the impression that at a more detailed level there have not been very great changes in financial arrangements and procedures. Interested readers will find excellent summaries in Goldsmith, *Financial Intermediaries*, and the monographs of Saulnier, Jacoby, Shapiro and other authors in the financial research and capital market studies of the National Bureau of Economic Research.

46. Those interested in pursuing these questions further will find a stimulating and perceptive analysis in the studies of Edward S. Shaw and John Gurley made at the Brookings Institution. See, for instance, J. G. Gurley and E. S. Shaw, "Financial Aspects of Economic Development," *American Economic Review*, 45: 515–538 (September 1955).

47. The ratio of the money supply to national income or gross national product has shown a persistent secular increase throughout the nineteenth and twentieth century. At least since the Civil War an increasingly large fraction of the total money supply has taken the form of bank deposits which are created by the banking system — one of the important financial intermediaries.

48. Goldsmith, *Financial Intermediaries* p. 279.

49. *Ibid.*, p. 304.

50. *Ibid.*, p. 221. The surprisingly high figure for 1923–1929 reflects purchases of $4.9 billion of equities (out of $16.7 billion issued) — a figure which includes investment company activity in the later part of the decade.

51. There was some resurgence of individual buying of corporate bonds in the years 1955–1957, particularly in the last year noted. This was doubtless related to the shifting yields between tax-exempts and corporates, and to the high and (during 1956–1957) unsettled condition of the stock market.

52. Goldsmith, *Financial Intermediaries*, p. 258.

53. *Hearings*, Subcommittee of the Committee on Interstate and Foreign Commerce, House of Representatives (1952), p. 956, and E. Raymond

Corey, *Direct Placement of Corporate Securities* (Cambridge, Mass., 1951), pp. 6, 106–107.

54. See J. K. Galbraith, *American Capitalism: An Analysis of the U. S. Economy* (Boston, 1956).

55. Goldsmith, *Financial Intermediaries*, p. 225. Small amounts of foreign holdings are included in the figures given, which range from 77.8 per cent to 79.5 per cent. According to the Federal Reserve Flows of Funds analysis, individuals, including personal trusts, held stock with market values of $276 billion in 1955, out of $317 outstanding. Raymond W. Goldsmith and Eli Shapiro, "An Estimate of Bank-Administered Personal Trust Funds," *Journal of Finance* 14: 11–17 (March 1959), estimate the holdings of such trusts at $43.5 billion, leaving $273 billion or 85 per cent, and this figure excludes foreign holdings, which are estimated separately by the Board.

56. Goldsmith, *Financial Intermediaries*, p. 225.

57. Private pension plans may be divided into two broad classes, those "insured," which are funded with life insurance companies and managed as part of the assets of these institutions, and "noninsured" plans, generally administered by the trust departments of large banks, although various other arrangements are found. Our interest here focuses on noninsured plans because the investments of insured plans are pooled with other insurance company assets and are subject to the same restrictions. See Note 69 below. For general information in this area the reader should consult the studies cited in later notes.

58. U. S. Securities and Exchange Commission, *Statistical Series*, Release no. 1533, June 8, 1958, and *Survey of Corporate Pension Funds, 1951–1954*. Reserves in insured plans have been growing relatively less rapidly in recent years and amounted to $14.0 billion in 1957.

59. The issues of investment companies are excluded in these comparisons.

60. The comparison stated in the text perhaps requires some explanation. More precisely it is the ratio of the net of funds supplied to the market by noninsured pension plans to the total net new issues of common stock during the period. Obviously a substantial part of the actual stock purchased by pension funds would be stock already available on the market, but we speak of them absorbing the net new issues because these funds they supply to the market will on balance be reinvested by others in the new securities issued.

61. See Victor L. Andrews, "Investment Practices of Corporate Investment Funds," Ph.D. thesis, Massachusetts Institute of Technology (1958), esp. pp. 133ff., and the references there cited, including *Institutional Investors and the Stock Market, 1933–55*, a Staff Report to the Committee on Banking and Currency, U. S. Senate (December 28, 1956).

62. For discussion of this issue (and the broader one of the effect of private pension plans or the volume of all other private saving) see George Garvy, "The Effect of Private Pension Plans on Personal Savings," *Review of Economics and Statistics*, 32: 223–226 (August 1950); Charles L. Dearing, *Industrial Pensions* (Washington, D. C., 1954); John J. Corson and John W. McConnell, *Economic Needs of Older People* (New York, 1956).

63. See Andrews, *Institutional Investors*, and Mooney.

64. Natrella, pp. 11–13. These estimates assume that benefit payments will more than double by 1965 and that interest rates will remain at 1957 levels. The same source estimates that insured pension plans will continue their marked growth over this same period, but at a somewhat slower rate. These need not concern us here since their assets are included with those of insurance companies and are not separately invested.

65. Natrella's estimate is $16 billion in common stock in 1965, or an increase of "only" $11 billion.

66. Berle, *Economic Power and the Free Society*, p. 9; also Corson and McDonnell; the Fulbright Committee study of *Institutional Investors and the Stock Market*, and Robert Tilove, "Pension Plans and Economic Freedom," prepared for the Fund for the Republic (to be published).

67. Berle, *Economic Power and the Free Society*, p. 11.

68. It is not clear whether Berle's figure of $70–$80 billion refers to all pension funds' assets, including those in so-called "insured" plans where the assets are managed as part of the life insurance company's own over-all portfolio, or refers only to the so-called "noninsured" plans. Only the latter are really relevant to the present issues. So far as the latter plans are concerned, the figures seem rather reasonable if one is looking into the 1970's and beyond.

Insurance companies are generally limited by law to high-grade non-equity securities. In 1951 the New York law (which is generally followed in other jurisdictions) was liberalized to permit life insurance companies to hold as much as 3 per cent of their assets in common stock, but total purchases in the next seven years totaled only $800 million. Insured pension plans would become directly relevant to the issues posed in the text if recent agitation for so-called "variable annuities" results in legislative approval and if most of the large companies begin vigorously to push such annuities in connection with their pension business. Many of the largest companies are now strongly opposed to receiving such authority, and in any event the impact would be delayed for many years while the assets of the variable plans for pensions were being built up. Also, much of any added growth of insured plans due to the variable annuity would probably be at the expense of the presently expected growth of noninsured plans.

69. Berle, *Economic Power and the Free Society*, p. 12.

70. SEC Release no. 1533 (June 8, 1958). The adjustment to exclude Sears-Roebuck stock was made by the author.

71. George Mooney, *Pension and Other Employee Welfare Plans* (New York, 1954), p. 28.

72. *Welfare and Pension Plans Investigation*, Final Report of the U. S. Senate Committee on Labor and Public Welfare, Subcommittee on Welfare and Pension Funds, 84 Cong., 2 Sess., April 16, 1956, pp. 360–361. The percentages are based on tabulations of 3191 noninsured plans.

73. Moody's *Industrials*, 1958. For the earlier history of this plan, see Boris Emmet and John E. Jeuck, *Catalogues and Counters, A History of Sears-Roebuck & Co.* (Chicago, 1950), esp. Appendix A, pp. 679–715.

74. These provisions require that no more than 5 per cent of assets may be invested in the securities of any one company and no more than 10

per cent of the voting securities of any one company may be held in 75 per cent of the aggregate portfolio. These limitations are currently being reviewed by the SEC.

75. Mooney, Table 4. In addition there were two real estate companies wholly owned by these pension funds in order to permit holding title to real estate.

76. There were: 12.6 per cent of General Bronze Corp., 6.95 per cent of J. C. Penney & Co., and 7.5 per cent of Manufacturers' National Bank, Detroit.

77. Of the ten companies, 0.92 per cent of total shares were held; 1.03 per cent of the market value was held.

Chapter 10. The Corporation, Its Satellites, and the Local Community

1. Clark Kerr, Lloyd Fisher, "Plant Sociology: The Elite and the Aborigines," Reprint no. 107, Institute of Industrial Relations (Berkeley, Calif., 1958).

2. Philip Selznik, *Leadership in Administration, A Sociological Interpretation* (White Plains, N. Y., 1957).

3. Carl Kaysen, "The Social Significance of the Modern Corporation," *The American Economic Review*, 23: 311 (May 1957).

4. Robert O. Schulze, "The Role of Economic Dominants in Community Power Structure," *American Sociological Review*, vol. 23 (February 1958).

5. John Barlow Martin, "The Blast in Centralia No. 5, A Mine Disaster No One Stopped," *Harpers Magazine*, 196: 193–220 (March 1948).

6. Anthony Harold Birch, *Small Town Politics: A Study of Political Life in Glossop* (New York, 1959).

7. R. R. R. Brooks, *When Labor Organizes* (New Haven, 1937).

8. Peter Rossi, "The Impact of Party Organization in an Industrial Setting," to be published in a forthcoming volume entitled "Community Political Systems," edited by M. Janowitz and H. Enlan, Chicago.

9. Cameron Hawley, *Executive Suite* (Boston, 1952).

10. C. Wright Mills, *The Power Elite* (New York, 1956).

11. Floyd Hunter, *Community Power Structure; A Study of Decision Makers* (Chapel Hill, 1953).

12. Andrew Hacker, "Politics and the Corporation," Occasional paper, Fund for the Republic, New York, 1958.

Chapter 11. The Body Politic of the Corporation

1. Thomas Hobbes, *Leviathan* (1651) (New York, 1924), p. 218.

2. Arthur Bentley, *The Process of Government* (Bloomington, Ind., 1935), p. 268.

3. Walton Hamilton, *The Politics of Industry* (New York, 1957). He says, "There has arisen, quite apart from the ordinary operations of state, a government of industry which in its own distinctive way has its constitution

and its statutes, its administrative and judicial processes, and its own manner of dealing with those who do not abide by the law of the industry" (p. 7).

4. Charles E. Merriam, *Public and Private Government* (New Haven, 1944), pp. 7–8.

5. C. Wright Mills, *The Power Elite* (New York, 1956), p. 165.

6. A. A. Berle, Jr., *The Twentieth Century Capitalist Revolution* (New York, 1954), p. 22.

7. A. A. Berle, Jr., *Natural Selection of Political Forces* (Lawrence, Kan., 1950), p. 24. Hamilton in speaking of politics said that "the word is used in the Aristotelian sense as an over-all term for the usages and traditions, for the arrangements and policies through which men are governed and through which men — usurping the function of the gods — attempt to shape destiny" (*The Politics of Industry*, p. 6). Some considerable time before either of the cited works of Berle and Hamilton, N. R. Danielian, using materials provided by the Federal Communications Commission investigation of the telephone industry, did a study of the American Telephone and Telegraph Company that was "Aristotelian" in its concept of politics. See *A. T. and T.* (New York, 1939).

8. Peter F. Drucker, *Concept of the Corporation* (New York, 1946), p. 21.

9. Otto Gierke, *Natural Law and the Theory of Society, 1500 to 1800* (Boston, 1957), p. lxvi. The reference is to the introduction by the translator, Ernest Barker, who examines various theories of the nature of the personality of the corporation and says that when we seek to discover what lies behind the legal Group-person, and constitutes its inner core, "We must not talk of 'fictions' which hover in a shadowy and unreal existence above a number of real individuals; we must not talk of 'collections' or 'brackets' or contractual nets, flung over so many individuals to bind them one to another in the bonds of an impersonal nexus." We must, in short, be prepared to accept an anthropomorphic superperson whose reality is as real as that of human beings. For a criticism of similar views stated by others, see Earl Latham, "Anthropomorphic Corporations, Elites, and Monopoly Power," *American Economic Review*, 57: 303–310 (May 1957).

10. Marshall E. Dimock, *Business and Government* (New York, 1949), p. 47.

11. Marshall E. Dimock and Howard K. Hyde, *Bureaucracy and Trusteeship in Large Corporations*, United States Temporary National Economic Committee, Monograph no. 11 (Washington, D. C., 1940).

12. Robert Aaron Gordon, *Business Leadership in the Large Corporation* (Washington, D. C., 1945). The text of this useful work uses the vocabulary of politics throughout much of the discussion of such concepts as hierarchy, leadership, power, coordination, and the like.

13. See, for example, Andrew Hacker, *Politics and the Corporation* (New York, n.d.), where the whole concept of corporate citizenship is confused with corporate employment, which is quite a different thing and is covered fully by William H. Whyte, Jr.

14. Leverett S. Lyons, Myron W. Watkins, and Victor Abramson, *Government and Economic Life* (Washington, D. C., 1939), I, 51–52.

15. William McDonald, ed., *Documentary Source Book of American History, 1606–1926* (New York, 1928), pp. 1ff.

16. *Ibid.*, p. 13. The jurisdiction of the "Treasurer and Company of Adventurers and Planters of the city of London for the first Colony in Virginia" was extended to Bermuda and other islands in 1612, but was soon revoked (*ibid.*, p. 15). The Virginia Company in its ordinance of 1621 established the pattern for the government of Virginia that was to be followed by the later English colonies (*ibid.*, p. 20). Thus the basic form of the public government in America derived from the provenance of a commercial corporation. The corporation created the government.

17. *Ibid.*, p. 22.

18. Lyons, Watkins, and Abramson, *Government and Economic Life*, I, 52.

19. At the end of a two-volume study of old corporations, John P. Davis in a chapter on modern corporations said: "Modern corporations seem to be substantially new bodies, modern not only in time but also in the nature of their activity." Second thought convinced him that the change was not fundamental, for "when a group of associated individuals is confirmed in its character as a group for the accomplishment of a public purpose through the pursuit by the group of private interest, the group is as much a corporation under the new definitions as it would have been under older ones." John P. Davis, *Corporations, Their Origin and Development* (New York, 1905), II, 248–249. Of the growth of corporations in the nineteenth century, Davis further said, ". . . the growth of corporations in western Europe and the United States signifies nothing less than a social revolution" (*ibid.*, p. 261).

20. *Ibid.*, p. 269. Lyons, Watkins, and Abramson point out that even as late as the ninth decade, the corporation had not entirely taken hold as the master form of business enterprise. Only half of the fourteen enterprises originally combined in the Standard Oil Trust Agreement of 1882 were incorporated (*Government and Economic Life*, I, 46).

21. Davis, *Corporations*, II, 269.

22. While safeguards for the public were being relaxed, protections for the corporation were being increased. Two key cases in the Supreme Court of the United States were decisive in the development of constitutionally vested interest. In Dartmouth College v. Woodward, 4 Wheaton 518 (1819), a corporate charter was held to be a contract under the protection of that clause of the Constitution that forbids a state to impair the obligations of a contract. And when the contract clause of the Constitution became eroded through state-favoring decisions under the police power doctrine, the Supreme Court held that corporations were persons under the protection of the due process clauses of the Fifth and Fourteenth Amendments. See San Mateo County v. S.P.R.R., 116 U. S. 138 (1885); Santa Clara County v. S.P.R.R., 118 U. S. 394 (1886). Justices Black and Douglas later argued that these cases should be overruled. See Connecticut Life Insurance Company v. Johnson, 303 U. S. 77 (1938) and Wheeling Steel Corporation v. Glander, 337 U. S. 562 (1949).

23. Lyons, Watkins, and Abramson, *Government and Economic Life*, I, 57.

24. See Carl J. Friedrich, *Constitutional Government and Democracy* (Boston, 1941), p. 128, for a discussion of the constituent power and the right of revolution.

25. U. S. Senate, Select Committee on Small Business, Subcommittee on Monopoly, *The International Petroleum Cartel*, Committee Print No. 6, 82 Cong., 2 Sess.; see summary of organization of the seven companies, pp. 32–33.

26. Berle, *Twentieth Century Capitalist Revolution*, p. 180.

27. The self-perpetuation of oligarchic control is aided by the membership in boards of directors of large numbers of operating officials. But even where "the active board is likely to be dominated by officer-directors who constitute a large minority or indeed even a majority of the board, the conclusion that the board does not typically serve to any marked extent as *an active and independent* participant in the leadership function holds with even greater force." Gordon, *Business Leadership in Large Corporations*, p. 134.

28. David Karr, *Fight for Control* (New York, 1956), p. 38.

29. The ICC, for example, by concerning itself with accounting procedure, the extension and withdrawal of facilities, rate-fixing, reorganizations, and other changes in the capital structure of the roads, "has much to do with the management of the railroads." Dimock and Hyde, "Bureaucracy and Trusteeship in Large Corporations," p. 36.

30. See Gordon, *Business Leadership in the Large Corporation*, pp. 189ff., for a discussion of the influence and leadership of active financial groups.

31. H. H. Gerth and C. Wright Mills, eds., *From Max Weber: Essays in Sociology* (New York, 1946), p. 196.

32. Bureaucracy, of course, is also a word of disparagement, suggesting ineptitude, insolence, extravagance, waste, nepotism, and other ills to which the institutional flesh is inclined. See the complaint of a distinguished economist who tried to get space on the "New England States," operated by the New York Central, and was told that the railroad was not interested in the business. Sumner Slichter, Letter to the Editor, *Boston Herald*, January 4, 1957.

33. James D. Mooney and Alan C. Reiley, *Onward Industry* (New York, 1931) and *The Principles of Organization* (New York, 1939).

34. Mills, *The Power Elite*, p. 133.

35. *Ibid.*, p. 134.

36. Chester I. Barnard, *The Functions of the Executive* (Cambridge, Mass., 1947), pp. 215ff.

37. *Ibid.*, p. 224.

38. *Ibid.*

39. Gordon, *Business Leadership in the Large Corporation*, p. 319.

40. *Ibid.*

41. *Ibid.*

42. United States Senate, Committee on the Judiciary, *Hearings* before the Subcommittee on Antitrust and Monopoly Pursuant to S. Res. 61, 84 Cong., 1 Sess., VII, 3609.

43. Joseph A. Schumpeter, *Capitalism, Socialism, and Democracy*

(New York, 1947), thought that the trend represented by General Motors, if widespread, might lead to the overthrow of capitalism by the managers, not in any revolutionary spirit, nor by any aggressive action, but by ousting the entrepreneur and by robbing the bourgeoisie of its function. Gordon, *Business Leadership in the Large Corporation*, notes the Schumpeter thesis, p. 319 n.

44. See Gordon, *Business Leadership in the Large Corporation*, p. 85.

45. Federal Trade Commission v. Cement Institute, 333 U. S. 683 (1948), by certiorari from the Seventh Circuit Court of Appeals, Cement Institute v. FTC, 175 F. (2d) 533.

46. Earl Latham, *The Group Basis of Politics, A Study in Basing-Point Legislation* (Ithaca, 1952), pp. 78ff.

47. *Boston Herald*, October 2, 1956.

48. United States Senate, Committee on the Judiciary, *Report of the Committee on the Judiciary Containing the Staff Report of the Subcommittee on Antitrust and Monopoly*, Senate Report 1879, 84 Cong., 1 Sess.

49. It was the final Board of Appeals in which dealers lost so drastically. Of 80 cases appealed to this Board between 1938 and 1952, 44 were settled without hearing by the Board, and of these in 34 cases the car division withdrew its decision not to renew, and granted the dealer a new selling agreement for a period of less than one year. But of a total of 53 cases heard by the final Board from 1938 to 1955, dealers won only 6. See Senate Subcommittee on Antitrust and Monopoly, *Hearings*, VIII, 4382 and 4383.

50. *Ibid.*, pp. 3332–3336.

51. Senate Report 1879, p. 11. Previous litigation against Ford and Chrysler had resulted in separation of their financial affiliates. *Ibid.*, p. 69.

Chapter 12. The American Corporation in Underdeveloped Areas

1. There are various technical problems associated with figures of this sort which condition their accuracy. But as rough orders of magnitude, these and other figures cited in the text are not misleading.

Chapter 13. The Private and Public Corporation in Great Britain

1. S. J. Prais, "The Financial Experience of Giant Companies," *Economic Journal*, 67: 249 (June 1957). "Industrial" includes manufacturing, building, and distribution.

2. National Institute of Economic and Social Research, *Company Income and Finance 1949–1953* (London, 1956).

3. P. E. Hart and S. J. Prais, "The Analysis of Business Concentration: a Statistical Approach," *Journal of the Royal Statistical Society*, ser. A, 119: 150 (1956).

4. I. M. D. Little and R. Evely, "Some Aspects of the Structure of British Industry 1935–1951," Manchester Statistical Society (February

1958). Concentration is here defined as the percentage share of trades, expressed in terms of employment, controlled by the three largest business units in each trade.

5. Prais; National Institute of Economic and Social Research.

6. Little and Evely, p. 15.

7. See "Who Control the Steel Industry?" British Iron and Steel Federation, *Steel Review* (October 1958), p. 1.

8. Nor necessarily, it is true, *maximum* profits; for a concentration on growth often leads to a level of output higher than the most profitable one. But the objective of rapid growth will generally require aggregate profits high enough to provide a high proportion of self-finance.

9. C. A. R. Crosland, *The Future of Socialism* (New York, 1957), p. 36. Many of the matters here discussed are more fully debated in that book.

10. Also they are often not fully maximized because maximum growth and maximum profit are in conflict.

11. I deal only with the "industrial" public sector, ignoring, for example, the Post Office and the National Health Service (which between them employ 840,000 workers).

12. One such minor improvement has already been made — the appointment of the Select Committee referred to earlier. This Committee may well play a useful role in unraveling particular problems, eliciting information not previously available (such as the existence of the "gentleman's agreement" on coal prices referred to above), and contributing to a better mutual understanding between Parliament and the Boards. But it can in no sense exercise effective, continuous control.

13. *Industry and Society* (Labour Party, 1957), p. 57.

14. *Industry and Society*, p. 48.

Chapter 14. Industrial Enterprise in Soviet Russia

1. V. Pareto, *Les Systèmes socialistes* (Paris, 1902), I, 107; Karl Diehl, *Über Sozialismus, Kommunismus und Anarchismus*, 2nd ed. (Jena, 1911), p. 7.

2. "The word socialist is one I never could well stomach. In the first place, it is a foreign word in itself and equally foreign in all its suggestions. It smells to the average American of petroleum, suggests the red flag, with all manner of sexual novelties, and an abusive tone about God and religion." Joseph Schiffman, "Mutual Indebtedness: Unpublished Letters of Edward Bellamy to William Dean Howells," *Harvard Library Bulletin*, 12:370 (Autumn 1958).

3. "Later on, as a university professor, I had frequent opportunity in my seminars to argue against the theories of Karl Marx who at that time was the students' highest authority. Time and again, a freshman would tell me with a condescending smile: 'But, professor, Marx is the last word of science'; to which I usually replied: 'How do you know it to be the ultimate and not the penultimate word of science?'" Prince Evgenii Nikolayevich Trubetskoy, *Vospominaniya* [*Memoirs*] (n.p., n.d.), pp. 46–47. The period referred to is the turn of the century.

4. G. Vico, *The New Science*, tr. T. G. Bergin and M. H. Fisch (Ithaca, 1948), p. 70.

5. Karl Marx, *Das Kapital*, Volksausgabe, III (Moscow-Leningrad, 1933), pt. 1, 425.

6. Marx, *Kapital*, Volksausgabe, I (Moscow-Leningrad, 1932), 193.

7. Marx, III, pt. 1, 422–423.

8. Karl Hilferding, *Das Finanzkapital* (Vienna, 1910), pp. 137ff.

9. Joseph A. Schumpeter, *Capitalism, Socialism, and Democracy* (New York and London, 1942), pp. 132–133.

10. *Ibid.*

11. V. I. Lenin, *Gosudarstvo i revolutsiya* [*State and Revolution*], *Sochineniya* [*Works*], 4th ed. (Moscow, 1949), p. 398.

12. Oskar Lange and Fred M. Taylor, *On the Economic Theory of Socialism* (Minneapolis, 1938).

13. *Ibid.*, pp. 77–85.

14. *Ibid.*, p. 75.

15. Marx, *Kapital*, Volksausgabe, I (Moscow, 1932), 624.

16. Cf. *e.g.*, *Ekonomika sotsialisticheskikh promyshlennykh predpriyatii* [*Economics of Socialist Enterprises in Industry*] (Moscow, 1956), p. 25.

17. In Austria and in Germany, for instance, such ideas became reflected in the institution of work councils or shop stewards. (Cf. for Austria "Gesetz betreffend die Errichtung von Betriebsräten," May 15, 1919, *Staatsgesetzblatt*, number 283, article 11), and for Germany the law of February 4, 1920 (Betriebsrätegesetz), and of February 5, 1921 (Bilanzgesetz). A. Shuchman, *Codetermination, Labor's Middle Way in Germany* (Washington, D. C.), pp. 79–81.

18. Cf. Fritz Naphtali, ed., *Wirtschaftsdemokratie, Ihr Wesen, Weg und Ziel* (Berlin, 1929).

19. Shuchman, chaps. ix, x.

20. I. V. Stalin, Speech, June 23, 1931, in *Sochineniya* [*Works*], (Moscow, 1951), XIII, 55–60. G. Bienstock, S. M. Schwarz, and A. Yugow, *Management in Russian Industry and Agriculture* (London, New York, Toronto, 1944), p. 37.

21. It is not necessary for the purposes of this presentation to go into detailed description of the administrative structure and to dwell on the different types of People's Commissariats beyond saying that for the bulk of the heavy industry the commissariats were of the "all-union" type which allowed of no intermediary organs in the constituent republics of the U.S.S.R. Light industries were controlled by the so-called "Union Republican" Commissariats, for which, at least in theory, the relations with the enterprises were channeled through People's Commissariats in the individual republics.

22. Georg Simmel, *Soziologie* (Leipzig, 1908), p. 135.

23. Cf. particularly David Granick, *Management of the Industrial Firm in the USSR* (New York, 1954), and Joseph S. Berliner, *Factory and Manager in the USSR* (Cambridge, Mass., 1957).

24. A Soviet journalist, Boris Polevoy — well but not always pleasantly known — recently crossed the United States from coast to coast without apparently finding anything to excite his admiration. But in Los Angeles,

he was shown through a Chevrolet assembly plant and was told that the plant received its materials from 12,000 different factories, some of them many hundreds of miles away from Los Angeles; still the assembly line moved on without interruption. This was so downright un-Soviet that Polevoy could no longer suppress a burst of enthusiasm. See *Amerikanskiye Dnevniki* [*American Diaries*] (Moscow, 1956), p. 214.

25. I. V. Stalin, Report to the 17th Congress, *Sochineniya* [*Works*], XIII, 315–317.

26. The first resolution in the matter was adopted by the Central Committee of the Communist Party on January 25, 1954. It was followed by the joint resolution on October 14, 1954, of the Central Committee and the Council of Ministers, which used little restraint in criticizing the bureaucratic confusion, inefficiency, and incompetence of the economic ministries and suggested and demanded various improvements without proposing yet any fundamental organizational changes. See *Direktivy KPSS i Sovetskogo Pravitel'stva po khozyaystvennym voprosam, 1917–1957 gody,* IV (Moscow, 1958), 155–156 and 311–317.

27. *Direktivy,* IV, pp. 451–457.

28. "Zakon o dal'neyshem sovershenstvovanii organizatsii upravleniya promyshlennost'yu i stroitel'stvom." *Direktivy,* pp. 732–738.

29. See A. N. Yefimov, *Perestroyka upravleniya promyshlennost'yu i stroitel'stvom v SSSR* [*Reorganization of Administration of Industry and Construction in the USSR*] (Moscow, 1957), *passim.*

30. Resolution of the Council of Ministers of the U. S. S. R. (September 26, 1957), *Direktivy,* IV, pp. 784–805.

31. Yefimov, p. 44.

32. *Pravda,* March 3, 1957.

33. *Sovetskaya Rossiya,* November 14, 1958.

34. On the close relation between decentralization and increase in managerial freedom, see a recent novel, *The Brothers Yershov* by V. Kochetov, currently a Soviet best-seller, directed against the so-called "revisionist" tendencies. There the point is emphatically made that merely increasing the number of economic ministries would have led indeed to a "more flexible and less cumbersome" organization; but "an unnatural centralization would remain and the managers' hands and feet would remain swaddled." V. Kochetov, "Brat'ya Yershovy," *Neva,* 7: 411 (1958).

35. It may be significant in this connection that the *theses* of Khrushchev's speech to the twenty-first Congress (the Seven-Year Plan) speak of increased local initiative on the part of labor and technical personnel, but fail to mention the need for managerial initiative. Thus the process of curtailment already may have begun. *Sovetskaya Rossiya,* November 14, 1958.

INDEX